ANCIENT INDIAN TRADITION & MYTHOLOGY

TRANSLATED BY

A BOARD OF SCHOLARS

EDITED BY

Professor J. L. SHASTRI

VOLUME 35

ANCIENT INDIAN TRADITION AND MYTHOLOGY SERIES

[PURĀṆAS IN TRANSLATION]

VOLUMES

ŚIVA 1-4
LIṄGA 5-6
BHĀGAVATA 7-11
GARUḌA 12-14
NĀRADA 15-19
KŪRMA 20-21
BRAHMĀṆḌA 22-26
AGNI 27-30
VARĀHA 31-32
BRAHMA 33-36

VOLUMES UNDER PREPARATION

BHAVIṢYA
BRAHMAVAIVARTA
DEVĪBHĀGAVATA
KĀLIKĀ
MĀRKAṆḌEYA
MATSYA
PADMA
SKANDA
VĀMANA
VĀYU
VIṢṆU
VIṢṆUDHARMOTTARA

BRAHMA PURĀṆA

PART III

TRANSLATED AND ANNOTATED BY

A BOARD OF SCHOLARS

MOTILAL BANARSIDASS • DELHI

UNESCO • PARIS

First Edition: Delhi, 1986

MOTILAL BANARSIDASS
Bungalow Road, Jawahar Nagar, Delhi 110 007
Branches
Chowk, Varanasi 221 001
Ashok Rajpath, Patna 800 004
6 Appar Swamy Koil Street, Mylapore, Madras 600 004

ISBN: 81-208-0196-2

UNESCO COLLECTION OF REPRESENTATIVE WORKS—Indian Series
This book has been accepted in the Indian Translation Series of the Unesco Collection of Representative Works jointly sponsored by the United Nations Educational, Scientific and Cultural Organization (UNESCO) and the Government of India.

PRINTED IN INDIA
BY JAINENDRA PRAKASH JAIN AT SHRI JAINENDRA PRESS, A-45 NARAINA INDUSTRIAL AREA, PHASE I, NEW DELHI 110028 AND PUBLISHED BY NARENDRA PRAKASH JAIN FOR MOTILAL BANARSIDASS, DELHI 110007.

PUBLISHER'S NOTE

The purest gems lie hidden in the bottom of the ocean or in the depth of rocks. One has to dive into the ocean or delve into the rocks to find them out. Similarly, truth lies concealed in the language which with the passage of time has become obsolete. Man has to learn that language before he discovers that truth.

But he has neither the means nor the leisure to embark on that course. We have, therefore, planned to help him acquire knowledge by an easier course. We have started the series of Ancient Indian Tradition and Mythology in English Translation. Our goal is to universalize knowledge through the most popular international medium of expression. The publication of the Purāṇas in English Translation is a step towards that goal.

PREFACE

This is the thirty-fifth volume in the series on *Ancient Indian Tradition and Mythology*. It contains Brahma Purāṇa, Part III (chapters 106-138).

The project was conceived in 1970 by the late Lala Sundar Lal Jain of Messers Motilal Banarsidass with the aim to disseminate the knowledge acquired by the ancient sages through the most popular international medium, viz. English. Hitherto the English translations of ten Purāṇas, namely, Śiva, Liṅga, Bhāgavata, Garuḍa, Nārada, Kūrma, Brahmāṇḍa, Agni, Varāha and Brahma (Parts I & II) have been published in the series.

Chapter 106 opens with an account of tortures inflicted on sinners in various hells. As many as forty-two hells have been named as against twenty-eight in most of the Purāṇas. A terrible picture of the tortures to which sinners are subjected has been drawn obviously with a motive to check the growth of crime. This is followed by an account of the reception accorded to the virtuous by Dharmarāja and his servants in chapter 107. Then chapter 108 describes the good and bad actions of the jīva and the *yonis* into which it is reborn as a result of them. The next chapter praises the gift of food as the best of charitable acts and then in the next three chapters details of the performance of Śrāddha for the departed are given. Chapter 113 contains a description of compulsory and optional duties prescribed for the householder together with various do's and dont's. Chapter 114 describes the special duties of the four castes (*varṇas*) and the four stages of life (*āśramas*). The next one is of a considerable sociological interest as it specifies the circumstances leading to upgrading and downgrading of castes. Chapters 118-120 are concerned with the superiority of god Viṣṇu, his worship and the benefits of singing songs in praise of Viṣṇu. Chapters 122-23 treat of the fate of men in Kali age and 'foretell' in what respects righteousness will decrease, what losses, difficulties and calamities will befall mankind. Various kinds of cosmic annihilation at the end of a *kalpa* etc. are described in chapters 124-25. It is really a terrible picture that has been drawn. The subject of the next one is human suffering and the means of getting rid of it for ever. Yoga as a means of ending the miseries and various restrictions to be observed during its practice is the topic of chapter 127. The principles of Sāṅkhya and Yoga are discussed in more details in chapters 128-32. Topics of religious and philosophical interest recur in the next five chapters. Sāṁkhya concepts find a prominent place in the philosophy of this Purāṇa.

Acknowledgement of obligations

It is our pleasant duty to put on record our sincere thanks to Dr. R.N. Dandekar and the UNESCO authorities for their kind encouragement and valuable help which render this work more useful than it would otherwise have been. We are extremely grateful to Shri T.V. Parameshwar Iyer for his valuable assistance in the preparation of this work. We also thank all those who have been helpful in our project.

—*Editor*

CONTENTS

PART III

ABBREVIATIONS

Common and self-evident abbreviations such as Ch(s)—Chapter(s), p—page, pp—pages, V—Verse, VV—Verses, Ftn—footnote, Hist. Ind. Philo.—History of Indian Philosophy are not included in this list.

ABORI	*Annals of the Bhandarkar Oriental Research Institute*, Poona
AGP	S. M. Ali's *The Geography of Purāṇas*, PPH, New Delhi, 1973
AIHT	*Ancient Indian Historical Tradition*, F. E. Pargiter, Motilal Banarsidass (MLBD), Delhi
AITM	*Ancient Indian Tradition and Mythology* Series, MLBD, Delhi
AP	*Agni Purāṇa*, Guru Mandal Edition (GM), Calcutta, 1957
Arch.S.Rep.	Archaeological Survey Report
AV	*Atharva Veda*, Svādhyāya Mandal, Aundh
Bd. P.	*Brahmāṇḍa Purāṇa*, MLBD, Delhi 1973
BG	*Bhagavadgītā*
Bh. P.	*Bhāgavata Purāṇa*, Bhagavat Vidyapeeth, Ahmedabad
Br.	*Brāhmaṇa* (preceded by name such as Śatapatha)
BS. P.	*Bhaviṣya Purāṇa*, Vishnu Shastri Bapat, Wai
BV. P.	*Brahma Vaivarta Purāṇa*, GM, 1955-57
CC	*Caturvarga Cintāmaṇi* by Hemādri
CVS	*Caraṇa Vyūha Sūtra* by Śaunaka; Com. by Mahidāsa
DB	*Devī Bhāgavata*, GM, 1960-61
De or GDAMI	*The Geographical Dictionary of Ancient and Mediaeval India*, N. L. De, Oriental Reprint, Delhi, 1971
Dh. S.	*Dharma Sūtra* (preceded by the author's name such as Gautama)
ERE	*Encyclopaedia of Religion and Ethics* by Hastings
GP	*Garuḍa Purāṇa*, ed. R. S. Bhattacharya, Chowkhamba, Varanasi, 1964

GS	*Gṛhya Sūtra* (preceded by the name of the author such as Āpastamba)
HD	*History of Dharma Śāstra*, P. V. Kane, G. O. S.
IA	*The Indian Antiquary*
IHQ	*The Indian Historical Quarterly*
JP	*Purāṇa* (Journal of the Kashiraj Trust), Varanasi
KA	*Kauṭilya Arthaśāstra*
KP	*Kūrma Purāṇa*, Veṅkaṭeśvara Press Edt., Bombay; also Kashiraj Trust Edt., Varanasi, 1971
LP	*Liṅga Purāṇa*, GM, 1960; also MLBD, Delhi, 1981
Manu.	*Manusmṛti*
Mbh.	*Mahābhārata*, Gītā Press, Gorakhpur, VS 2014
MkP	*Mārkaṇḍeya Purāṇa*
MN	*Mahābhārata Nāmānukramaṇī*, Gītā Press, Gorakhpur, VS 2016
MtP	*Matsya Purāṇa*, GM, 1954
MW	Monier Williams' *Sanskrit-English Dictionary*, MLBD, Delhi, 1976
NP	*Nāradiya* or *Nārada Purāṇa*, Veṅkaṭeśvar Press, Bombay
PCK	*Bhāratavarṣiya Prācina Caritrakośa*, Siddheshwar Shastri, Poona, 1968
Pd.P.	*Padma Purāṇa*, GM, 1957-59
PE	*Purāṇic Encyclopaedia*, V. Mani, English version, MLBD, Delhi, 1975
PR or PRHRC	*Puranic Records on Hindu Rites and Customs*, R. C. Hazra, Calcutta, 1948
ṚV	*Ṛg-Veda*, Svādhyāya Mandal, Aundh
Śat.Br.	*Śatapatha Brāhmaṇa*
SC or SMC	*Smṛti Candrikā* by Devanna Bhaṭṭa
SEP	*Studies in Epics and Purāṇas*, A.D. Pusalkar, Bharatiya Vidya Bhavan (BVB), Bombay

CHAPTER ONE HUNDRED AND SIX*

Tortures in Hell

The sages said :

1. O ascetic, how do the sinners go to that city by the southern path? We wish to hear. Recount it in detail.

Vyāsa said :

2-3. I shall recount that extremely terrible and awful doorway which is infested with many beasts of prey. It is resonant with the sounds of hundreds of vixens. It abounds in shrieking and howling sounds. It is impassable. It makes the hairs stand on their ends. It is surrounded by goblins, ghosts, evil spirits and other Rākṣasas.

4. On seeing such a terrible doorway, those who have committed sins faint and lose consciousness suddenly. They begin to babble and prattle due to fear.

5. Then the servants of Yama bind them with chains and nooses and drag them ruthlessly. They beat them with sticks and threaten them again and again.

6. After regaining consciousness they go towards the southern door faltering at every step. They are smeared with blood.

---

*The chapter opens with the account of tortures inflicted on sinners or punishment for their sins. Quite a terrible picture is drawn by the narrator to create horror with a view to check the growth of crime. The descriptions of hells and the torments suffered by the sinners are motivated by this purpose. The Purāṇas refer to a number of hells by their names which differ from Purāṇa to Purāṇa. The Brahma Purāṇa mentions as many as forty-two hells while generally most of the Purāṇas mention twenty-eight hells in all.

See Devī Bhāgavata, Skanda and Viṣṇu Purāṇa Part 2, ch.6. The Purāṇas refer to twenty-eight hells. They are : (1) Tāmisra, (2) Andhatāmisra, (3) Raurava, (4) Mahāraurava, (5) Kumbhīpāka, (6) Kālasūtra, (7) Asipatra, (8) Śūkaramukha, (9) Andhakūpa, (10) Kṛmibhojana, (11) Taptamūrti, (12) Śālmali, (13) Vajrakaṇṭakaśāli, (14) Vaitaraṇī (15) Pūyodaka, (16) Prāṇarodha, (17) Viśasanam, (18) Lālābhakṣa, (19) Śārameyāśana, (20) Avīci, (21) Ayaḥpāna, (22) Kṣārakārdama, (23) Rakṣobhakṣaṇa, (24) Śūlaprota, (25) Dandaśūka, (26) Vaṭarodha, (27) Paryāvartanaka, & (28) Sūcīmukha.

7-9. The miserable ones move ahead along the path where there are sharp thorns. It is full of gravel. There are pebbles with keen edges resembling those of razors. In some places the path is full of mud. There are unfathomable moats too. In some places there are tooth-like edges with sharp points like those of iron needles. In some places big trees have fallen down from the mountain ridges and blocked the path. In some places there are burning coals.

10-16. In some places there are dangerous ditches and pits. In some places there are slippery lumps of clay; in some places there are red hot sand particles; there are sharp pointed pikes in some places. The cross-roads are covered with iron plates which are red-hot. In some places there are forest fires. Some places are covered with hot rocks. Some places are covered with snow. In some places there are sands so loose that the pedestrians slip down therein upto the neck. In some places there is defiled water. Other places are filled with the fire of burning husk.

The pedestrians are tortured by the following, viz. lions, wolves, tigers, terrible biting insects, big leeches, huge pythons, awful flies and bees, massive poisonous snakes, wicked elephants that are intoxicated by their strength and kill, great bulls with sharp-pointed horns digging up the path, infuriated buffaloes with huge horns, that are mad and that devour persons, hideous and terrible Dākinī witches, Rākṣasas and very terrible ailments. Harassed by these pedestrians, the dead go ahead along that path.

17-21. They are struck by fierce gusts of wind mixed with huge columns of dust and striking by a great shower of pebbles. They find no place of shelter. As they go along, they are torn and shattered by the fall of thunderbolt. Everywhere they are cut and split by huge showers of arrows.

They are burned by thunderbolts and terrific meteors falling in multitudes as well as burning coal. A great shower of dust particles covers them up and they cry in agony. They are frightened by the repeated terrible sounds of clouds. They are pounded and smashed by showers of arrows. They are sprinkled and sprayed with solutions of acid as they go ahead.

22. When the extremely rough, coarse and chill wind blows against them they shrink, shrivel and become frozen.

23-24. Thus those men are led along the path without repast and rest. They do not get water to drink. The path is impassable. Thus the embodied souls, the deluded perpetrators of sinful crimes are forcibly led along that path by the terrible emissaries of Yama whose behests they carry out.

25-32. They are lonely and without friends or kinsmen. They are subject to other's will and helpless. They bewail their lot and lament continuously.

Those forbidden persons (?) turned into ghosts find their throat, lips and palates parched up. They are emaciated and terribly afraid. They are burnt by the fire of hunger. Some are bound with fetters with their legs raised up. Even as they are parched up thus, they are dragged and pulled by the emissaries of Yama of manifest strength.

These men with their faces down and others are also dragged by the servants of Yama. They are extremely miserable. Deprived of food and drink they beg for it saying "Give, please give" in a voice choked with tears.

On seeing various foodstuffs and beverages in plenty, these wretched persons afflicted by hunger and thirst request for the same with palms joined in reverence. They see cooked rice mixed with curds, milk and ghee; they observe various articles with sweet odour, they notice various kinds of fragrant and cool beverages. On seeing these, they begin to request for the same. Thereupon, the servants of Yama rebuke them with harsh words. Those terrible fellows with the tips of their eyes red with anger threaten the pedestrians and say :—

Yama's servants said :

33-38. You have not performed sacrifices at the proper time. You have not offered gifts to the brahmins. Moreover, when something was offered to brahmins you had actively prevented it. The time for the reaping of the fruits of that sin has arrived, O base men, your assets were not burnt by fire nor did they perish in water. They had not been seized by kings or robbers. Where are they now? Why were they not handed over to brahmins? These mountain-like heaps of cooked rice that are seen here have been kept ready for those good men by whom charitable gifts of Sāttvika type have been made. There are various good stuffs and beverages—those that should be chewed and masticated, those that should be swallowed, those that should be licked and those that should be squeezed of their juice. You will not get these since nothing has been given by you before. Cooked rice is always brought and kept here for the sake of those persons by whom gifts are given in charity, Homas are performed, sacrificial ceremonies are celebrated and brahmins are worshipped. O hellish beings, how can others' fruits of piety be given away by us to you?

Vyāsa said :

39. On hearing the words of Yama's servants they lose their taste therein. They are afflicted by hunger and thirst (all the more). Thereafter they are tortured by the servants of Yama with terrible weapons.

40-41. The ruthless emissaries af Yama attack them from the rear with iron clubs, iron-rods, javelins, tomaras, paṭṭiśas, bhindipālas and parighas. They are bit and pierced by arrows, axes and maces. The sinners are attacked from the front by lions, tigers etc. and are eaten up by them.

42. They do not get the opportunity of either getting in or coming out. They are in a highly wretched state. Those sinners are overwhelmed by their own actions. They lament piteously.

43. After restraining and afflicting them much the sinners are taken by the servants of Yama to that place where Yama himself is present.

44-45. Lord Yama is a virtuous soul. He causes piety. He restrains evil. The deceased persons who reach the city of the dead through the very difficult path are brought in front of Yama after duly informing him. Then those evil doers see that terrible person.

46-56. The eyes of the sinners are obstructed by sins. They had a wrong notion and idea of the soul before. Such sinners see Yama face to face. His face appears terrible due to the curved fangs. His eyebrows are coorked as he sees furiously. His hairs are lifted up. He has great moustache. His lower lip throbs. He has eighteen arms. He is infuriated. He resembles the blue mass of collyrium. All types of weapons shine in his hands. He is equipped with a dreadful rod. He rides on a great buffalo. His eyes resemble the blazing fire. He wears red garlands and garments. He is as lofty as the great cloud. His voice is as loud as the rumbling sound of the cloud at the time of dissolution. He appears to drink the great ocean, swallow the three worlds and vomit fire. Near him the sinners see Death whose lustre is like that of black fire. They see the Annihilator too who is terrible and who resembles the fire at the time of dissolution. Then there is the fierce Mahāmārī (great smallpox) and the terrible Kālarātri (Nightmare). There are also different ailments terrible and of different forms. They hold javelins, tridents, goads, nooses, discuses and swords. They are terrible with thunderbolt and rod of chastisement. They hold daggers, quivers and bow. The emissaries of Yama are innumerable. They are ruthless and they resemble collyrium in lustre. They have great prowess. They have all types of weapons lifted up in their hands. Yama is surrounded by these excessively terrible attendants. The worst sinners see Yama and the terrible Citragupta. Yama rebukes those sinners severely. Lord Citragupta enlightens them by words of virtue.

Citragupta said :

57-58. O perpetrators of evil deeds, O misappropriators of other men's wealth, O outragers of other men's wives, O sinners, arrogant due to beauty or prowess! What is done by you must be endured and experienced by yourselves. Then why were evil deeds committed by you all only to ruin your own souls?

59. Now, when you are being afflicted by your own actions, why do you repent and bewail? Experience your own miseries. It is not the fault of anyone else.

60-61. O ye rulers of Earth who have come near me! You are of evil intentions, arrogant due to your strength you have come here for your own terrible deeds. O kings, of evil conduct, you are the causes of destruction of your subjects. Why was sinful action committed by you for your kingdom lasting for a short time?

62. Due to your greed for the kingdom, due to delusion

the subjects were unjustly and forcibly punished by you. O kings, now experience the result thereof.

63. Where is your kingdom? Where is your wife, for whose sake sins have been committed by you? Leaving all that you are now stationed here in isolation !

64. We do not see all that strength of yours whereby the subjects have been destroyed. You are being hit and pierced by the emissaries of Yama now. Now see, what have you gained?

Vyāsa said :

65-70. Thus they are rebuked by Yama too by means of various words. Repenting over their sinful deeds, the kings stay there silently. After telling them the activities of the kings Dharmarāja himself spoke thus in order to rectify their sins.

Yama said :

O Caṇḍa, O Mahācaṇḍa, take away these kings. Purify them of their sins gradually in the fires of hell.

Vyāsa said :

Then the emissaries of Yama rise up quickly, catch hold of those kings by their feet and whirl them with force. They throw them up and seize them again. In accordance with the magnitude of their sins they strike them against the rocky slab in the manner of the thunderbolt hitting a great tree. Shattered thus the embodied one discharges blood through the blood vessels. Then he becomes senseless and motionless too.

71. Touched by the wind he slowly regains life. Then they throw the man into the ocean of hellish life.

72. O leading brahmins, the emissaries intimate to Yama about the people engaged in sinful activities who are now extremely miserable.

Yama's emissaries said :

73. O lord, at your behest, this man who is averse to virtue, who is much deluded and who is interested in sinful activities has been brought by us.

74. This man is greedy. He is of evil conduct. He commits

sins of various types, big and small. He is impure and he is engaged in violence.

75. This man has had sexual intercourse with forbidden women. He is a wicked man. He is a person who stole away other men's wealth. He has sold his daughter. He is a perjuror. He is ungrateful. He has deceived friends.

76. Virtue and piety has always been censured by this proud follow. A sinful deed has been committed by this wicked man in the mortal world.

77. Now, O lord of Devas, mention the modes of restraining or blessing this fellow. Our lord must be competent to lay down action against him. We will be only hindering if we do anything ourselves.

Vyāsa said :

78-83. After intimating this to the lord of Devas and placing the sinner in front of him, the servants go to fetch other men from among hundreds and lakhs and crores of hellish beings.

When the crime committed has been accepted, Yama gives instructions to his deadful servants to punish the sinners in accordance with the injunctions of Vasiṣṭha and other law givers in regard to their restraints and punishment.

The infuriated servants of Yama destroy sins. The sinners are hit and pierced with goads, iron clubs, batons, hatchets, javelins, tomaras, swords and tridents also.

The sinners, thousands, hundred, hundred thousands and crores of them, are afflicted by the servants of Yama through the faults and sins acquired by their actions. Now listen to the nature and forms of hells. They are terrible.

84-89. Listen to the names and extent of these hells as well as to the cause whereby men fall into them.

The hell, well known as Mahāvīci, is flooded with blood. It is strewn over with adamantine thorns. It extends to ten thousand Yojanas. The man who kills cows is immersed into that bloody river. He is split and torn against the adamantine thorns. This terrible ordeal lasts for hundred thousand years.

The terrible hell Kumbhīpāka extends to ten million Yojanas. It contains blazing sand full of copper jars and burning coal. It is here that the slayer of a brahmin, one who illegally takes possession of lands and one who misappropriates amounts kept in trust—are hurled and burnt until the dissolution of all living beings.

The hell Raurava is strewn with adamantine darts and shafts that blaze. It is sixty thousand Yojanas in length and extent. In that hell, men are pierced and torn by these blazing darts and shafts.

90-97. Those who commit perjury are crushed and pounded in that hell like cane stumps in the machine.

The hell named Mañjūṣā is known as one which consists of a blazing iron box. Men brought as prisoners are placed in it and burnt.

The hell named Apratiṣṭha is full of pus, urine and ordure. One who harasses a brahmin falls into it topsy turvy.

Lākṣāprajvalita is a terrible lubricous and slippery hell. O excellent brahmins, those who are addicted to wine are put into it and burnt. The hell Mahāprabha is a lofty one with blazing tridents. Those who create split between husbands and wives are pierced with tridents in that hell. There is the hell Mahāghora. There is an iron block there resembling a rocky slab. It is named Jayanti. The sinner who habitually approaches other men's wives is struck with this iron block.

The hell named Śālmala contains blazing sturdy thorny shrubs. The woman who lives with many men has to embrace these thorny shrubs. She becomes wiserable thereby.

The tongues of those who lie always, wounding the sensitive feelings of others are plucked by the servants of Yama, who are entrusted with this task. The eyes of those who view other men's wives with lustful glances are pierced with darts by the servants of Yama.

98-105 Those who outrage the modesty of their own mothers, sisters, daughters, and daughters-in-law, and those who kill women, children and old men undergo tortures in hell for the duration of the reign of fourteen Indras.

The hell named Mahāraurava is very terrible. Clusters of fiery flames spread everywhere. This hell extends to fourteen thousand Yojanas.

The deluded man who commits arson on cities, fields, houses and villages is burnt in that hell for the period of a Kalpa.

The hell that is well known as Tāmisra extends to a hundred thousand Yojanas. It is very terrible. Swords and iron clubs named Paṭṭiśas and Mudgaras always fall therein. Men who steal are put therein and beaten by the servants of Yama. They are tortured with tridents, javelins, maces and swords for the period of three hundred Kalpas.

The hell named Mahātāmisra is twice as large as Tāmisra. It is full of leeches and serpents. It is devoid of light and it yields great misery. Men guilty of matricide and fratricide and those who kill friends who have trusted them remain in this hell as long as the Earth lasts. They are pared and pierced.

The hell named Asipatravana yields much misery.

106-113. It extends to ten thousand Yojanas. It is infested with blazing swords. With these swords falling in hundreds, the person who is guilty of treachery to friends is cut, struck and pierced until the dissolution of all living beings.

There is a hell named Karambhavālukā. It is in the shape of a well and it extends to ten thousand Yojanas. It is covered with blazing sands and coals and thorns. The person by whom people are continuously burnt with terrible means under false pretext is burnt or pierced for a hundred and ten thousand three hundred years in this hell.

The hell named Kākola is flooded with putrescent fluid infested with germs. Those wicked persons who partake of sweet food alone (without sharing it with others) are hurled into that hell.

The hell named Kuḍmala is filled with faeces, urine and blood. Men, who do not perform the five Yajñas and other holy rites are cast into that hell.

The hell Mahābhīma (exceedingly terrible) is full of foul smell and is contaminated by flesh and blood. Base men who are interested in eating forbidden food fall into that hell.

The hell Mahāvaṭa (the great cavernous pit) is infested with worms and germs. It is filled with corpses too. The man who sells his daughter falls into it with face downwards.

There is an exceedingly terrible hell named Tilapāka where

persons who are engaged in afflicting others are crushed and powdered like sesamum seeds.

114-119. There is a hell named Tailapāka where boiling oil floods the ground. He who kills friends or those who seek refuge in him, is cooked there.

There is a hell named Vajrakapota. It contains an admantine chain. Those who sell milk are ruthlessly tortured there.

There is a hell called Nirucchvāsa. It is blindingly dark and devoid of wind. He who prevents a charitable gift from being given to a brahmin is rendered motionless and hurled into it.

The hell named Aṅgāropacaya is dazzling with burning coal. He who promises a gift to a brahmin but does not give it to him is burnt there.

The hell named Mahāpāyī extends to a hundred thousand Yojanas. Those who always utter lies are hurled into it with faces downwards.

The hell named Mahājvāla is very terrible and is very bright due to flames. A man who is intellectually inclined towards sins is burnt there for a long time.

120-125. There is a hell named Krakaca. Men who indulge in sexual intercourse with forbidden women are tortured there with saws and hatchets the edges of which are keen and adamantine.

There is a hell named Guḍapāka. It is full of boiling eddies of treacle and molasses. A man responsible for mixture in castes is thrown into it. He is burnt therein.

The hell Kṣuradhāra is full of keen-edged razors. Men who illegally seize the lands of brahmins are cut off and pared there for the duration of a Kalpa.

The hell called Ambarīṣa is kindled with the fire of dissolution. He who steals gold is burnt there for a period of a hundred crores of Kalpas.

The hell known by the name Vajrakuṭhāra is agitated by thunderbolts. Sinners who cut off the umbrellas (upper branches and leaves) of trees are tortured there.

The hell called Paritāpa is rendered blazing by the fire of dissolution. A sinner who administers poison or steals honey and wine is cooked there.

126-131. The hell Kālasūtra is made of adamnatine wires. Those who cut off and plunder the vegetable products of others wander there. They are cut, pierced and tortured therein.

The hell named Kaṣmala is full of phlegm and nasal mucus. The man who takes interest in wine and flesh is cast into that hell and kept there for the period of a Kalpa.

The hell Ugragandha is full of saliva, urine and faeces. Those who do not offer balls of rice unto the Pitṛs are thrown into it.

The hell named Durdhara is infested with leeches and scorpions. A man who swallows bribes stays there for ten thousand years.

There is the hell named Vajramahāpīḍa. It is made of adamant. Those who take away other people's wealth, food-grains or gold are thrown into this hell, burnt and tortured by the servants of Yama.

132-136. Those thieves are cut off into bits by razors by the emissaries of Yama.

Those deluded persons who kill living beings and eat them like crows and vultures are compelled to eat their own flesh by the servants of Yama. Those who take away the seat, bed and garments belonging to others and those who commit perjury are crushed like sugarcane.

The hell Āyasa is remembered as constituted by iron. It blazes. Those who are engaged in imprisoning persons are thrown into it and are burnt.

There is a hell named Atratiṣṭha. It contains putrescent urine and faeces. Those who censure Smṛtis and the Vedas fall into it with faces downwards.

There is a hell named Pārilumpa. It is infested with vultures, dogs and wolves. Those who kill children and old people are scorched in this terrible hell.

137. There is a hell named Karāla. It is terrible and infested with dead bodies and ghosts. He who inflicts pain on a brahmin is eaten by Rākṣasas in this hell.

138. The hell Vilepana is terrible with boiling melted lac. O excellent brahmins, those who imbibe wine and liquor are immersed therein and burnt.

139. There is a hell named Mahāpreta. It contains a blazing trident of great height. Those who create split between husbands and wives are pierced with that trident.

140. There is a hell Mahāghora where there is an iron block like a rocky slab. It blazes. A sinner who hovers round other men's wives is dragged with that iron block.

141. There is a hell named Śālmali where there is a blazing sturdy thorny bush. A man engaged in the attack of vulnerable points in others is compelled to embrace this thorny bush. He becomes miserable thereby.

142. The tongues of those who take false pledges and speak words that wound the sensitive spots in others are plucked by the servants of Yama, who are the members of the assembly.

143. Those who carnally approach the daughters-in-law are hurled over the heaps of burning coal and burnt by the servants of Yama.

144-147. Those deluded persons who spoil the holy rites, or take away the abode and gold belonging to others, are split and crushed by the emissaries of Yama by means of javelins and iron clubs.

The evil-minded persons who steal even fruits and leaves of other men are burnt by the infuriated emissaries of Yama through grass fires. A blazing trident is fixed into the heart of that evil-minded man who is enamoured of other men's wives and properties. The emissaries of Yama torture such men thus.

Those who are averse to virtue mentally, verbally and physically undergo excessively terrible tortures in the world of Yama.

Thus there are hundreds, thousands, millions and crores of hells. Men who commit sins go to them.

148-152. By committing even the smallest act of inauspicious nature here a man undergoes tortures in the terrible hells in the world of Yama. Deluded men do not pay heed to the excellent speech made by Dharma. As a retort that say thus—"Who has seen this with his own eyes ?"

Those who assiduously perform sinful deeds every day and night do not perform virtuous deeds even erringly. They are deluded. Those who enjoy the fruits here itself and are averse to the other world are base men. They fall into terrible hells.

A life in hell is very terrible. A residence in heaven yields happiness. It is by doing virtuous or vicious deeds that heaven or hell is attained by men.

CHAPTER ONE HUNDRED AND SEVEN

The Goal of the Virtuous

The sages said :

1-2. Alas ! the great and terrible misery in the path of Yama has been recounted by you. O excellent one, the terrible hells and the entrances to the abode of Yama have also been recounted.

O brahman, is there any means whereby men can traverse the terrible path of Yama comfortably and go to Yama's abode ? Please tell us.

Vyāsa said :

3-4. I shall recount to you how righteous men traverse that path along with their wives and sons. Men of righteousness, who are engaged in non-violence, who are interested in serving the preceptors and elders, and who worship Devas and brahmins traverse that path from the mortal world.

5. Served by heavenly damsels they go the city of Dharmarāja travelling by different divine aerial chariots rendered splendid by diamonds and gold.

6. Those who devoutly give the brahmins gifts of various forms go comfortably along that great path.

7-8. Those who offer with great devotion to the brahmins well consecrated cooked rice, particularly to the brahmins well versed in the Vedas, go to the city of Dharmarāja by means of well adorned aerial chariots. They are assiduously served by excellent young women.

9. Those who speak truth, those who are devoid of impurities inwardly and outwardly, go to the abode of Yama by serial chariots. They resemble the immortal beings in lustre.

10-11. Those persons who are conversant with what is virtue and who make over sacred gifts of cows to good men who are poor and whose activities are befitting the poor go to the glorious city of Dharmarāja by means of aerial chariots having divine lustre and colour, and embellished with jewels. The gifts must be made to them with the idea that they are representatives of Viṣṇu. Such devotees are seized by groups of celestials.

12-13. Those who give away a pair of sandals, an umbrella, bed, seat, garments and ornaments, go to the divine city of Dharmarāja embellished and equipped with horses, chariots, elephants and golden or silver umbrellas.

14-15. Those who with devotion and pure mind, give the worthy brahmins water, sweetened with treacle as well as cooked rice, go to the abode of Yama, on golden vehicles of various kinds. In accordance with their desire they are again and again served by excellent women.

16-17. Those who give the brahmins well consecrated milk, ghee, curds, jaggery and honey assiduously and with purity, go to the abode of Yama by means of golden aerial chariots drawn by ruddy geese. They will be attended upon by Gandharvas with their instrumental music.

18. Those who give fruits and fragrant flowers go to the city of Dharma sitting on aerial chariots drawn by swans.

19-20. Those who are endowed with faith and give to the brahmins, well-versed in the Vedas, gingelly seeds, tiladhenu or ghṛtadhenu go by spotless vehicles resembling the lunar disc. Gandharvas sing songs in their praise in the city of Yama.

21-22. Those who build tanks, wells, lakes, ponds, big oblong tanks, lotus ponds and cold water reservoirs (for the general public) go by means of vehicles that have the lustre of golden moon and that are resonant with divine bells. They have great lustre and they are fanned with handmade palmleaf fans.

23-26. Those people who have temples and shrines of wonderful features dazzling with jewels, charming and splendid go to the beautiful city of Dharmarāja full of various people by means of aerial chariots that have the speed of the wind. They are accompanied by the guardians of quarters.

Those who give water that constitutes the main sustenance of all living beings go to the city of Yama comfortably without the (inconvenience of) thirstiness by means of aerial chariots of great velocity.

Those who give charitable gifts of wooden sandals, vehicles, stools and seats to brahmins go along the path very comfortably.

27. Keeping their feet on excellent golden pedestals embellished with jewels they travel in aerial chariots beautified by the presence of heavenly nymphs.

28-29. Those men who grow wonderful parks with flowers and fruits thereby helping men go (along that great path) (after duly resting) in beautiful and cool shades of trees. They are well bedecked and attended upon by excellent women to the accompaniment of songs and instrumental music.

30. Those who make gifts of gold, silver, corals or pearls, travel in aerial chariots shining like furnished gold.

31-35. The donors of land gifts become brilliant. All their desires are fulfilled. They travel by means of extremely resonant aerial chariots shining like the rising sun.

Those who give an embellished virgin as gift, as worthy of being given to a brahmin, go to the abode of Yama in aerial chariots and surrounded by celestial virgins.

O excellent brahmins, those who are endowed with great devotion and give to the brahmins sweet scents, agallochum, camphor, flowers and incense go to the abode of Dharma by means of wonderful vehicles. They are well adorned. They emit sweet odour. The are well dressed and they are lustrous.

Those who make gifts of lamps go along the path by means of vehicles. They brighten the ten quarters. They are brilliant with vehicles resembling the sun. They shine like fires.

36. Those who make gifts of houses and residences go to the abode of Dharmarāja (making use of) rest houses embellished in gold and resembling the rising sun.

37. Those who make gifts of water pots, different types of vessels such as Kuṇḍikā, Karaka etc. go (along the path) by means of lordly elephants. They are honoured by celestial damsels too.

38. Those who give to brahmins oil for applying over the feet or on the head, those who give water for bath and drink unto the brahmins, go to the abode of Yama by riding on horses.

39. Those who accord rest to brahmins who are travel-worn and emaciated go comfortably along the path in a vehicle drawn by ruddy geese.

40. He who greets and honours a brahmin offering him welcome and befitting seat goes along that path comfortably. He becomes excessively delighted.

41. He who salutes Hari saying "obeisance, O lord, favourably disposed to the brahmins" and he who salutes a cow saying "O dispeller of sins", goes along that path comfortably.

42. Those who take meals after the guests have taken and those who are devoid of arrogance and untruthfulness, go along that path by means of vehicles drawn by Sārasas (waterfowls).

43. Those who take only a morsel of food (each day) and are devoid of obstinacy and arrogance go to the abode of Yama comfortably by means of aerial chariots drawn by swans.

44. Those who have conquered the sense-organs and sustain themselves on a single morsel of food once in four days, go to the city of Dharma in vehicles drawn by peacock.

45. Those who regularly do virtuous deeds and take food once in three days go to that region by means of vehicles and divine chariots fitted with elephants.

46. He who takes cooked rice once in six days, has conquered the sense-organs, and always maintains cleanliness, goes like the consort of Śacī seated on an elephant.

47. (He goes to) the beautiful city of Dharmarāja embellished with jewels, resonant with different notes and voices as well as the shouts of victory.

48. Those who observe fasts for a forthnight go to the city of Dharmarāja in vehicles drawn by tigers and attended by Devas and Asuras.

49. Those who have conquered their sense-organs and observe fasts for a month go to the abode of Yama in vehicles as refulgent as the sun.

50. He who is steadfast in the observances of religious vows and undertakes the long journey of death with concentration

goes to the abode of Yama in vehicles as lustrous as the sun. He is attended upon by Gandharvas.

51. He who sanctifies the body with the inner soul devoted to Viṣṇu goes to heaven in a chariot as refulgent as fire.

52. He who is devoted to Nārāyaṇa and enters fire goes to the abode of Yama in an aerial chariot refulgent like fire.

53. He who remembers Viṣṇu and casts off his vital airs without resorting to destructive weapons goes to the city of Dharma by means of a vehicle that has the refulgence of the sun.

54. He who enters water and casts off his vital airs, goes comfortably in a vehicle resembling the lunar disc.

55. The devotee of Viṣṇu who gives up his body to the vultures, goes to the abode of Yama in a splendid chariot made of gold.

56. He who meets death in a battle ensuing upon his attempt to resist the abduction of a woman or capture of cows goes along shining like the sun and attended upon by celestial girls.

57. Those devotees of Viṣṇu who have conquered their sense-organs and undertake pilgrimages to holy centres go along that terrible path by comfortable vehicles.

58. The excellent brahmins who worship, performing sacrifices wherein monetary gifts are generously distributed go comfortably by means of aerial chariots resembling molten gold.

59. Those who refrain from inflicting pain on others and those who sustain their servants, go comfortably in aerial chariots shining like gold.

60-61. Those who forgive all living beings, those who ensure freedom from fear to all living beings, those who are devoid of anger and delusion, those who have restrained their sense-organs and those who have no pride, go to the city of Yama by means of an aerial chariot as refulgent as the full moon. They have great lustre and are served by Devas and Gandharvas.

62. Those who worship Viṣṇu, Brahmā, the three-eyed lord Śiva and the sun with the same emotional fervour go there immediately with a pure mind.

63. Those who are devoted to truth, cleanliness and mercy and do not eat flesh go to the city of Dharmarāja comfortably.

64. There is nothing sweeter than meat among the food-stuffs, edibles etc. Hence no one shall eat meat, for happiness does not come from sweet things.

65. Formerly, Brahmā, the most excellent one among the knowers of the Vedas, said thus :—He who makes a gift of a thousand cows and he who abstains from eating meat—these two are on a par with each other.

66. O brahmins, the benefit resulting from the avoidance of meat-eating is the same as that of the pilgrimage to all holy centres and of the performance of all Yajñas.

67. Thus the virtuous ones engaged in charitable gifts and religious vows go comfortably in vehicles to the world of Yama, the lord who is the son of the sun.

68. On seeing those virtuous persons lord Yama will honour them by offering them greetings of welcome, seats and pleasing water for washing feet and materials of worship.

69-71. "O great souls, you are blessed. You have done what is conducive to the welfare of your souls; meritorious deeds have been done by you for the achievement of divine happiness. Get into this aerial chariot and go to heaven that is unparalleled and equipped with all desirable things. Rejoice with the divine ladies there. Enjoy all great pleasures there. At the end when merit gets exhausted and there still remain some evil deeds to be recompensed experience the result thereof here".

72. Men who have magnificence of meritorious deeds find Dharmarāja very gentle, as though he is their father himself.

73. Hence virtue should be resorted to always. It yields the benefit of salvation. From virtue result wealth, love and liberation.

74. Virtue is our mother, father, and brother. Virtue is our lord and friend. Virtue is our master, friend, saviour, creator and nourisher.

75. From virtue one gets wealth; from wealth one realizes one's desire and gets all sensual enjoyments. Virtue gives prosperity, and the greatest goal of heavenly pleasures results from virtue.

76. O brahmins, if one resorts to it, virtue saves one from great dangers. One shall undoubtedly attain divinity and brahminhood by means of virtue.

77. O excellent brahmins, when the previously accumulated demerit of men dwindles, their mind turns to virtue.

78. If, after thousands of births in the other species one attains the rare birth as a human being, but still one does not practice virtue, he is a deceived persons indeed.

79. The following should be known as persons devoid of virtue—Despicable persons, ugly ones, impoverished men, sick men, foolish ones and those who serve others.

80. Virtue has been practised previously by the following persons :—those who live long, the heroic ones, scholars, those who have wealth, those who are free from ailments and those who are beautiful and handsome.

81. O brahmins, those who are engaged in righteous activities attain the highest state. Those who resort to sin and evil are born as animals and low creatures.

82. Yama is not competent to harm those men who are devoted to lord Kṛṣṇa, the slayer of Naraka. He does not see them even in dreams.

83. Those who always bow to the lord who has neither birth nor death and who slays Daityas and Dānavas, do not see Yama.

84. Those who have sought refuge in Viṣṇu in their thoughts, words and deeds get the benefit of salvation. Yama is not able to harm them.

85. O brahmins, those people who continuously bow to Nārāyaṇa, the lord of worlds, do not go anywhere else other than the abode of Viṣṇu.

86. By bowing to Viṣṇu, (the devotees) do not see those emissaries, Yama, that city or that path. They never see hells.

87. Although those who are deluded may commit sins, still if they are devoted to Hari, the destroyer of sins, they do not go to hell.

88. Those who remember the lord even roguishly, go to the world of Viṣṇu, free from ailments, after casting off this mortal body.

89. He who is excessively angry with Hari but sometimes does mention or recite his name shall obtain liberation after his defects perish just as the king of Cedi (Śiśupāla) did.

CHAPTER ONE HUNDRED AND EIGHT

The cycle of worldly existence

Lomaharṣaṇa said :

1. After hearing about the path of Yama and the tortures in the hells the excellent sages asked Vyāsa again to clear their doubts.

The sages said :

2-3. Who is the ally of a man? (Can it be) his father, mother, son, preceptor, kinsmen and relatives or friends? People leave off their houses and the bodies like a log of wood or a lump of clay. They go to the other world. Who follows them ?

Vyāsa said :

4-6. O brahmins, man is born alone and alone he dies. Alone he surmounts difficulties and alone he faces adversities with no one to assist him.

Father, mother, brother, son, preceptor, kinsmen, relatives and friends—all appear to cry for a short while. Then they leave off the dead body like a log of wood or a lump of clay. They turn their faces away.

7. The body is left off by them. But Dharma alone follows him. Hence Dharma is the ally. It should always be resorted to by men.

8. A creature equipped with Dharma will attain the greatest heavenly goal. Similarly, one defiled by sins attains hell.

9. Hence, the wise one should not be delighted by riches acquired through sins. Dharma alone has been described as the sole ally of men.

10. Even a well-read man commits unworthy acts on being deluded by covetousness for wealth of others. He may commit sins due to greed, delusion, sympathy or fear.

11. Virtue, wealth and sensual pleasure are the three objectives that a living man strives after. These three should be acquired after avoiding sins.

The sages said :

12. The virtuous words of Your Holiness have been listened to. They are greatly conducive to our welfare. Now we are inclined to know about this assemblage (of parts) called body.

13. The dead body of men becomes subtle. It passes into an unmanifest state. It reaches a state where it cannot be seen. How does Dharma follow it ?

Vyāsa said :

14. The earth, wind, ether, water, fire, mind, intellect, soul—all these collectively see Dharma always.

15. They are the witnesses unto all living beings by day or by night. Along with these, Dharma follows the individual soul.

16. O excellent brahmins, the skin, bone, flesh, semen and blood all these leave off the body bereft of living soul.

17. Then the individual soul equipped with Dharma attains happiness, both in this world and in the other world. What else shall I tell you ?

The sages said :

18. How Dharma follows (the soul) has been indicated by Your Holiness. We wish to know how semen begins to function.

Vyāsa said :

19-21. The divine beings who are stationed in the body, (the elements) earth, wind, ether, water, fire, and mind, partake of the cooked rice (the food intake). O brahmins, when they are satiated, when the five elements with the mind as the sixth are contented, the great energy, the semen, is generated. It is the pure Ātman.

Thereafter, O brahmins, by the union of woman and man the foetus develops. Thus everything has been recounted to you. What else do you wish to hear?

The sages said :

22. O revered one, you have told how an embryo is formed. Please let us know how a person comes into being.

Vyāsa said :

23. When the soul is enveloped by the elements he comes into being. When the elements separate he dies.

24. When he is enveloped by the elements, he comes to life again. Then the presiding deities of the elements watch his good and evil deeds. What else do you desire to hear?

The sages said :

25. Bereft of skin, bones, flesh and devoid of the elements too where does the being station himself and experience joys and sorrows?

Vyāsa said :

26. The being enveloped by his Kārmic Saṁskāras enters the womb of the mother when he is born in course of time.

27. (After death) the being undergoes suffering and torture at the hands of the attendants of Yama. He enters the cycle of births and deaths, attended by misery and distress.

28. O Brāhmaṇas, the jīva enjoys the fruits of action which he performed during his worldly existence.

29. If his actions are pious throughout his existence, he will enjoy pleasures as a man during the course of his life.

30. But, if while doing acts of piety, he takes recourse to impious deeds, he gets joys and sorrows succeeding each other.

31. If his activities are absolutely unholy, he goes to Yama's region (Hell) where he suffers misery and distress and therefore, is born in lower species as a beast etc.

32. Now, listen, in which particular life or existence, a deluded person is born and for what action of his.

33. It is recorded in the holy treatises—Śāstras and Vedas

—that the dreadful world of Yama is interlinked with the world of mortals.

34. O Brāhmaṇas, there are spots as holy as celestial regions. These are progressive and specially designed for the mortals.

35. O Brāhmaṇas, in the world of Yama which equals the world of Brahmā, the jīva, bound by the fast chains of his actions reaps the fruits thereof.

36. I shall, now, tell you about those actions which cause a person to assume an ugly form.

37. A Brāhmaṇa though well versed in the Vedas is born as an ass if he receives charity from a fallen person.

38. O Brāhmaṇas, he is born and lives as an ass for full fifteen years. Dying as an ass he becomes a bull and in the form of a bull he lives for seven years.

39. Dying as a bull, he is born a Brahma-Rākṣasa and in the form of a Brahma-Rākṣasa he lives for three months. Then he is born a Brāhmaṇa.

40. If he officiates at a sacrifice performed by a low person, he is born a worm and in the form of a worm he lives for fifteen years.

41-43. Released from the form of worm he is born an ass and in the form of an ass he lives for five years; in the form of a cock for five years; in the form of a jackal for five years; then he is born in the form of man; then a jealous person; then an animal. On betraying confidence he is born a fish.

44. He remains in that form for eight years. Then he is born a fawn, O Brāhmaṇas. He remains in that form for four months. Then he is born a goat.

45. He remains in that form for one year. Then he is born as an insect, then a man.

46-47. He who steals unwittingly rice, sesamum seeds, bean, gram, linseed, chick-pea, legumimus seed, kidney bean, wheat, lamp or other corns, is born a rat, O noble sages.

48-50. Afterwards, he is born as a boar. As soon as born, he dies of some disease. Then, afterwards, he becomes a dog, then a dumb person, then again a dog for five years. Then in the form of man he copulates with another man's wife and is born as a wolf, then a dog, a jackal, a vulture, a snake or a tiger, a heron, a crane.

51. He who out of delusion, with a guilty mind, seduces the wife of his brother is born a male cuckoo and remains in that form for a year.

52-54. Overpowered by the sex-instinct, if he seduces the wife of his friend or preceptor or the ruling monarch he is born as a boar and remains in that form for five years, as a crane for ten years, as an ant for three months, as a worm for a month. Having passed through these births he is born as a worm. He lives in that form for fourteen years.

55-57. When his sins are exhausted he is born as a man. If a person consents to wed his daughter to a youth but then changes his mind and intends to give her to another person, if a person, being stupid, acts contrarily to the wishes of his preceptor, he enters three wombs. O Brāhmaṇas, first of all, he is born as a dog, then a carnivorous demon, then an ass. Passing through these forms, he is born a Brāhmaṇa.

58-60. If a pupil, prone to sinful deeds, sexually approaches the wife of his preceptor, not actually but mentally, he is born, by the perversity of his sinful mind, a dog. He lives in that form for full one year. Then after death he is born in the form of a Brāhmaṇa.

61. If a preceptor kills his pupil who is no less than his son without any rhyme or reason, but just at his own sweet will, he is born in the form of a ferocious animal.

62-63. Being a son if he disregards his parents, O Brāhmaṇas, he is born an ass. As an ass he lives for ten years. Then he is born a thief and lives as a thief for a year.

64. He with whom his parents are angry or he who is not attentive to the instructions of his teacher is born an ass.

65. As an ass he lives for two years. As a cat he lives for seven months, then he is born as a man.

66-67. If he reproaches his parents he is born as a female parrot. If he strikes his parents he is born as a porcupine. He lives in that form for three years. Then he is born as a snake. He lives in that form for six months. Then he is born as a man.

68. If he joins the king's service but is in league, he, the

deluded one is born a monkey. He remains a monkey for ten years, as a rat for seven years, as a dog for six months. Then he is born a man.

69-70. He who mis-appropriates a deposit goes to hell. Then passing through a series of births and deaths he is born a worm.

71-72. O Brāhmaṇas, he remains for fifteen years in that form. When the consequences of his evil deeds are exhausted he is born a man. If otherwise he is born a worm. O best of brāhmaṇas, he lives in that form for thirteen years.

73. When he is released from the results of his unrighteous deeds he is born a man.

74-77. If he fails to perform rites due to manes or deities, if he does not offer libations of water or balls of rice to the deities, he is born a crow. He remains in that form for one hundred years, then he becomes a cock. He is born as a snake and remains in that form for a month. He is born a man. He who disregards his elderly brother, who is no less respectable than his own father, is born a heron. He lives in that form for ten years. Then he is born a cakora bird, then a man. If a Śūdra approaches a Brāhmin woman he is born a worm.

78-80. Then he is born a boar. As soon as born he dies of a disease, O Brāhmins. As a result of his sinful acts he becomes a dog. When the fruits of his acts are exhausted he becomes a man. He generates progency from the womb of a woman. Then he is born a rat. O Brāhmaṇas, as an ungrateful wretch he goes to the region of Yama.

81. He is bound by the cruel agents of Yama who beat him with canes, clubs, tridents, fire-sticks.

82. He suffers from various sorts of pains in hell, coming in contact with leaves as sharp as swords, or in hell full of hot sands, or in hell where the wicked are tortured with sharp swords.

83-84. He undergoes sufferings and is born as a worm. He remains in that form for fifteen years. He then enters the womb but dies there.

85-93. He then undergoes a series of births and deaths. He then becomes an animal. Then he undergoes suffering for a number of years. Then he is born as a tortoise. By stealing curd he is born a crane or a frog; by stealing unroasted fish he is born a honey-bee. By stealing fruits, radish or sweet bread he is born an ant. By stealing corn he becomes a rat. By stealing rice boiled in milk he is born a partridge; by stealing powdered bread he is born an owl. By stealing water he is born a crow; by stealing copper he is born a pigeon. By stealing silver vessel he is born a dove. By stealing gold vessel he is born a worm. By stealing silk garment he is born an osprey. By stealing a silken upper garment he is born a parrot. By stealing a lower silken garment he is born a swan.

94-98. By stealing a cotton cloth he is born a heron. By stealing a woollen or a silken cloth he becomes a hare or a peacock. By stealing red cloth he is born a cakora. By stealing paints and perfumes, a greedy person is born a musk-deer. He lives in that form for fifteen years. After exhausting the fruits of his wicked actions he is born a man. By stealing milk he is born a crane. By stealing oil he is born a tailapāyī (?) (the drinker of oil).

99-104. If a person with weapon kills one with no weapons for monetary gains or out of enmity he is born an ass. He lives in that form for two years; he is then killed by weapons. He is born in the form of a deer and suffers from grief. He lives in that form for a year and is then killed. He then becomes a fish and is caught in the net. He is then born a tiger. In the form of a tiger he lives for ten years. Then after death, when the fruits of his karmas are exhausted and he is awakened intellectually he is born as a man.

105-114. By stealing musical instruments he is born hairy. By stealing food inclusive of oil-cake he is born a brown hairy rat biting people. By stealing butter he is born a crow or a low-class person. By stealing the flesh of a fish, he is born a crow. By stealing salt he is born a cricket. By denying or misappropriating deposit he is born a fish. Born a man, he commits sin after sin. Then after his death he is born an animal. He does not know what Dharma is nor about the right means of knowledge. He who commits sin after sin and discards vows is struck by grief and suffers from disease or is reduced to a naked state or degraded to a low caste. This is said of those who are of sinful character, greedy and passionate.

Those who do not commit sins since their very birth remain free from disease and are possessed of beauty and wealth.

115. Even women in association with the sinful men incur sins.

116-118. O best of Brāhmins, this in brief I have narrated to you. In another context, you will hear more. O revered ones, thus I have heard from the mouth of Brahmā when he was addressing the assembly of gods and sages. I put questions too, now and then. I too have narrated to you in entirety. O best of sages, you hear the same and be interested in Dharma.

CHAPTER ONE HUNDRED AND NINE

Gift of food the best of all charitable acts

The sages said :

1. O lord, you have addressed us on the course of adharma. now let us know about the course of dharma too.

2. Having done sinful deeds, how do people meet with disaster ? By what righteous activities do the people attain prosperity ?

Vyāsa said :

3. Having performed evil actions, having come under the control of adharma, with his mind averse to dharma, man goes to hell.

4. He who out of ignorance performs acts of impiety but repents afterwards with his mind concentrated on his self never comes to grief.

5. Inasmuch as his mind dislikes performing evil deeds, in the same proportion is his body released from the control of adharma.

6. O Brāhmaṇas, if he confesses his guilt before the pious Brāhmaṇas, he is soon released from the guilt accruing from adharma.

7. Inasmuch as he confesses his guilt with his mind concentrated on himself he is released from that guilt.

8. As a snake casts off his slough, so he casts off guilt incurred previously. By giving charitable gifts of all sorts and with his mind concentrated on his self he attains heaven.

9-10. O best of Brāhmins, I shall let you know about the gift by which a man attains piety, though he may have done evil deeds.

11. Of all the gifts, the gift of food is the best. The upright honest person who is eager to follow the path of piety should give all sorts of food in gift. Food is the breath of people. A person is born of food.

12. People abide in food. Food is praised therefore. Gods, sages and manes praise food itself.

13-17. By gifting food man goes to heaven. The best sort of food earned by just means should be given as gift to the educated Brāhmaṇas with mind full of joy.

If he invites ten Brāhmaṇas to eat at his house, though he feeds them once, with his joyous mind, he is never born as an animal. If he feeds ten thousand Brāhmaṇas, even a hard sinner, ever engaged in sinful acts is released from impiety. If a person proficient in the Vedas collects food by begging and gives it to a Brāhmaṇa who is engaged in studies, he obtains happiness.

18-27. If a Kṣatriya spares the wealth of Brāhmaṇas, guards the same as the rules of law permit, if he gives his surplus money and food to the people of three castes who have learnt Vedas, he is purified and released from the fruits of his evil deeds.

By giving to the twice-born a portion of the produce of cultivated field, after it has been taxed at the rate of production, a Vaiśya is released from sins.

By giving to the twice-born, the food earned at the risk of life, by emaciating his body, a Śūdra is released from sin.

He who earns food by the sweat of his brow, and that too without violating the right of others, never succumbs to trouble. If a person joyously gives food earned by him lawfully to a person well-versed in the Vedas, he is released from sin. By giving food which invigorates men, the person becomes invigorated. If he follows the path of the good he is released from sins.

The path is made by those who know the benefits of gifts. The wise go by that path. There too, those who gift food. There too those who follow tradition.

In all circumstances, the food that is earned by right means has eternal value. By giving such food a man attains the highest position. He is blessed with the fulfilment of all desires. Thus the person attended by merit is released from all sorts of sins.

28. Thus the food not attained by unlawful activities should be gifted. He should, first of all, pour offerings of food into the fire with the formula Prāṇāya Svāhā and then eat food.

29-30. A man should not render the day unproductive but should make gift of food. If a person feeds a hundred of topmost knowers of Veda, Nyāya, Dharma and Itihāsa, he does not go to a dreadful hell nor does he enter transmigration.

31. He attains the fulfilment of all desires and then after death he gets happiness. Thus performing good actions and devoid of fever he enjoys life. He is blessed with beauty, fame and wealth.

I have thus told you the fruit of gifting food as well as the basis of all these dharmas and donations.

CHAPTER ONE HUNDRED AND TEN

On the performance of Śrāddha and the associated legend

The sages said:

1. How should sons and relatives perform Śrāddha for the manes who have departed to the other world and who are abiding in the region assigned to them according to their actions ?

Vyāsa said :

2. I bow to Varāha, lord of the universe, creator of the people. Listen, I shall tell you all about Śrāddha, as was recorded afore.

3. In days of yore, the lord uplifted the manes who were drowned in the waters of Kokā river, by performing Śrāddha for their sake, O best of Brāhmaṇas.

The sages said :

4-5. Why were the fathers drowned in the waters of the Kokā river ? How were they uplifted by Varāha, O best of Brāhmins in that holy place of pilgrimage that grants fruits in the form of worldly enjoyment as well as release ?

We wish to hear about it. Tell us all in detail. It is a matter of great curiosity to us all.

Vyāsa said :

6. In the intervening period of Tretā and Dvāpara Yugas, the diverse human beings—the manes, stood in the company of Viśvedevas at the top of Meru mountain.

7. Once, they were sitting (as usual) there (at the top of Meru). A beautiful divine girl born of Soma appeared before them with hands joined in reverence. Among the manes who had assembled there, those shining with refulgence spoke to her.

The pitṛs said:

8. O auspicious lady ! Who are You ? Who is your lord ? Please tell us.

Vyāsa said:

9. She said to the refulgent manes. I am Kalā, born of the Moon, You are my lords whom I can choose, if you so desire.

10. My first name is Ūrjā; second is Svadhā; third is Kokā. This latter name you have given me this very day.

11. The manes, the divine beings heard her speak this. They fixed their eyes on her face but were not satisfied.

12. When Viśvedevas saw that they were gazing at the face of the girl and had fallen off Yoga, they left their company and went to heaven.

13. When the holy god Moon did not see his daughter Ūrjā, he was upset. Where she may have gone ? He thought to himself.

14. The Soma came to know the facts. He knew that manes were after her, that they were sexually inclined to her and had accepted her by the virtue of their penance.

15. The Moon was overcome with anger. He cursed the manes, "Fall off from your Yoga, be confounded".

16-17. Since you passionately desired my daughter, without my permission; since, she of her own accord accepted you as her husbands, disregardful of me, her father; since she transgressed the dictates of Dharma and acted independently, let her become a river by name Kokā and resort to Mount Himālaya.

18. Thus cursed by the Moon, the manes, the divine men were deprived of yoga and fell off at Mount Himavat.

19-20. Ūrjā fell off at the top of Himavat mountain, at the confluence of seven rivers. She was called Kokā. By flowing along with hundreds of rivers over the peak of the mountain she came to be known as Sarit.

21-23. Then those manes fallen off yoga assumed the forms of Brāhmins. They saw the river Kokā of cool water but they could not recognize her as the beautiful-eyed girl they once loved. Then the mount Himālaya observed that the manes who were cursed to assume the form of human beings were very hungry.

He arranged for their sustenance, the cow 'Badari' yielding sweet honey, milk, the sweet waters of Kokā river and the berry fruit.

24. O best of sages, the manes living on that sustenance passed ten thousand years as it were a single day.

25. Thus, when the world was deprived of the services of manes and of Svadhā, the asuras, yātudhānas and rākṣasas became powerful.

26. Then the asuras, yātudhānas and rākṣasas found that the manes were estranged from Devas and they fell upon them.

27. The Brahmins stationed on the bank of Kokā (who were formerly manes) saw asuras and yātudhānas pouncing upon them. The infuriated brahmins caught hold of a lofty slab.

28. The fast-flowing Kokā saw them holding the slab. She concealed the manes in her waters which overflowed Himālaya.

29-30. The asuras, yātudhānas and rākṣasas found that they were concealed. They ascended the peak Vibhītaka and disappeared. Meanwhile the manes felt hungry and thirsty. Distressed by hunger and thirst, the manes sang songs of praise in favour of Viṣṇu.

The manes said :

31. Victory to Govinda : O the abode of the universe, O Keśava, be pleased to favour us with Victory. O Janārdana of pure and spotless impression, uplift us from the cavity of waters.

32. O lord, Viṣṇu, O Boar, Vaikuṇṭha, Nārāyaṇa, lord of lords, lotus-navelled, worthy of praise, we are afraid of asuras, of dreadful sight; protect us, O lord, and grant us victory.

33. O Viṣṇu, the younger brother of lord Indra, O Yogin, the slayer of Madhu and Kaiṭabha demons, O Endless, of steady disposition, Vāsudeva, holding bow, discus, lotus and conch in your hands, O lord of Devas, protect us from rākṣasas.

34. O Śambhu, you are the father of universe, the dreadful asuras are unable to assail you. Hence, we come to your shelter.

35. As soon as your name is uttered, the asuras fly away, the evil-doers disappear, the enemies are destroyed. Dharma, Truth etc. attain eminence.

Vyāsa said :

36. Thus praised by the manes, the lord in the divine form of a boar, the sustainer of this Earth saw the manes, merged in the waters of Kokā carrying slabs over their head.

37. Lord Viṣṇu, in the form of a boar, saw the manes hidden in the waters of Kokā out of fear from the asuras and thought of uplifting them to the Earth.

38. The boar cast away the slab with the tip of his tusks and brought up the manes to the Earth.

39-40. The manes, when they came into contact with the boar (incarnate of Viṣṇu) looked splendid. Made fearless by Viṣṇu, they stood at Kokāmukha. Having uplifted them thus the lord poured libation of water for the manes at Lohārgala.

41-46. Then, with a handful of Kuśa grass produced from his hair and the Sesamum seed grown up from his sweat, Keśava made a fire-brand. He made a torch as bright as the light of the sun and a vessel. He stood under a wish-fulfilling, holy, tall, banyan tree. He took up the sacred waters of Gaṅgā and the juices of sacrificial herbs from the lofty peak of the mountain. He brought honey and milk and fragrant substances such as odorous flowers, perfumes and sweet-smelling unguents; he brought forth a cow from the lake and the gems from the ocean; he scratched the earth with his tusk and sprinkled and smeared the same with drops of perspiration, scratching it up again, encircling it with the fire-brand and sprinkling it up again and again. He took up a handful of Kuśa grass, with their tips pointed to the east while their ends were stuck into the pores of hair. He then invited the sages and asked their permission, saying "I shall like to pour libations of water to the manes".

47. They said : "You may" The Lord then invoked all gods and on their arrival gave them seats.

48. Adorned with discus and mace, he planned out their protection with the unbroken rice.

49. The unbroken rice and the barley seeds are born of parts of all-gods. These ward off calamities from all sites; they are produced for the sake of protection.

50. In this mobile and immobile world, none among Devas, Dānavas, Daityas, Yakṣas and Rākṣasas is able to effect their destruction.

51-52. As they are not broken by any, they are called akṣatas. Of yore, they were appointed by Viṣṇu to guard the people. The Boar incarnate of Viṣṇu, propitiated all of them with the holy Kuśa grass, incense and barley seeds. He poured libation of water to all goḍs and then said :

53. "I invoke the manes, both divine and mortals." When they agreed to be invoked, he invoked them.

54. He held a handful of sacred grass together with the

sesamum. He put his left hand on the left knee and gave each of them a seat.

55. Similarly, he put his right hand on the right knee and the sacred thread on the right side and invited them with the mantra 'āyāntu naḥ'.

56. Varāha recited the mantra 'apahatā' and warded off the asuras from the site. He then transferred his sacred thread to the right. Uttering the names and gotras he invoked the pitṛs by the personal and gotra names.

57. Varāha then uttered the mantras 'āpyāyayantu' and 'saṁvatsaraiḥ' and poured arghya to the Pitṛs who as a result of the curse had assumed the form of Brahmins.

58-59. He uttered the mantra 'yās tiṣṭhatyamṛtā vāco yanmā' and poured water mixed with Kuśa, incense, sesamum seed and flowers to the Pitṛs while he wore the sacred thread on the right side. He repeated the mantra 'yanmā' and poured water for the grand-father. Again, he repeated the mantra 'yanmā' and poured water for the great-grandfather.

60. Varāha (incarnate of Viṣṇu) repeated the same procedure for the maternal grandfather. He propitiated them again with incense etc. and offered them perfume with devotion.

61-63. The lord of the universe uttered the mantra 'Āditya Vasavo Rudrāḥ' He then held food and butter mixed with sesamum seeds and Kuśa grass and put the same in the vessels as previously. He then asked the permission of the sages, "shall I make offering in the fire". Permitted by them he made three offerings to the fire. One to Soma, one to Fire and one to Yama. He repeated the seven mantras of the Yajurveda beginning with "Ye māmakā".

64. The residue of the sacrificial material he offered thrice to each of the Pitṛs, by their personal and gotra names.

65. The residue of the material such as "food" he put into the vessel wherein the rice-ball was kept. Then, he gave the tasty food together with the rice boiled in milk.

66-70. He served Brāhmaṇas with fresh and tasty meals, with less vagetables, abundance of fruits, with six flavours, nectar-like. He put the same anointed with butter and sprinkled with honey in the rice-ball vessel meant for Pitṛs, preceded by Devas, by reciting the mantra beginning with Pṛthivī and the three ṛcas :Madhuvātā ṛtāyate etc. When the Brāhmaṇas started eating, he recited the five mantras beginning with the mantra 'yat te'. He also recited the three Madhu and three Suparṇa portions from the Bṛhadāraṇyaka, the mantra of solar deity and *Puruṣa Sūkta.* When the Brahmins had finished meals he asked them, "are you satiated".

71. On their reply, "we are satiated", he gave them water for breaking silence. He gave the rice-ball vessel to Chāyā.

72. He divided food into two parts. Then each into three parts. Varāha scratched the Earth and covered the same with the particles of Kuśa grass.

73-74. He turned the tips of Kuśa grass to the South, put the seat (āsana) on the Kuśa grass, for, the Pitṛs like to sit upon Kuśa grass uprooted from the very root and on which the sesamum seeds have been spread. He placed incense, flowers etc. over the rice-ball and recited the formula 'Pṛthivī dadhi' and gave the rice-balls to grandfather, great-grandfather, maternal grandfather.

75-76. The residue of the rice-ball material was offered to the paternal ancestor in the fourth, fifth and sixth degree. He repeated the formula 'Etad Vaḥ Pitar' with the mind full of devotion and offered fresh white pieces of cloth to the Brahmins. He gave them incense and flowers and circumambulated them.

77-79. He should sip water from the palm of his hand, also make the Brahmin pitṛs sip at first and then Devas too. He should sprinkle the place with water mixed with flowers and rice. He should give water mixed with the sesamum seeds to the Pitṛs at first, then to Devas mixed with rice. He should recite 'akṣayyam naḥ,' for the pitṛs and 'Prīyatām' to Devas.

80. Having pleased them thus, he should move aside, repeat aghamarṣaṇa thrice. Withdrawing himself, he should repeat 'yan me'.

81-82. O Pitṛs, give us residence abounding in grains and riches. Repeating the formula 'Ūrjaṁ Vahanti', he put the rice ball, the ring of Kuśa grass and rest of the material consisting of cold milk, honey and sesamum seeds into the Arghya vessel. Then he offered libation of water to the Pitṛs.

83-84. When the officiating Brāhmaṇas had said: "Welfare to you", and they felt gratified on the Amāvāsyā day, Varāha incarnate of Viṣṇu gave silver-fee (*rajata-dakṣiṇā*) to each of the Brāhmaṇas. When he asked "Is the rite completed", they said, "Yes". When he asked "may you be pleased", they said: "We are already pleased". When he asked them about the remaining food, they said, "You may partake of it together with your people".

85-86. He caught hold of the Brāhmaṇas by his hand and led them outside the ritual altar repeating the formula 'Vāje-Vāje'.

87. Then sprinkling the massive heap of hair with the collected waters of holy rivers he begged blessings of Brāhmaṇas.

88-91. The Brāhmaṇas blessed him, saying, "May our patrons prosper in riches". Varāha circumambulated them; touching their feet with reverence; he offered them seats to take rest. He held the middle ball of rice and gave the same to Chāyā. That beautiful lady took hold of the rice-ball and said : "May the Pitṛs enter the womb". She then bowed at the feet of the Brāhmaṇas. Then the boar-incarnate Viṣṇu thought of letting the Pitṛs go.

92-94. Then Kokā and Pitṛs spoke out their self-interest. We were formerly stationed in heaven when we were cursed by the Moon, "You fall off from Yoga and descend to the nether region". We were falling to the nether regions but are saved by you. Being fallen off from Yoga, we were deserted by the guardians. Now, may all-gods protect us again.

95. O lord Boar, by your favour, we shall go to heaven. Let Soma (the Moon-god), the observer of Yoga be our guardian.

96-99. May Soma, the source of Yoga, protect us. Through Yoga may we live in heaven as well as on earth. May some of us attain prosperity within a month, in the firmament. This Ūrjā known by her popular name Svadhā endowed with Yoga, be the mother of Yoga (roaming) in the middle region.

Thus requested by the manes lord Varāha addressed the river Kokā and the manes : Whatever you have asked will indeed be accomplished.

100. Let Yama be your deity; Moon the preceptor; Fire the priest.

101. Let Fire, wind and Sun be your abodes; Brahmā, Viṣṇu and Rudra be your guardians.

102. Let Āditiyas, Vasus and Rudras be your forms. Let Yogīs, embodying Yoga make yoga as your basis and observe vows.

103-105. Let you move at will bestowing fruits of actions upon the people at large. Let you elevate by the strength of your Yoga both the mobile and immobile stationed in heaven, hell and earth.

This Ūrjā, daughter of the Moon, fashioned by flesh and wine will be born as the daughter of Dakṣa, Svadhā by name. This good-faced lady will be your wife.

106. Known as Kokā, she will resort to Himālaya. She will be as efficacious as the crores of holy places all together.

107. I shall stay in Kokā from this very day, smashing sins of all mankind. The sight of lord Boar is holy. His worship grants worldly pleasures and salvation.

108. Drinking the water of Kokā destroys sins. The plunge yields merit. The fast leads to heaven.

109. Charity gives imperishable fruit; it destroys sins of birth, death and old age.

110-111. In the dark fortnight of the month of Māgha, on the Amāvasa night, when there is no moon, one should come to Kokāmukha and stay there for five nights. During the time, the person who offers libation of water to the pitṛs will reap the fruit of the same. There is no doubt in this. I shall be staying here on the eleventh and twelfth tithi always.

112. He who fasts here reaps the fruit thereof as mentioned previously. O blessed ones, you are now free to go to your places at your will.

113. "I too shall rest here", saying this lord Boar disappeared. When lord Boar had gone, the pitṛs took leave of Kokā and went away.

114-115. Kokā took up her abode on that mountain. Chāyā, the Earth conceived by lord Boar generated asura Naraka known also by the name Bhauma. Lord Viṣṇu gave him Prāgjyotiṣa, the capital city of Kāmarūpa.

116. Thus have I described at Kokāmukha the Boar incarnate of Viṣṇu who confers boons to the people. On hearing this description, a man is purified from dirt, becomes devoid of sins, and obtains the merit of performing Aśvamedha Sacrifice.

CHAPTER ONE HUNDRED AND ELEVEN

The details of the Śrāddha ritual

The sages said :

1-2. O sage, tell us further in detail about the ritual of Śrāddha. O ascetic, let us know how it was performed, at what place, when and by whom ?

Vyāsa said :

O great sages, hear in detail about the ritual of Śrāddha, how it was performed, where, when, in which nakṣatras or tithis, in what region and by whom ?

3. Brāhmaṇas and Vaiśyas should perform Śrāddha each following one's own dharma and reciting mantras.

4. Women and Śūdras too should perform the same under the direction of Brāhmaṇas. But there should be no recitation of mantras or ritual of sacrifice.

5-13. Śrāddha should be performed in holy places as Puṣkara, or meritorious spots, peaks of mountains or sacred regions, in streams of holy waters, rivers or lakes, in the confluence of rivers or in any one of seven oceans or in one's own home purified or smeared with cowdung or spots enjoined by the Śāstras, at the root of holy trees or in lakes worthy of sacrifice. One should hold Śrāddha at such places. Śrāddha is prohibited among Kirātas, Kaliṅgas, Koṅkaṇas, Kṛmis, Daśārṇas, Kumāryas, Taṅgalas, Krathas, on the northern bank of Sindhu, on the southern bank of Narmadā, to the east of Karatoyā. Śrāddha should be performed every month on the Amāvasa day. In Ṛkṣagocarya (?) Śrāddha should be performed on Pūrṇamāsī for the manes as well as Devas. Nitya Śrāddha is performed for gods. There are other Śrāddhas performed for the attainment of desired objects. O Brahmins, they should be done every year. Vṛddhi Śrāddha should be performed on such occasions.

14. When the sun enters zodiac Kanyā, there are fifteen days exclusively meant for Śrāddha.

15-33. Pratipat is for riches, Dvitīyā for progeny, Tṛtīyā for sons, Caturthī for destroying foes, Pañcamī for obtaining wealth, Saptamī for lordship, Aṣṭamī for intelligence, Navamī for conjugal relations, Daśamī for fulfilling desire, Ekādaśī for acquiring Vedic knowledge, Dvādaśī for victory, Trayodaśī for increase in progeny, animals, intellect, independence, prosperity, longevity and supremacy, Caturdaśī for those who died in youth or who were killed by weapons and Amāvāsyā for fulfilling all desires including the attainment of heaven as an abode for eternity. O best of sages, I shall now tell you the material for food which pleases the pitṛs and the period of propitiation.

If in the Śrāddha, the sacrificial food is offered to the Brahmins, the Pitṛs are fed for a month. If the flesh of a fish is offered, the Grandfathers are fed for two months. If a goat's flesh is offered, the Pitṛs are fed for three months. If a hare's flesh is offered, the Pitṛs are fed for four months. If a bird's flesh is offered, the Pitṛs are fed for five months. If a hog's flesh is offered, the Pitṛs are fed for six months. If a ram's flesh is offered the Pitṛs are fed for seven months. If black deer's flesh is offered the Pitṛs are fed for eight months. If ruru deer's nine months; if cow's for ten months; if ram's for eleven months. If cow's milk or rice cooked in cow's milk for one year; if of rhinoceros or of rohita fish for endless period of time. So also food for progeny. He who offers Śrāddha at Gayā with sesamum seeds mixed with sugar, honey or honey-mixture obtains endless stock of corn. The Pitṛs say : "May there be born one in our lineage who may give us oblation of water, rice cooked in milk and mixed with honey, during the rainy season, in Maghā nakṣatra." One should wish for many sons. If even one of them goes to Gayā or marries a girl of eight years or releases a blue-coloured bull or worships Pitṛs in Kṛttikās he obtains heaven.

34-42. One who performs Śrāddha in Rohiṇī gets progeny, in Saumya splendour, in Ārdrā valour, in Punarvasu fields for cultivation, in Puṣya eternal wealth, in Āśleṣā longevity, in

Maghā progeny and prosperity, in Phālgunī, good fortune, in Uttarā-s progeny and benevolence, in Hastā proficiency in Śāstras, in Citrā beauty, splendour and progeny. Śrāddha performed in Svātī bestows gains in merchandise, in Viśākhā gives sons, in Anurādhā sovereignty, in Jyeṣṭhā Lordship, in Mūla good health, in Āṣāḍhā attainment of fame, especially in Uttarās, in Śravaṇa fulfilment of auspicious desires, in Dhaniṣṭhā abundant riches, in Abhijit the knowledge of the Vedas, in Vāruṇa efficiency in medicine, in Prauṣṭhapadī skill in goats and sheep, in Uttara Bhādrapada cows, in Revatī a vessel of brass, in Aśvinī horses, in Bharaṇī longevity. The performer of Śrāddha obtains the result in these nakṣatras. O Brahmins, thus are the Śrāddhas performed for the attainment of particular desire.

43. When the sun has entered the Kanyā Zodiac, the performer of Śrāddha in that period obtains whatever desire he has in his mind. Nāndīmukha should be performed during the same period. It should be done in Pūrṇimā as stated in Varāha Purāṇa.

44-47. When the sun entered the Kanyā zodiac, the Pitṛs mobile or immobile, living in heaven, earth or firmament, wish for the rice-ball. The first sixteen days of the month, when the sun has entered Kanyā, one should propitiate Pitṛs with the libation of water, vegetable and roots. He gets the rare fruit desirable from the performance of Rājasūya and Aśvamedha sacrifices.

48-56. If a person propitiates Pitṛs, when the sun has entered Uttarā or Hastā, he goes to heaven.

When the sun enters Hastā asterism, Pitṛs leave home at the command of Yama. They remain out till the sun enters the sign Scorpion of the Zodiac.

When the sun has passed through Scorpion, Pitṛs return to their abode, together with Devas, sobbing and cursing their progeny.

In the ages of Manu, the Śrāddha should be performed in Aṣṭakas and Anvaṣṭakas. It should start serially beginning with the Mother. During the period of eclipse, in Vyatīpāta at the confluence of the Sun and the Moon, on the day of natal star, during the oppression caused by the planet, he should perform Pārvaṇa Śrāddha.

During the interval between the solstices, on the day of equinox or at the sun's equinoctial passage, Śrāddha should be performed without offering the rice-ball. On the third of Vaiśākha, on the ninth of Kārttika, on the Pūrṇimā day, the Śrāddha should be performed as at the equinoctial passage.

On the thirteenth day of the Bhādrapada month, on the amāvāsyā day of the month of Māgha, one should do Śrāddha by means of rice cooked with milk in the manner it is performed at the winter solstice.

57. When a Brahmin versed in the Vedas and the fire-rituals comes to the house, he alone should be considered as worthy of Śrāddha.

58. When the material for Śrāddha approved by the experts is available, he should perform Pārvaṇa Śrāddha with the help of Brahmins well versed in the Śrāddha.

59. One should celebrate the anniversary of one's departed parents, also of the uncle and elder brother if they died sonless.

60-62. In Pārvaṇa offerings should begin with Devas. In Ekoddiṣṭa no offerings should be made to Devas. In Śrāddha pertaining to Devas, he should offer two Piṇḍas, in that pertaining to Pitṛs three or a single piṇḍa should be offered to each. Similarly, in regard to maternal grandfather.

When a person is dead his son should offer rice-ball with libation of water with Kuśa grass and sesamum seeds outside the village on the bank of a river or a pond. On the third day, they should collect the bones.

63. If the deceased is a Brāhmaṇa, the purification of relatives of the same gotra is effected after ten days, if Kṣatriya, after twelve days, if Vaiśya after fifteen days, if Śūdra after a month.

64. After purification, they enjoin Ekoddiṣṭa, on the twelfth day, or after the expiry of a month or at the end of three fortnights.

65. O Brahmins, Śrāddha should be performed every month, for a year. Then he should perform sapiṇḍīkaraṇa rite after a year. When that is done, he should perform Pārvaṇa. The deceased then change their states as Preta to that of Pitṛs.

66. Pitṛs are twofold : mūrta and amūrta. Nāndīmukhas are amūrta and Pārvaṇas are mūrta. Pretas receive Ekoddiṣṭa, Pitṛs receive Pārvaṇa Śrāddha.

CHAPTER ONE HUNDRED AND TWELVE

The details of Sapiṇḍikaraṇa Rite

The sages said :

1-3. How should the rite of Sapiṇḍīkaraṇa for the dead be performed, O best of Brahmins, according to the Śāstras? O best of speakers, let us know all.

Vyāsa said :

O Brahmins, listen, I shall tell you how the rite of Sapiṇḍīkaraṇa should be performed. Herein no offering is made to Devas. A single libation of water is enjoined. One ring of Kuśa grass is sanctioned. No offering in the fire. No invocation. A single brahmin is fed in that rite.

4. This rite is to be performed, every month, for a year. Listen attentively. I shall tell you what is additional to this rite.

5. There should be four vessels, three for the Pitṛs, mixed with sesamum seeds, incense and water and one for the Preta.

6. In each of the three vessels some water from the Preta pātra should be poured. In each case, he should recite the mantra "Ye samānā".

7. In regard to women also, the same procedure should be adopted. But sapiṇḍīkaraṇa need not be performed if the deceased woman had no sons.

8. In case of women sapiṇḍīkaraṇa should be done every year by men. The rite should be performed on their death anniversary, as enjoined by the śāstras.

9. If there be no son, this should be performed by the relatives connected by the offering of rice balls. If there be no such relatives, brothers should do the same. If there be no brothers, grandsons or great-grandsons should perform the sacrifice.

10. The daughter's son should perform the rite for his maternal grand-father. They are named dvyāmuṣyāyaṇa (for they are linked to both : the maternal grandfather and the paternal grandfather).

11. They should propitiate both, by Nitya and Naimittika Śrāddhas. If none of the aforesaid is there, the women should perform the rite but without mantras.

12-13. If there are no women too, the king should get the funeral rite done by his distant relatives or in their absence, he should do the same by himself, because the king himself is the relative of all. O Brahmins, thus I have told you Nitya and Naimittika rites.

14. I shall now tell you other sorts of Nitya and Naimittika rites. Darśa Śrāddha, performed on the Amāvasa day is Naimittika, for it is linked with the diminution of the moon.

15-32. Nitya is the fixed period of time, when one should do this rite as prescribed by Dharma.

After the rite of Sapiṇḍīkaraṇa has been performed, the great-grandfather of the father forfeits the right of receiving piṇḍa. He can receive only the residue of the piṇḍa. This fourth one loses importance in relationship. Hence his share in the rice-ball is reduced to residue.

The trio, father, grandfather, great-grandfather, are the rightful recepients of the rice-ball. Further, the three beginning from the grandfather of the grandfather are the sharers in the residue of the rice-ball. The seventh is the performer of sacrifice himself. Thus the relationship link is sevenfold as told by the sages.

After yajamāna (the performer of the ritual) the Pitṛs cease to have the right of partaking piṇḍa. Even distant relatives whether placed in hell or born in low species or transformed into evil spirits, imps, devils and the like become well fed with the leavings of food scattered on the ground. O Brahmins, the water dropped from the edge of bathing costume quenches the thirst and allays the hunger of those who are transformed into trees. Those who have reached divinity receive nourishment from the fragrant drops of water fallen from the rice-ball. Similarly, those who are born into animal creation receive nourishment by drinking drops of water fallen from the rice-balls.

The infants who are dead before teething, the youths who are forbidden to perform ritual and have died without any rite get their hunger and thirst allayed by the water used in wiping floors or used in cleansing the feet of brāhmaṇas.

Whatever particles of water or leavings of food, pure or impure, are dropped by yajamāna or the brahmins, by that the departed spirits, whatever form of existence they have attained, get nourishment. By the Śrāddha performed with the riches acquired through unfair means, the low class of people—caṇḍālas etc. get nourishment. Thus, one should perform Śrāddha for the departed in the family, even by means of vegetables (in the absence of other materials) as prescribed in the Śāstras. By the drops of water and bits of food, dropped from the rice-ball, he alleviates thirst and hunger, not only of his close relatives but also of distant kins born in different species of existence.

33-35. By performing Śrāddha no one comes to grief in the family. Only those of the Brahmins should be invited at Śrāddha who possess self-control, who are accustomed to agnihotra, who are pure in deeds, who are learned in Śāstras as well as in the Vedas. The invitee should be the one who thrice kindles the Naciketā fire, who knows the three verses beginning with Madhu or Suparṇa, who knows six ancillaries of the Veda, who is devoted to his parents, who has sisters, knows Sāman. The performer of Śrāddha should feed the priest who officiates at the sacrifice, the family priest, the spiritual guide or a teacher.

36-37. The following should be invited to dine at Śrāddha —the maternal uncle, father-in-law, brother-in-law, a relative, the family teacher or the teacher in society, one who is expert in interpreting the Purāṇas, not greedy or with a little greed, not accustomed to charity. Brahmins with these qualities should be invited at Śrāddha. They are purifiers of society.

38. The list of Brahmins as mentioned above should be invited a day before Śrāddha. Whether the rite pertains to gods or manes, he should appoint them accordingly.

39-41. The invitees to the Śrāddha should control their sense-organs. If the person performs Śrāddha and then after taking meals copulates with woman, his deceased ancestors sleep in that semen for a month. Again, if a person copulates with the woman, then partakes of Śrāddha, his deceased ancesters live upon semen and urine for that month. Hence, the performer of Śrāddha should invite the Brāhmaṇas on the day of Śrāddha or a day before. Those who are addicted to women should be excluded.

42-43. If, on the day of Śrāddha, the yatis of controlled mind come for alms, he of controlled mind should propitiate them with respectful homage and then feed them liberally.

44-68. The pitṛs have yoga as their base. The yogīs should always be honoured therefore.

If among a thousand brāhmaṇas, there be a single yogī, he alone can take Yajamāna and the invitees across the ocean of existence, as a boat in the river.

Those versed in the Vedic lore recite a verse in the context, which was formerly sung in the assembly of king Aila.

"When in our family will there be born a son to one of the members who will give us rice-balls, when the yogīs have taken meals? We desire in Gaya, a rice-ball, flesh of rhinoceros, oblation, Kāla-śaka (?) butter mixed with sesamum seed or Kṛsara (?) pertaining to Viśvadeva and Samya. We desire the flesh of rhinoceros from the feet to the head."

One should give Śrāddha on Trayodaśī in Māgha according to the prescription of the Śāstras in the winter solstice. He should offer rice cooked in milk as also honey and butter. Therefore, the performer should propitiate the Pitṛs, out of devotion. Satiated with Śrāddha, the Pitṛs will fulfil all desires of the performer, bring freedom from sins and set Vasus, Rudras, Ādityas, constellations, planets and stars to favourable desposition.

Propitiated with Śrāddha, the Pitṛs confer longevity, progeny, riches, knowledge, happiness, sovereignty, heaven and Mokṣa.

Pitṛs prefer noon to forenoon. When the brāhmaṇas reach the house, he should welcome them, honour them. While he is wearing kuśa-ring, he should give them water to sip and ask them to sit comfortably on the seat. He should perform Śrāddha accordingly to Śāstraic injunctions and let the best of Brāhmaṇas feed on sweet dishes and then dismiss them with sweet words and obeisance devotedly. He should follow them to the gate and return with their permission. Then he should perform his daily routine and then let his guests take meals. Some pandits hold that the rites to the Pitṛs should be performed everyday. 'Not so to the pitṛs', say others. Other rites should be performed as usual. He should take meals in the company of his family. Thus he should perform śrāddha attentively, as prescribed in the Dharmaśāstra, in the manner as it pleases the learned Brahmins.

Now I shall tell you the sort of people who are forbidden to receive Śrāddha: one who deceives friend, one who has diseased nails, one who is impotent, one who is suffering from tuberculosis, one who is suffering from jaundice, one who lives by trade, one who has dark-brown teeth, bald-headed, one-eyed, blind, deaf, dull, dumb, lame, cripple, eunuch, of bad skin, deformed, leper, red-eyed, hump-backed, pigmy, ugly, indolent, friend's enemy, of bad family, a herdsman, despised, one who has married before his elder brother, an unmarried elder brother whose younger brother is married, the son of Parivedanikā, son of a woman whose husband has married before his elder brother, the husband of a śūdra woman and their son too, one who has officiated at the religious ceremony of the Śūdra's son, one who has not married, one who has married the widow of his brother, one who is salaried teacher or one who is taught by a salaried teacher, one who partakes of food from the family in pollution, one who is a hunter, one who trades in soma, one who is under curse, a thief, a fallen one, a usurer, a rogue, backbiter, one who has abandoned the injunctions of Veda, one disinclined to charity, sacrifice, the king's priest, the king's servant, devoid of knowledge, jealous, ill-disposed to the elderly people, one who is short-tempered, harsh, stupid, an attendant upon an idol, an astronomer, maker of an arrow or the wearer of a foreign dress, one who officiates as a priest at the sacrifice of a person who is not worthy of holding sacrifice. Those of low class should not be invited to Śrāddha since they defile the social circle.

69. Where the wicked are honoured and the good are dishonoured, the terrible divine punishment befalls the people immediately.

70. Contrary to the Śāstraic injunction and in violation of the customary laws, if the performer of Śrāddha feeds a stupid person, he comes to grief.

If the holder of Śrāddha excludes the family brahmin and feeds another he is consumed by the fire of his grief.

71. If the holder of Śrāddha does not gift clothes, his performance of Yajña and penance, and his knowledge of Veda are of no avail. Therefore, he should give clothes especially on the occasion of Śrāddha.

72. He who gives fresh garments, made of silk or cotton, obtains the fulfilment of his desire.

73-74. Just as a calf finds out its mother from among several cows, similarly, the Pitṛs obtain food from the bellies of the brahmins who have partaken of Śrāddha meals.

75. The Pitṛs receive food offered to the brahmins who utter the Pitṛ's name, gotra and mantras. Although they are not present in physical forms they get satiated thereby.

76. Homage to Deities, Pitṛs and Yogins. Homage to Svāhā, Svadhā for ever and for ever.

77. At the beginning and the end of Śrāddha, he should repeat the same thrice. At the offering of the rice-ball as well, he should recite this attentively.

78. Pitṛs come very soon. Rākṣasas fly away. They get propitiated in the three worlds. This mantra, indeed uplifts them.

79. He should gift a fresh thread, silken, hempen, cotton, one made of patrorṇa, patka or kauśeya. Variety should be avoided.

80. The wise man should avoid that piece of cloth which in spite of its being full has no fringe. The aforesaid variety does not propitiate the Pitṛs and the donor too comes to grief.

81. Piṇḍa is not to be given to one who is alive. He should be fed with the meals of his taste according to Śāstraic injunctions.

82. With faith and devotion he should offer ball into the fire. If he is in need of progeny, he should give it to his wife, reciting the mantras.

83. If he wishes for brilliant splendour, he should offer it to the cows. If he wishes for wisdom, fame and renown he should offer the same into waters.

84. If he wishes for longevity he should give it to the

crows. If he wishes for children, or a house, he should give it to the cocks.

85. Again, some brahmins opine that Piṇḍa should be lifted by the front. He should do so when the Brahmins have said: "Now, lift it up please".

86. Therefore, Śrāddha should be performed as the sages of yore have stated. Otherwise, he incurs sin, and the Pitṛs do not receive the essence thereof.

87-88. The following should be given in Śrāddha: barley, rice, sesamum seeds, beans, wheat, chick pea, kidney bean, śyāmaka variety of corn, mustard, wild rice, hasti-śyāmaka, priyaṅgu, prasātika (a kind of rice) along with the grains.

89-91 The mango-fruit, hog plum, bilva, pomegranate, bījapūraka, old myrobalan, milk, fruits of coconut, parūsaka, vatsaka trees, dates, grape, wood apple of blue colour, a fruit of patola tree, vine, fruit of jujube tree, berry, vaikaṅkata, orange, bījapūra—these fruits should necessarily be given in Śrāddha.

92-99. Treacle, sugar, juice of the sugar-cane, juice of other plants, mūrmuras, cow's milk, curd, butter, oil squeezed from sesamum seeds, salt produced from ocean or lake should be offered in Śrāddha. He should offer essence of fragrant substances, sandal paste, aloe, suffron, Kālaśāka, Taṇḍulīya, Vāstuka, Mūlaka, wild vegetables, and the following flowers: jasmine, Campaka, Lodhra, Mallikā Bāṇa (Blue flower), Barbarī, Vṛntakāśoka, Tulasī, Tilaka, Pāvantī, Śatapatrā, fragrant Śephālikā, Kubjaka, Tagara, Mṛga, wild Ketakī, Yuthikā, Atimuktā. O Brahmins, these flowers are worth offering in Śrāddha. Moreover, day-lotus, night-lotus, white lotus, blue lotus, red water-lily, white water-lily, Kostus (Kuṣṭa) Māṁsī, Bālaka, Kukkuṭī, Jātipatraka, Nalikā Uśīra, Mustā and Granthiparṇī—these and other fragrant substances are worthy of Śrāddha.

100. Guggulu, sandal paste, Śrīvāsa, Aguru, and such other instances as are available.

101. Beans, Caṇakas, Masuras, Koradūṣakas, Vipruṣas, Markaṭas, Kodravas should be avoided.

102. He should avoid milk, curd, ghee produced from Mahiṣa, Camara, Mṛga, Avikā, Ekaśaphā (an animal whose hoof is not cloven) (as a horse, ass etc.), the breasts of women, camel.

103. Tāla, Varuṇa, Kākola, Bahupatra, Arjunīphala, Jambīra, red Bilva, and the fruit of Śāla should be avoided.

104-110 He should avoid fish, boar, tortoise and cows especially. Pūtika, musk, Gorocanā, lotus-paste, Kāleyaka, Ugragandha, Turuṣka, Pālaṅka, Kumārī, Kirāta, Piṇḍamūlaka, Gṛñjana, Cukrikā, Cukra, Varumā, Canapatrikā, Jīva, Śatapuṣpā, Nālikā, Gandha-Śūkara, Halabhṛtya, Sarṣapa, Palāṇḍu, Laśuna, Mānaskanda, Viṣaskanda, Vajrakanda, Gadāsthika, Puruṣālva, Sapiṇḍālu—these should not be used.

He should also leave Alābu, Tiktaparṇī, Kuṣmāṇḍa, three sorts of Kaṭukas, Vārtāka, Śivajāta and the hairy Vaṭas, Kālīya, Crane of red colour.

Similarly, the fruit of Vibhītaka, Āranāla, partially broken conch shell and stale food.

111-131. Things of bad odour should not be given in Śrāddha. Similarly, Kovidāra, Śigruka, that which is sour, picchila, rūkṣa, vātayāma should not be given. Similarly, that which is devoid of taste or emits smell of wine should be cast off. Hiṅgu of bitter smell, Phaṇiśa, Bhūnimba, Nimba and Rājikā, Kustumburu growing in Kaliṅga, sour Vetasa, pomegranate, Māgadhī, Nāgara, Ārdraka, Tittiḍī, Āmrātaka, Jīvaka, Tumburu—these are not prohibited. Similarly, rice cooked in milk, Śālmalī, Mudga and sweet balls should be included. Drinks made of mango juice and cow's milk should be included. So also those which are in common use, sweet and oily, though a little sour and bitter. Those which are extremely sour, bitter and tasteful to Devas should be used in Śrāddha. The meat of goat, quail, partridge, hare, jackal, Lāvaka or Rājīva fish should be used.

Besides, the flesh of rhinoceros, red jackal, a fish having scale, a fish named Siṁhatuṇḍa, osprey should be used in Śrāddha. Though Manu has allowed the flesh of Rohita, it should not be used. This is my considered opinion which is supported by Varāha. If he feeds on things prohibited in Śrāddha, he will go to Raurava hell. O ascetics, Varāha has prohibited the following which are forbidden to the twice-born. They should not be offered to the Pitṛs :

Rohita fish, pig, tortoise, iguava, swan, the Cakra bird, Madgu (diver bird), fish without scale, osprey, snakes, Vāsahāri, Kukkuṭa, Kalaviṅka, Mayūra, Bhāradvāja, Śārṅgaka, Nakula,

Ulūka, Mārjāra, Lopas, others which are not easily available, Ṭiṭṭibha bird, jackals, tiger, bear, hyena—if a stupid person eats the flesh of these and other prohibited animals or birds, he having incurred a great sin goes to the Raurava hell. If that sinner includes the prohibited flesh in Śrāddha, he will let his Pitṛs, though stationed in heaven, fall into hell.

If he eats Kusumbha-śāka (vegetable mixed with safflower), Jambīra, Śigruka, Kovidāra, Piṇyāka, Vipruṣa, Masūra, Gṛñjana, Śaṇa, Kodrava, Kokilākṣa, Cukra, Kambuka, Padmaka, Cakora, flesh of Śyena, Vartula, Alābu, Tālinī and the fruit of tall trees, he goes to hell. If he gives these to the Pitṛs, he falls along with them in Pūyavaha. Therefore by all means, a wise person should not partake of them.

132-135. Varāha has said that they should not be offered to the Pitṛs. Better feed upon one's own flesh rather than partake of the forbidden meat.

If out of ignorance or negligence, one has eaten the forbidden things, he should perform the rite of expiation or atonement.

If he eats what is prohibited he should, for the atonement thereof, feed upon fruits, roots, curd, milk, buttermilk mixed with water, cows' urine, yāvaka—one each day for a week.

136-143. Thus should transgression be corrected, especially by the devotees of Viṣṇu. O ascetics, the forbidden things as mentioned above should be excluded. The material necessary for Śrāddha should be collected according to the capacity of the performer. Thus, if the person performs Śrāddha according to the prescribed rules and his resou ces, he will remain happy so long as he lives upon this earth.

The sages said :

If the father is alive, grandfather and great-grandfather are dead, how will he perform Śrāddha? Please tell us in detail.

Vyāsa said :

The son should offer Śrāddha to the departed who could duly receive the same from his father. There is no infringement of duty—secular or Vedic in regard to that.

The sages said :

If the father is dead but the grandfather is alive, how will he perform Śrāddha? You will kindly explain.

Vyāsa said :

He should offer Piṇḍa to the father and feed the grandfather who is alive. This is the judgement of Śāstras.

The Piṇḍa should be given to the dead, food should be given to the alive. He should not perform Sapiṇḍīkaraṇa or Pārvaṇa in that case. If the son performs Pitṛmedha, he is blessed with sons, riches and longevity.

144. He who recites this section on Pitṛmedha at the time of Śrāddha, O Brahmins, his Pitṛs feed upon his food for a number of years lasting for three yugas.

145. Thus I have told you the section on Pitṛmedha which destroys sins and increases merit. Men with controlled mind should hear it attentively and recite the same during the period when the Śrāddha is being performed.

CHAPTER ONE HUNDRED AND THIRTEEN

Conduct of the Good

Vyāsa said:

1. Thus the Deities and Manes are to be duly worshipped by the householder by means of the Havya and Kavya offerings. The guests and kinsmen should be honoured with cooked rice.

2. The living beings, the servants, animals, birds and even ants; the mendicants who beg for alms and all other travellers who come to the house are to be received hospitably.

3. Brahmins observing the disciplined conduct of life of the good should be honoured by the good householder.

The sages said :

4-5. O brahmin, the Nitya and Naimittika rites have been

recounted by you. Human activities are three-fold: Nitya, Naimittika and Kāmya. O sage, even as you recount we wish to hear the rules of good conduct by pursuing which a man attains happiness here and hereafter.

Vyāsa said:

6. Good conduct should always be preserved by a householder. There is no welfare here or hereafter to one who is devoid of good conduct.

7. Sacrifices, charitable gifts and austerities are not conducive to the prosperity of the person who transgresses the rules of good conduct.

8. A person who maintains good conduct attains the longevity of Brahmā (?) Virtue and good conduct should always be maintained. Virtue is the symbol of good conduct.

9-10. O brahmins, I shall recount the form and general outline of good conduct. One shall maintain it with great concentration. Endeavour should be made by a householder in achieving the three-fold aim of life. The achievement of the householder here and hereafter depends on the realisation thereof.

11-12. With one-fourth of one's wealth the self-possessed man shall achieve the other-worldly welfare. With half of his wealth he shall sustain himself as well as perform the Nitya and Naimittika rites. With the remaining one-fourth one shall increase one's original capital. O brahmins, if one pursues thus, one's wealth becomes fruitful.

13-16. Similarly, for the sake of dispelling sins, virtuous rites should be performed by a learned man. Thus the other Dharma which has the fruit of welfare in the next world should be made fruitful here itself. The three (Dharma, Artha and Kāma) are of two types each. One type causes sinful offence; the other type is not antagonistic. One shall think about these as mutually complementary. O excellant brahmins, know them to be conducive to the contrary result. (For example) the wealth that is conducive to virtue is intrinsically virtuous. That which does not afflict the soul is virtue. Kāma (Desire) is split into two (?) by the other two : Dharma and Artha; and the other two are split into two by it (i.e. Kāma).

17-18. One shall get up in the Brāhma Muhūrta and think about virtue and wealth. After getting up, one shall perform the Ācamana rite. After taking both and making himself pure one shall worship the Sandhyās. The early Sandhyā (i.e. dawn) he shall worship even when the stars are seen. He shall worship the late Sandhyā (i.e. dusk) even when the sun is visible. He shall perform Sandhyā prayers duly. Unless in extreme case of emergency he shall not forsake it.

19. O brahmins, one shall avoid evil utterances, falsehoods and harsh words. He shall eschew ignoble scriptures, evil arguments and service of ignoble persons.

20. One shall perform Homa both in the evening and in the morning, with perfect restraint over the self. He shall not see sunrise and sunset directly.

21. The following activities should be performed in the forenoon :—Washing the teeth, applying collyrium, embellishing the hair, looking into the mirror and the Tarpaṇa rite to the deities.

22. Faeces should not be discharged on the path leading to the rural residences, holy centres and fields, nor in a ploughed field, nor in a cowpen.

23. One shall not look at the naked wife of another man; one shall not look at one's own ordure. (One shall avoid) seeing, touching and talking to a women in her menses.

24. One shall not discharge urine or faeces into the waters (of a tank etc.). Nor should one indulge in sexual intercourse under water. One shall not stand on faeces and urine nor on hairs or ashes. One shall not stand over the sharp edge of any cutting instrument.

25. An intelligent man shall not stand on scattered husk, burning coal, bits of ropes, clothes etc. on the road or in a ground.

26. After performing the rite of worship of the Pitṛs, Devas, human beings and other living beings, the householder deserves to take food in accordance with his affluence.

27. After performing the Ācamana rite, after restricting unnecessary talk, the man shall remain pure. He shall sit facing the East or the North and take food with the mind therein. He shall keep the hands between the knees.

28. Except in the case of utter destruction of food, the wise man shall not complain about the defects of food at the time of taking it. One shall avoid taking salt directly (i.e. salt should be mixed with food and then taken in). He shall avoid the leavings of food also.

29-31. The self-possessed man shall not discharge urine or faeces, while standing or walking. He shall not eat anything defiled by the leavings of food. If one is defiled by the leavings of food, one shall not speak anything. He shall avoid reciting the Vedas too. One shall not look at the sun, moon or the stars as one pleases. One should avoid using a seat, bed or a vessel if it is broken. One should honour and greet elderly persons by standing up and offering them seats.

32. An intelligent man shall talk in a way favourable to them (i.e. elderly persons). He shall follow them. He shall not act against them.

33-34. No intelligent man shall take food, worship the deities or invoke them with a single cloth on. O brahmins, no intelligent man shall perform a sacrifice, if there is no fire. No man shall take bath or lie down completely naked. One shall not scratch head simultaneously with both hands.

35. Head-bath should not be repeatedly undertaken by the intelligent men without cause. One who has already had head-bath should not touch any limb with oil.

36. One shall avoid studying the Vedas during the holidays. One shall never disregard or insult brahmins, fires, cows and the sun.

37. One shall discharge faeces and urine facing the north during the day and facing the south during the night. During distress he shall discharge them as he pleases.

38. One shall not speak out the misdeeds of the preceptor. If he is angry, one shall propitiate him. One shall not listen to others who slander him.

39-41. Priority in access to the path shall be given to the brahmins, to the king, to one who is miserable, to one of superior learning, to a pregnant woman, to one who is afflicted by sickness, to a greater person, to the deaf, mute or blind, to one who is elated and to one who has become mad.

A learned man shall circumambulate a temple, a tree in a monastery, cross-roads, and the preceptor who is of superior learning. One shall never wear shoes, clothes, garlands etc. worn by others.

42. One shall avoid taking oil bath or indulging in sexual intercourse with women on the eighth, fourteenth and fifteenth lunations as well as on Parvan days.

43. No wise man shall ever stand with arms and upper leg (?) raised up. One shall not throw up the feet. One shall not keep one leg over another.

44. One shall avoid reviling, wounding the sensitive spots of and slandering an unchaste woman or a boy who has indulged in an unworthy act (?) or a fallen fellow.

45-46. A clever man shall never be arrogant, proud and harsh. One shall not laugh at or find fault with a fool, a mad fellow, a person in distress, ugly persons, persons with deficient limbs or poor people. One shall not lift up another man's stick to chastise a disciple or a son.

47. A wise man should not drag a seat with his leg and sit thereon. One shall not prepare a cake of wheat flour or a dish of rice and peas mixed together or meat solely for oneself.

48-52. Food should be taken in the evening and in the morning after worshipping the guests.

O brahmins, one shall always clean the teeth sitting silently facing the east or the north. One shall avoid the forbidden creeper. No man shall ever sleep with his head placed towards the north or the west. One shall place one's head towards the south or the east.

One should never take one's bath in scented water, especially in the morning. If at all, one has to take one's bath at other times during the day it should be only during the eclipse. The limbs should not be wiped off with the edges of cloths or with one's hands.

One shall never shake tresses or the clothes. No learned man shall ever apply unguents before taking bath.

53. One shall never wear a red, or a black cloth nor one of variegated colour. No one shall exchange clothes or ornaments (with others).

54. A cloth should be abandoned if it is excessively worn out and the threads come off, if it is defiled by worms and hairs or if it is touched by dogs.

55. One shall avoid the following types of meat : if it is licked by a dog; if it is defiled after the essence has been taken away; the meat of the back; or the forbidden meat.

56. A man shall never take in salt directly. O brahmins, a foodstuff that has been left over for a long time, that has become dry or that has become stale should be eschewed.

57. O excellent brahmins, the resultant products of sugarcane juice, milk, vegetable and flour as well as the products of gravy need not be abandoned even if they are left over for a long time.

58-59. One shall avoid lying down at the times of sunrise and sunset. A man shall never take food : if he has not taken his bath; if he is sleeping; if his mind dwells on other things; if he is seated on the bed or on the bare ground or if he has not given a part of it to his servants. While taking food he shall not make sounds.

60-63. One shall take food only after taking bath in the morning as well as in the evening.

Other men's wives should not be carnally approached by a learned man. Sexual intercourse with other men's wives destroys the merits of Iṣṭāpūrta and also longevity. A thing so destructive of the span of life of a man does not exist in the world, so destructive as the outraging of the modesty of other men's wives.

It is only after duly performing the rite of Ācamana that one should perform the holy rites of Devas, Pitṛs and fire-god. The obeisance to the preceptor as well as the routine of taking food shall be performed only after the Ācamana rite. The water used for the Ācamana rite should be clear. It should be devoid of smell and foam. No sound should be made at that time. It should be eagerly performed.

64-68. One shall sit facing the east or the north and then perform the rite of Ācamana. Before that rite one shall wash his hands and feet after applying clay. The clay taken for this purpose shall not be any of these five : Clay taken from under the water; that taken from residential localities; that taken from the ant-hill; the clay from the rats' den and the clay that remains after performing the purificatory rites. One shall avoid these five types of clay. With great concentration and keeping the hands between knees, one shall perform the Ācamana rite three or four times. After wiping off the limbs and whirling the water round the head, and after performing the Ācamana rite perfectly, the pure man shall perform the other holy rites. One shall perform the Ācamana rite after sneezing, licking, breaking the wind, spitting etc. After touching what should not be touched, (and as an expiation thereof) one shall look at the sun or touch the right ear.

69. These rites are in accordance with their availability. If the previous one is not available the later one is sought; when the previous is present the later is not used.

70. One shall not grind one's teeth, nor beat one's own body. While sleeping, meditating or taking food, one shall eschew the self-study of the Vedas.

71-72. One shall avoid sexual intercourse and journey during Sandhyā (Dusk). One shall perform Tarpaṇa rite unto the Pitṛs with full faith, in the early afternoon. The head bath and the holy rites unto Devas and Pitṛs also shall be done in the afternoon. One shall get the shaving done facing the east or the north.

73. For matrimony one shall avoid a girl with crippled limbs or one wanting a limb even if she is free from ailments or born of a noble family. One shall marry a girl removed by (not less than) seven generations on his father's side and (not less than) five generations on his mother's side.

74. One shall protect one's wife. One shall avoid jealousy as well as sleeping and indulgence in sexual intercourse during the day. One shall eschew infliction of pain on animals, and all other activities that cause distress and sorrow to others.

75. In the case of the people of all castes, a woman in her monthly course should be avoided for the first four nights. To prevent the birth of a female child, one shall avoid the fifth night also.

76. Thereafter he shall carnally approach her on the sixth night or other excellent nights even in number. Boys will be

born (if intercourse is carried out) on even nights and girls on nights odd in number.

77. Unrighteous persons indulge in sexual intercourse on Parvan and other days and impotent persons during dusk time. A clever man shall avoid Riktā days.

78. Even if rude people speak a lot, one shall never lisen to them.

An honourable seat should not be offered to a person who is not magnificent.

79. After shaving, vomitting or sexual intercourse with a woman an intelligent person shall take bath along with the clothe worn. He shall take bath also after going to the cremation ground.

80-84. O brahmins, one shall not make slanderous remarks about the following nor laugh at them: Devas, Vedas, brahmins, noble and truthful persons, preceptor, chaste women, Brahman, Yajñas and ascetics.

One shall be in perfectly auspicious dress, clad in white garments and embellished with white flowers. One shall never be inauspicious in dress and features. He shall not be in friendly terms with arrogant persons, mad fellows, the foolish and impolite, persons of no good conduct, those who are defiled by the defects of age and caste, those who habitually spend much, those who are enemies, those who are censured, those who are inefficient in their work, those who are in contact with lecherous persons, those who have no money, those who are solely interested in arguing and other base men.

85. One shall stand up while meeting friends, persons who are initiated, kings, religious students who have finished studies and become householders and the father-in-law. When they come to one's house one shall greet them in accordance with one's affluences.

86. O brahmins, after honouring and worshipping them in accordance with his capacity he shall bid them farewell to their respective places, after they had stayed for a year.

87-94. One shall then offer worship. He shall offer oblations into the fire in due order. The first oblation shall be offered to

Brahmā; then to Prajāpati; the third to the Gṛhyas; next to Kaśyapa. After offering oblation to Anumati he shall offer the (domestic oblation).

The holy rite that had been recounted by me before at the time of laying down the rules regarding the Nitya rites, shall be performed then. The Vaiśvadeva rite shall be done thereafter. O brahmins, even as I recount it, listen. After allotting the different divisions in the abodes (and places) in regard to Devas the devotee shall offer three oblations in the water jar to Parjanya, Āpaḥ (waters) and Dharitrī (Earth) (?). To Vāyu he shall offer oblation in every quarter; he shall offer to the quarters beginning with the east and in due order. Then he shall offer to Brahmā, to the firmament and to the sun in due order. Subsequently, with purity he shall offer oblations to the Viśvedevas, to all living beings, to Uṣas (dawn) and to the Bhūtapati (the lord of living beings). In the south he shall offer oblation to the Pitṛs after saying "Svadhā ca namaḥ" making it anticlockwise. He shall duly offer the water mixed with the remnant of cooked rice in the south-east, uttering "Yakṣma etat te". Thereafter he shall perform the rite of obeisance to Devas and to Brahmins.

95-98. The line at the root of the thumb of the right hand is known as the Brāhma Tīrtha for the rite of Ācamana.

The spot between the index finger and the thumb is cited as the Pitṛ Tīrtha. Except in the case of Nāndīmukha type of Pitṛs, water libation shall be offered by means of this spot to the Pitṛs. The Tīrtha pertaining to Devas is at the tip of fingers. The holy rite unto Devas is by means of Pitṛtīrtha. The Tīrtha of Prajāpati should be assigned at the root of the little finger. Thus by means of these Tīrthas alone should all the rites be performed to the respective deities along with the Pitṛs. They should never be performed through the Tīrthas of others.

99-100. The rite of Ācamana by means of Brāhma Tīrtha is excellent. The rites of Pitṛs shall always be performed by means of Pitṛ Tīrtha; the rites of Devas by means of Deva Tīrtha and the rite of Prajāpati by means of the Tīrtha of Prajāpati. With the same one shall perform the rites of water libation and offering the ball of rice unto the Nāndīmukha variety of

Pitṛs. Everything connected with Prajāpati shall be performed by means of Prājāpatya Tīrtha.

101. No shrewd man shall hold water and fire together. One shall not stretch one's legs in front of one's preceptors, Devas, Pitṛs and brahmins.

102. One should not look at a cow suckling her calf; one should not drink water with the palms joined together to form a cup; an intelligent man shall not cause delay in the short and long periods of cleaning. One shall not blow fire with the mouth.

103. O brahmins, one should not stay in a place where the following four are not present, viz. one who offers debt; a physician, a brahmin well-versed in the Vedas and a river abounding in water.

104. An intelligent man shall always stay there where the king is strong, interested in virtue and has conquered his servants. Whence can one have happiness if the king is bad.

105. It is conducive to happiness to stay at a place where the citizens are united, where they abide by justice, where they are peaceful and where they rival with one another (to work for the welfare of all).

106. A shrewd man shall live in that country where the husbandmen are generally not very arrogant and where all medicines are available.

107. O brahmins, one shall not stay in that place where the following three exist together : one who is eager to conquer; a previous enemy and people who continuously celebrate the festivals.

108. A learned man shall stay among his fellow travellers of very good conduct. One shall always stay at a place where the king cannot be thwarted and where the earth yields plenty of vegetables.

109. Thus, O brahmins, everything has been mentioned by me for the welfare of you all. Henceforth I shall state the rules of procedure regarding the food-intake.

110. Cooked rice, though stale, can be taken in if it is soaked in oil. It can be kept thus for a long time. Wheat products, barley products and milk products, kept for a long time can be eaten even if they are devoid of oiliness.

111. The following can be eaten : hare, tortoise, alligator, porcupine and the fish with darts (?) The village boar and the cock should be avoided.

112. In the following circumstances, even if one eats meat, one is not defiled : if it is the remnant of offerings unto the Pitṛs, Devas etc. or if it is cooked in Srāddha at the request of the brahmins and is sprinkled with holy water or if it is taken as a medicine.

113-114. The following articles can be cleaned with water : conch, rock, gold, silver, rope, garments, vegetables, roots, fruits, baskets of split bamboos, hides, jewel-studded cloth, coral pearl, (ordinary) vessels and vessels used for drinking Soma juice.

115. The cleansing of stony vessels may be with water or by scrubbing with a stone. The cleansing of oily vessels is by means of hot water.

116-117. The sieves, deer skins, mortars and pestles, or clothes in a bundle are cleaned by just sprinkling (water over the bundle). The cleansing of all types of bark-garments is by means of clay and water. The cleasing of wool and all types of hairs is done in this manner :—

118-119. It shall be cleansed with the Kalka (paste) after being boiled well of white mustard or sesamum seeds. The purification of all articles likely to get destroyed is always thus. The cleasing of cotton dress shall be with water and ash; that of wood, ivory, bones and horns is through paring.

120-122. The purity of pots made of clay is effected by baking it again. What is received by way of alms, the hand of an artisan and the mouth of the harlot—these are pure. The following are pure : the perfect knowledge and passage through the street, that which is consecrated by the servants, that which. is praised at the outset, that which is past after a long time, that which is hidden by many, that which is light, that which has many boys within, that in which old people are active, the chambers of barn and storage for sugarcane, grain etc. and the two breasts of a woman.

123. The flowing waters devoid of odour are pure. A plot of land becomes pure by the efflux of time, by being burnt, by being swept or when herds of cows pass over it.

124-136. (The ground becomes purified) by smearing (with cowdung), by scraping, by sprinkling (with water), by sweeping. Clay, water and ash must be put over cooked rice in the following circumstances for the sake of purity: if it is defiled by hairs or worms, if it is sniffed at by a cow or if flies settle on it.

The purity of (a vessel) made of Udumbara tree, tin or lead is effected by means of alkaline water (?). The purity of bell, metal vessels is effected by means of water mixed with Bhasman (ashes). If a liquid is defiled by contact with impurities, it is to be filtered or its foul smell is to be dispelled by means of clay and water. One shall remove the colour and the (bad) odour of other materials too (similarly). The (piece of) meat dropped down by a Caṇḍāla, beasts and birds of prey etc. is pure (intrinsically). Oil etc. that is spilt on the street is pure. The water that gives satisfaction to a cow is pure. Dust particles, fire, the shadow of horses and cows, rays (of the sun), wind, earth, sprays (of water) flies etc. are not defiled by means of their contact with (other) defiled things. Goats and horses are pure in their mouths but not the mouths of cows and calves. The flow of milk of the mother is pure. A bird felled down by an arrow is pure. Seats, beds, vehicles, river banks, grasses etc. are purified by the rays of the sun and the moon, and by the wind like the articles of trade.

One shall duly perform the rite of Ācamana after traversing through streets, after a bath and during the activities of hunger and drinking. One shall perform Ācamana after wearing a cloth.

The purity of those who are touched by the foul marshy water of the street is effected by contact with wind. So also the purity of platform built of baked bricks.

One shall take away the upper part of the cooked food defiled much, and leave it off and sprinkle the remaining part with water along with clay (?). The means of purity of the person who partakes of a defiled food is fasting for three nights and performing the rite of Ācamana by means of water. This atonement is prescribed when the partaking is due to ignorance. If it were to be with full knowledge that defect does not subside.

After touching a woman in her monthly course or a woman who has come into contact with her or a woman who has given birth to a child and persons belonging to the meanest caste, one shall take bath for purity. So also one shall take bath after touching persons who have borne a dead body. If a brahmin touches a human bone he can become pure by taking an oil bath.

137-138. If he does not take oil bath he shall perform the Ācamana rite, touch a cow and look at the sun. (He shall then become pure.)

One shall not tread on spittle or vomitted matter.

The leavings after food, faeces, urine, and water used for washing the feet shall be cast out of the house.

Without concluding the rite of offering five Piṇḍas one shall not take bath in the water belonging to others.

139. One shall take bath in natural water reservoirs (literally, those dug by gods), in eddies and Gaṅgā (and other) rivers.

An intelligent man shall never remain in gardens and other places at wrong times.

140-147. One shall never converse with those persons who are hated by the people as well as women bereft of sons.

One becomes purified by looking at the sun if one touches or converses with the persons who speak in contempt of deities, manes, scriptures, performance of sacrifice and saintly persons.

This selfsame purificatory rite should be performed by intelligent persons after looking at the following persons etc. : a woman in her monthly course, a dead body that has been left abandoned and lying (unattended), persons devoid of righteousness or persons of other religions, a woman who has given birth to a child, a eunuch, a naked man, a man of the lowest caste, persons who have carried a dead body and those who are enamoured of other men's wives.

A person who is conversant with righteousness becomes purified by taking a bath if he touches these : a medicant who is not worthy of being fed (?), a heretic, a cat, an ass, a cook, a fallen man, an outcaste (a person ostracised), a Caṇḍāla and those who bear dead bodies, a country pig and a woman in her monthly course. Similarly one has to take bath for purification if one touches any one of these : persons defiled by a woman who has given birth to a child or a person who has the pollution due to child birth or a person who fails to perform his daily round of duties at home or he who is abandoned by brahmins or the meanest man who commits sins by his (indiscriminate) eating.

One shall never fail to perform the daily duty of observing rituals. I shall mention the occasions when they need not be performed. On the occurrence of a death or a birth (in his family) a brahmin shall refrain from the rites of performing sacrifice, offering sacrificial fee, etc.

148. (In similar circumstances) a Kṣatriya shall remain without performing the Nitya rites for twelve days, a Vaiśya for half a month and a Śūdra for a month.

149-150. Thereafter all these shall perform their duties duly.

Water (libation) should be offered to the dead man by the members of his Gotra after going out of the house. The bones of a dead person shall be collected on the first, fourth, seventh or the ninth day. They should be gathered by the members of his Gotra on the fourth day.

151. After the rite of Sañcayana (collection of bones after cremation) the touch of their limbs is laid down in the Śāstras. The rites should be performed by the members of the Gotra, after the rite of Sañcayana.

152-156. (Defective) On the day of death two Sapiṇḍas can touch each other, for they are related to each other. If death takes place due to weapons, hanging, fire or enemy the prescription is the same as mentioned afore. If death takes place due to protest fasts or starvation, men are purified immediately. But the Sapiṇḍas will have pollution for three days. When a Sapiṇḍa dies after the death of another (i.e. immediately thereafter), a single purificatory rite is sufficient. The routine daily rites should be performed there. The same is the procedure when a birth takes place during the postnatal pollution due to a person's birth in the case Sapiṇḍas and Sodakas.

According to injunctions the father shall take bath at the birth of a son. He shall take bath along with clothes he is wearing at the time of the birth.

157-158. Even in the case of (post-natal pollution) if another birth taken place while a pollution is current, the purity is mentioned as having been effected in the course of days of the previous birth. The castes shall duly perform their duties and rituals after ten, twelve, fifteen or thirty days have passed.

159. Thereafter the rite of Ekoddiṣṭa Śrāddha should be performed by learned men in regard to the dead man and gifts should be given to the brahmins.

160. Whatever was pleasing unto, whatever was liked by him in the house, should be given to a worthy Brahmin by the person who wishes that the same should be inexhaustible.

161. When the days are completed the people shall touch water by their vehicles and weapons. After giving water libations and Piṇḍas to the dead men people of all castes would have fulfilled all their due rites.

162. They shall perform all rites maintaining purity for prosperity here and hereafter. The Vedas should be studied everyday. One should try to be a learned scholar.

163-167. One should earn and amass wealth righteously. One should assiduously perform sacrifices whereby the Ātman will not be infuriated. O brahmins, it shall not be treated with contempt. Without hesitation one shall perform that rite which need not be concealed by great men.

O brahmins, if a householder practises the foregoing conduct of life thus, he attains virtue, wealth and love. It is splendid for him here and hereafter.

This is an esoteric secret. It is conducive to longevity and affluence. It increases intellect. It dispels sins. It is meritorious. It bestows glory, health and nourishment. It is auspicious. It confers fame and renown. It increases splendour and strength. It is a means of attainment of heaven. It should always be practised by men, O excellent sages. It should be practised by Brahmins, Kṣatriyas, Vaiśyas and Śūdras.

168-170. This should be known carefully by those who desire prosperity. He who understands and practises it on all occasions shall be rid of sins. He is honoured in the heavenly world. O excellent brahmins, this is the essence of all essences that has been related. It is the virtuous path mentioned in Śrutis and Smṛtis. This secret should not be imparted to anyone, least to an atheist, a defiled mind. Nor should it be imparted to an arrogant fellow, a foolish person or a prattler of unsound arguments.

CHAPTER ONE HUNDRED AND FOURTEEN

Assignment of duties to different castes and stages of life

The sages said :

1. O holy one, we wish to hear about the special duties of different castes. O excellent brahmin, recount the duties of four Āśramas also.

2. Listen with restraint to the duties of different castes, Brahmins, Kṣatriyas, Vaiśyas and Śūdras in due order as they are being recounted by me.

3. A Brahmin shall be devoted to (the practice of) sympathy, charitable gift, austerities, sacrifice unto the gods and study of his own branch of the Vedas. He shall regularly perform water libations. He shall maintain sacrificial fires.

4. For his livelihood he shall perform sacrifices on behalf of others. He shall teach Vedic lore to the twice-born. O brahmins, for performing sacrifices he shall accept monetary gifts with discretion.

5. O brahmins, he shall do everything beneficial to the world. He shall not perform what is detrimental to anyone. Friendliness to all living beings is the excellent asset of a Brahmin.

6. O brahmins, he shall view a cow and another man's precious gem as equal. O brahmins, his carnal approach to his wife during the permissible period after the days of menstruation, is commended.

7. A Kṣatriya shall give charitable gifts to the brahmins as much as they wish. O brahmins, he should perform different sacrifices and read the Vedas.

8. He shall maintain himself through his weapons. Protection of Earth is his excellent means of livelihood. Sustenance of Earth is his primary duty.

9. Rulers of men (kings) are content only by due sustenance of the Earth, since the protection of the king himself is accomplished by such holy rites as sacrifice.

10. By chastising the wicked and protecting the good, the king attains desired worlds. He is one who establishes and stabilises different castes.

11. O excellent sages, Brahmā, the grandfather of the worlds, granted breeding of cattle, trading activities and agriculture as means of livelihood unto a Vaiśya.

12. For him the following activities too are recommended: Reading of the Vedas, sacrifice, charitable gifts, practice of piety and the performance of compnlsory and optional rites.

13-14. The holy rites of a Śūdra depend upon the collaboration of the twice-born. For that purpose he supports and nourishes them through riches earned by purchase and sale of articles or by practising arts and crafts. A Śūdra shall offer charitable gifts. He shall worship by means of Pākayajñas (offering cooked food unto gods). He shall perform rites unto the Pitṛs.

15-18. There are certain virtuous observances common to the four Varṇas. All of them can accept gift for sustaining their dependents. O excellent brahmins, they should carnally approach their own respective wives during the permissible period after the days of menstruation. The following are recounted as the noble characteristics of all the Varṇas, O excellent brahmins: Kindness and sympathy towards all living beings, forbearance, absence of over-exertion (?), auspiciousness, loving gentle speech, friendliness, absence of desire, abstention from miserliness and being devoid of jealousy. O brahmins, these alone are the characteristics common to all stages of life. There are special qualities and subsidiary duties of the Brahmins and others.

19. In times of adversity the vocation of a Kṣatriya or a Vaiśya is recommended for a Brahmin; the vocation of a Vaiśya to a Kṣatriya and the jobs of a Śūdra to both Kṣatriyas and Vaiśyas.

20. O brahmins, in case of incompetence that shall be avoided. That alone shall be pursued during adversity, but chaotic mixing up of jobs shall not be effected.

21. Thus, O brahmins, the duties of a Brahmin have been mentioned by me. Understand now the respective duties of the people of various stages of life even as I explain them well.

22-23. A boy who has been invested with the sacred thread shall be devoted to the acquiring of Vedas. Residing in the abode of his preceptor, O brahmins, a religious student shall be mentally pure. He should be devotedly engaged in the practice of cleanliness. Service should a rendered to the preceptor. He shall maintain devotional observances and grasp the Vedas intelligently.

24. O brahmins, with concentration and purity of mind he shall make obeisance to the sun-god and fire-god at dawn as well as at dusk. He shall salute the preceptor too.

25. O excellent brahmins, he shall stand when the preceptor remains standing. He shall follow when the preceptor goes ahead. When the teacher is seated he shall be seated on a lower level. He shall avoid what is contrary to the preceptor.

26. He shall sit in front of him. Without his mind dwelling on anything else he shall repeat the Vedic text recited by the preceptor. Thereafter, on being permitted by him, he shall partake of the cooked food received as alms.

27. He shall take bath in the water wherein the preceptor has taken bath. Early in the morning everyday he shall fetch water for libation and sacrificial twigs for the preceptor.

28. Having learnt the requisite Vedic texts he shall pay fees to his preceptor. On getting his permission he shall enter the stage of a householder.

29. He shall duly acquire a wife. O brahmins, after earning wealth by his own work he shall perform the duties of a householder.

30-31. The householder propitiates the Manes by means of oblations, Devas by sacrifices, guests by cooked food, sages by regular recitation of Vedic texts, the spirits and other living beings by oblations etc., and the entire world by the truthfulness of words. Thus he attains celestial regions by his own actions.

32. The recluses and religious students who sustain themselves by cooked food received as alms depend on the householder. Hence the stage of householder is the noblest.

33-34. O brahmins, some brahmins are engaged in disseminating the Vedic knowledge. Some wander over the Earth for pilgrimage, taking holy dips in sacred waters. Some wander visiting different countries of the world. These have no abode of their own. They do not prepare their own food. To these people the householder offers a home and rest in the evening. Hence it is said that the householder sustains and supports them.

35. The householder should welcome them. He should speak sweet words always. He shall give them gifts. He shall offer seats, food and beds to those who come to his house.

36. A guest returning disappointed from a person's house goes, after taking his merits and handing over his own sins.

37. For a householder the following are despicable : Dishonouring (others), egotism, arrogance, slandering, attacking and speaking harsh words to others.

38. The householder who duly adheres to what is thus enjoined becomes liberated from bondage and attains the most excellent worlds.

39. At a ripe old age, O brahmins, the householder who has duly fulfilled his duties shall entrust his sons with the duty of looking after his wife and himself retire and go to the forest. Or he can allow his wife to accompany him.

40. O brahmins, there he shall stay as a sage sustaining himself with leaves, roots and fruits. He shall let the beard and facial hairs grow. He shall have matted hairs on his head. He shall sleep on the bare ground. He can be the guest of anyone.

41. O excellent brahmins, his wearing apparel and upper garment shall consist of leather, Darbha grass or Kāśa plants. Taking head bath thrice a day (in rivers or lakes) is recommended for him.

42. The following are highly recommended in his case: Worship of the deities, offering ghee into the fire, greeting and honouring visitors and guests, begging alms and offering oblations.

43. Massaging his limbs by means of oil obtained from forest products is also commended. O leading brahmins, ability to bear the extremes of chilliness and heat is a form of penance unto him.

44. The forest-dwelling recluse who regularly preforms

duties fixed for him shall burn off his defects like fire. He shall attain the eternal worlds.

45. O excellent ones, follow me even as I relate the nature and general characteristics of the stage of a mendicant sage, that is called the fourth stage by the wise.

46. O excellent brahmins, a mendicant shall eschew affection and attachment unto his sons, wife and assets. He shall enter the fourth stage of life after eschewing competitive spirit and rivalry.

47. O excellent brahmins, he shall leave off the enterprises of the three Varṇas. He shall behave alike unto the friends and others. He shall be friendly to all creatures.

48. He shall maintain Yogic practice. He shall never injure the oviparous, viviparous and other creatures mentally, verbally or physically. He shall refrain from all attachments.

49. He shall never stay in a single place permanently. In a village he shall stay for a single night. In a city he shall stay for five successive nights. He has neither pleasurable attachment nor hatred unto the lower creatures and birds.

50. For sustaining himself he shall visit, begging for alms, the houses of men of noble caste where coal has ceased to burn but the inmates have not yet taken food.

51. He shall not be dejected when nothing is obtained. He shall not be overjoyous when something is obtained. He shall have that much which is necessary to maintain his life. He shall be out of all attachment to quantities.

52. He shall have absolute contempt for over-cherished acquisitions. Even the liberated sage is bound (again) by overcherished acquisitions.

53. Eschewing such defects as passion, anger, arrogance, greed, delusion etc., the full-fledged saint shall be free from all possessions.

54. After offering freedom from fear to all living beings he shall wander over the Earth. Liberated from his physical body he shall have no cause of fear anywhere.

55. By means of sacrificial offerings such as ghee acquired through begging the brahminical sage shall perform the symbolic Agnihotra in his own body. He shall perform Homa unto

the bodily fire through his mouth. He attains the other worlds through the funeral pyre.

56. He who is pure and endowed with good conceptions and intellect and passes through the stage of life pertaining to salvation in the manner mentioned above becomes calm like the fire wherein no fuel is put. That twice-born attains Brahma world.

CHAPTER ONE HUNDRED AND FIFTEEN

Characteristics of mixed castes

The sages said :

1-3. O highly blessed one, you are omniscient. You are engaged in activities beneficial to all. O sage, there is nothing past, present or future that is not known to you. O highly intelligent one, by what activities does the downward fall of the Varṇas take place? By what activities does their upward progress take place? Tell us. We wish to hear how and by what means does a Śūdra attain the status of a Brahmin and a Brahmin that of a Śūdra.

Vyāsa said :

4-6. The beautiful peak of the Himālayas is embellished by different minerals. It is covered by various trees and creepers. It is endowed with wonderful features. The three-eyed lord of Devas, that Supreme god, the destroyer of the three cities, was seated thereon. The goddess of charming eyes, the daughter of the king of mountains, bowed down to the lord, O brahmins, and put this question formerly unto him. O excellent sages, I shall describe that. Listen.

Umā said :

7-11. O three-eyed lord, O destroyer of the eyes of Bhaga, teeth of Pūṣan and the sacrifice of Dakṣa, I have this great doubt (to be cleared). The arrangement (of the people) into four castes had been formerly brought about by the self-born lord. What are those activities, as a result of which a Vaiśya attains the status of a Śūdra? By what means does a Kṣatriya or a Vaiśya become a Brahmin or a Ksatriya ? O lord, how can Dharma be made to recede in such a reverse activity? By what activity is a Brahmin born in the womb of a Śūdra lady? O lord, by what activity does a Kṣatriya attain the status of a Śūdra? O lord, O lord of goblins, please clarify this doubt of mine. How do the persons of the three Varṇas attain Brahminhood naturally ?

Maheśvara said :

12. O goddess, brahminhood is very difficult to attain. The Brahmins are naturally auspicious, the Kṣatriyas, Vaiśyas and Śūdras are not auspicious.

13. The Brahmins fall off from their status by performing evil deeds. For the same reason one is forced down again even after attaining the most excellent of castes.

14. One who adheres to the characteristics of a Brahmin, whether a Kṣatriya or a Vaiśya, attains Brahminhood.

15. He who forsakes brahminhood and resorts to the activities and features of a Kṣatriya incurs a downfall from the status of a Brahmin and is born of a Kṣatriya womb.

16-17. Even after attaining the rare distinction of being a brahmin, if he becomes greedy and deluded with deficient intellect and resorts to the activities of a Vaiśya, that Brahmin attains Vaiśya caste. A Vaiśya (in similar circumstances) attains Śūdra caste. A Brahmin deviating from his duties shall thereafter attain Śūdra caste.

18. That person who has fallen off from his Varṇa attains hell. He who falls from the world of Brahmā is born of the womb of a Śūdra lady.

19-20. O highly blessed lady of sacred acitivities, if a Kṣatriya or a Vaiśya eschews his own duties and resorts to the occupation of a Śudra, he falls off from his original status and becomes one of mixed castes. A Brahmin or a Kṣatriya or a Vaiśya on becoming one of mixed castes, attains Śūdra caste.

21. A Śūdra who maintains his own duties, who is endowed with wisdom and perfect knowledge, who is conversant

with piety and who is engaged in holy activities attains the fruit of those holy activities.

22. O goddess, this too, another thing pertaining to the Ātman has been cited by Brahmā. Eternal achievement is resorted to by those who are desirous of righteous activities.

23. O goddess, the food cooked by the mixed caste Ugra is despicable. The food collectively cooked, the food pertaining to Śrāddha, the food defiled by pollution due to the birth or death of someone in the family and the food that is loudly proclaimed should not be eaten. The food cooked by a Śūdra should never be eaten.

24. The food cooked by a Śūdra is despised by gods and noble men, O goddess. That which is uttered by Brahmā is authoritative.

25. A Brahmin, a person who maintains sacrificial fires and one who performs sacrifice attain the goal of Śūdras if they were to die with the remnants of the food cooked by a Śūdra within the stomach.

26. A Brahmin, who has been ousted from Brahmā's abode by the remnants of food cooked by a Śūdra attains the state of a Śūdra. This is certain.

27. A Brahmin takes birth in the womb of a lady of the same caste as the person whose food he uses for sustenance or the remnants of whose food remain undigested in his stomach at the time of his death.

28. After happily attaining the rare privilege of being born as a Brahmin, if anyone slights it or if he partakes of forbidden food, he falls off from the status of a Brahmin.

29-30. A Brahmin falls off from his status if he is a wine-addict, a brahmin-slayer, a thief, a robber, one who has violated the vow of holy observances, an unclean one who refrains from regular study of the Vedas, is a sinner, a greedy person, one who indulges in misdemeanour, is a knave, one who does not observe religious vows, is the husband of a Śūdra woman, one who has taken food for sustenance from a bastard, one who sells Soma juice and one who serves a mean person.

31. A Brahmin who defiles the bed of his preceptor, who hates his preceptor, who delights in despising his preceptor or who is hostile to Brahmins, falls from Brahminical birth.

32. O goddess, by preforming these splendid holy rites a Śūdra attains Brahminhood and a Vaiśya the status of a Kṣatriya.

33-36. A Śūdra attains the status of a Vaiśya in the following circumstances : He performs his duties justly and in accordance with his injunctions. He is hospitable to all and he partakes of the food left by them. He assiduously renders service to and attends upon the persons of superior castes. He is not dejected or disheartened in his attempt. He remains an excellent man. He clings to the path of the good. He honours and worships the twice-born and the gods. He observes hospitality to all as a holy rite. He approaches his wife only on the permissive nights after the period of menstruation. He is regular in habits and taking food. He is an expert. He seeks good persons for companionship. He partakes of the food left by others. He daes not partake of meat without consecrating it.

37-40. A Vaiśya becomes a Brahmin in the following circumstances: He is truthful in speech and an expert in the employment of peaceful means. He is not affected by mutually opposed extremes. He does not boast about himself. He performs daily sacrifices. He is devoted to the study of the Vedas. He maintains purity. He controls his sense organs. He honours Brahmins. He is not envious of any of the four Varṇas. Taking meals twice a day he observes the duties of a householder. He does not hesitate to eat remnants of food. He controls his diet. He is devoid of passionate desire. He is not arrogant. He performs Agnihotra carrying out Homas in accordance with injunctions. He entertains everyone as his guest and partakes of their learning. He duly maintains the three sacrificial fires.

41-42. That Vaiśya who is pure is reborn in a noble family of Kṣatriyas. That Vaiśya who is reborn as a Kṣatriya shall be purified by performing the consecratory rites beginning with his maturity. After the investiture with the sacred thread he shall be devoted to all holy observances. Thus consecrated he becomes a Brahmin. He gives charitable gifts and performs sacrifices with rich monetary gifts. Always seeking refuge in the three sacrificial fires and continuing the study of the Vedas, he shall hope to achieve heaven.

43-51. A Kṣatriya shall study the Vedas with a desire for the attainment of heaven. He shall seek refuge in the three sacrificial fires. He shall always make gifts so that his hands remain wet. He shall protect the subjects righteously. He shall be truthful. He shall perform truthful deeds, with his vision on purity for ever. By self-imposed righteous punishments he shall burn off his sins. He shall acquire virtue, love and wealth. He shall be self-controlled by his organs of action. He shall partake of only a sixth of the produce of his subjects. He shall be shrewd in monetary dealings. He shall not indulge freely in licentious activities. He shall be virtuous. He shall carnally approach his wife only during the prescribed periods after the days of menstruation. He shall be strict in the observance of fasts and other holy rites. He shall be engaged in the study of the Vedas. He shall be pure. Even in his house he shall always sleep in the well protected apartments free from strangers. He shall be hospitable to all in regard to three aims of life: virtue, love and wealth. He shall be pure in mind. To the Śūdras who are desirous of food he shall say, "Well, it is ready". He shall not look at anything with selfishness or passionate love. He shall gather all the things necessary for the manes, gods and guests. He shall duly perform worship, in his abode, even by resorting to alms (?). He shall duly perform Agnihotra twice everyday. He shall face even death in battle for the welfare of cows and brahmins. Such a Kṣatriya shall become a Brahmin. He shall purify himself by reciting Mantres for the maintenance of three sacrificial fires. He shall become richly equipped with perfect knowledge and wisdom. He shall consecrate himself. He shall master the Vedas.

52. O gentle lady, a virtuous Vaiśya shall become a Kṣatriya by performing his own duties. By the fruits of these activities of a lower birth he can become so.

53-65. Even a Śūdra who is richly endowed with the knowledge of the Vedas shall become a Brahmin and cultured. Even a Brahmin shall forfeit his Brahminhood and become a Śūdra if his conduct is base and if his diet and culture is base. Brahmā himself has said that even a Śūdra should be resorted to like a Brahmin, O gentle lady, if he is virtuous, purified by holy rites or if he has conquered his sense-organs. A Śūdra who clings to his duties, should be considered purer than the twice-born ones. Neither the womb of birth, nor the consecratory rites, neither the Vedic knowledge nor the lineage can be the cause of Brahminhood. Conduct is the real cause. All men are Brahmins if their conduct is pure. Even a Śūdra who strictly adheres to good conduct attains Brahminhood. O lady of splendid hips, the inherent quality of a Brahmin is the same everywhere. He is a Brahmin, in whom the attributeless, faultless, pure Brahman resides. O gentle lady, those persons who are free from impurities are the exponents and guides of good conduct. These are mentioned by Brahmā himself, the bestower of boons, as he was creating the subjects. The Brahmin is, as it were, a great mobile field that has feet. If any one sows seeds therein it fructifies after death. A person who desires prosperity shall always be contented. He shall always cling to the path of the good. He shall abide by the Brahminical path. He shall be a householder regularly studying the Saṁhitās at home. He shall regularly study the Vedas but should not have the same as his means of livelihood. A Brahmin who is like this, who abides by the path of the good, who maintains the sacrificial fire and who studies the Vedas regularly becomes competent to attain liberation. O gentle lady, after attaining Brahminhood the man of controlled self shall protect it by holy rites such as acceptance of monetary gifts from worthy persons. O lady of pure smiles thus the secret doctrine has been recounted to you as to how a Śūdra becomes a Brahmin or how a Brahmin, falling off from virtue, attains the status of a Śūdra.

CHAPTER ONE HUNDRED AND SIXTEEN

Review of Virtue

Umā said:

1. O lord of all living beings, O lord saluted by Devas and Aśuras, O powerful lord, please clear my doubts in regard to the notions of piety and sin among men.

2. All embodied beings are bound by three kinds of bonds, viz. thought, speech and physical action. How are they released therefrom ?

3. O lord, by what habitual practice, by what holy rite, by what sort of conduct and good quality do men go to heaven?

Maheśvara said:

4. O goddess Umā of perfect knowledge of the principles of piety, O gentle lady of permanent adherence to virtue, your question is conducive to welfare and wisdom of all living beings.

5. Persons of tranquillity, engaged in truth and piety and devoid of all external symbols are free from doubts. They are fettered neither by piety nor by blasphemy.

6. Those persons who are omniscient, who are conversant with the principles of creation and annihilation, who see everything and who are devoid of passionate attachment are released from the bonds of Karmans.

7. Those who do not injure anything whatsoever, mentally, verbally or physically, those who are not involved in anything, are not bound by Karmans.

8. Those who refrain from violence to lives, who possess good conduct and mercifulness, and who are equally amiable to others' hatred and love are released from the bondage of Karmans. They have self-control.

9. Those who are merciful to living beings, who are worthy of being trusted by living creatures and who have eschewed violent activities go to heaven.

10. Those who are indifferent to others' assets, who always avoid other men's wives and who enjoy the riches virtuously acquired by themselves go to heaven.

11. Those men who always associate with other men's wives as though they were their own mothers, sisters and daughters, go to heaven.

12. Those who cling to their own wives, who carnally approach them only during the prescribed period after the days of menstruation and who never indulge themselves in vulgar lechery, go to heaven.

13. Those who desist from stealth, who are content with their own wealth and who enjoy their own good luck go to heaven.

14. Those who view other men's wives with eyes enveloped by chastity, who have conquered their sense organs and who value good conduct very much, go to heaven.

15-16. This divinely evolved path should be resorted to by men. Only a path untarnished by sins should always be resorted to by wise men. Only a path that never needlessly harms others should be resorted to by wise men. A path of such holy rites as charitable gifts and austerities, a path of good conduct, cleanliness and mercy should be resorted to by those who wish to attain heaven. No other path shall be resorted to.

Umā said:

17. O sinless lord of living beings, recount to me those activities wherein a man is fettered verbally but is again released therefrom.

Maheśvara said:

18. Those who never utter a sin-based lie either for their own sake or for others' sake go to heaven.

19. Those who never utter falsehood either for livelihood, or for virtue or out of desire for the same go to heaven.

20. Those who welcome others speaking sweet, sinless and polished words with clearly pronounced syllables, go to heaven.

21. Those who never speak harsh, incisive and cruel words and who never indulge in slanderous gossip are good men who go to heaven.

22. Those who do not speak calumnious words or words that antagonise their friends or inflict pain on others, go to heaven.

23. Those who eschew harshness and malice to others and those who are calm and who mete out equal treatment to all living beings go to heaven.

24. Those who desist from knavish blabber, those who avoid antagonistic activities and those who speak gently go to heaven.

25. Those, who, out of anger do not utter words that wound the heart, those who attain peace in not being angry, go to heaven.

26. O gentle lady, this act of piety relating to speech, should be resorted to by men. False (speech) should be eschewed by wise men who possess the auspicious quality of truthfulness.

Umā said :

27. O highly blessed lord of gods, O Pināka-wielding lord, tell me those mental-acts whereby a man is held in bondage.

Maheśvara said :

28. O lady of weal, those who possess virtues of thought do always go to heaven. Listen, even as I narrate them.

29. O lady of splendid countenance, man is held in bondage by the mind led asray. Listen how his inner working binds him.

30. When another man's property is seen kept in a forest or a lonely place (good men) do not even think of appropriating it. They go to heaven.

31. Good men do not become overjoyed on seeing other men's property left in a lonely place whether in the village or in the house (nor do they think of appropriating it). They go to heaven.

32. Similarly, good men do not even think of molesting lecherously the wives of others (on meeting them) in lonely spots. They go to heaven.

33. Good men mentally view friends and enemies alike. They have a friendly attitude towards them. They go to heaven.

34. Good men are learned, merciful, pure and truthful; they are contented with their own riches. They go to heaven.

35. Good men are devoid of enmity. They do not overstrain themselves (?) They always maintain a friendly attitude. They are merciful towards all living beings. They go to heaven.

36. They possess knowledge. They perform holy rites. They are fond of their friends. They understand piety and sin. They go to heaven.

37. Good men, O gentle lady, are indifferent to the accumulating fruits of auspicious and inauspicious deeds. They go to heaven.

38. After attaining prosperity good men are devoted to gods and learned brahmins. They shun the sinful. They go to heaven.

39. They go to heaven due to the splendid results of holy rites. O gentle lady, those who tread the path of heaven have been enumerated by me. What more do you wish to hear ?

Umā said :

40. O great lord, I have a certain doubt concerning mortals Hence it behoves you to explain it fully.

41. O lord, by means of what holy rite does a man attain a long life ? By what type of penance, O lord of gods, does he obtain a great span of life ?

42. By means of what activity does man on Earth get longevity reduced ? O uncensured lord, it beloves you to narrate the consequences of actions.

43. Differences are observed in men. Some are highly fortunate. Others are less fortunate. Some are born noble and others are ignoble.

44. Some are very odious in appearance as if they are made of wood. Others are very pleasing to behold.

45. Some appear to be evil-minded. Some appear to be highly learned. Others have highly developed intellect with pure wisdom and prescience.

46. O lord, some are men of few words. Others are highly eloquent. Hence it behoves you to explain this diversity.

Maheśvara said :

47-50. O gentle lady, I shall explain upto you the outcome of the fruits of actions whereby all men in the mortal world deservedly experience their respective benefit. If a man raises weapon and kills host of living beings he is sure to fall into hell. Even a leader of Yogins (?) goes to hell if he injures living beings. A man ruthless to all living beings, one who causes heartburn even unto germs and worms, one who is extremely merciless and one who never affords refuge (unto others) falls into hell. One who is not like this is a pious soul and he is reborn in human form (?)

51. A man of violent nature goes to hell. A nonviolent man goes to heaven. The man who goes to hell undergoes terrible and unbearable torture in hell.

52. If anyone, by any means, survives and comes out of hell and attains human birth, he becomes short-lived.

53. O gentle lady, one who commits sinful actions, violence etc. is inimical to all living beings and becomes short-lived.

54-57. On account of his splendid activity, O gentle lady, a good man eschews slaughter of living beings. He lays aside his weapons. He does not mete out punishment (to others). He never injures others. He neither kills nor abets slaughter. He does not encourage killing. He does not make anyone kill anyone. He is friendly to all living beings. He views others as himself. A man of this type, O gentle lady, attains divinity. He enjoys pleasures and happiness deservedly. He rejoices, if ever he happens to be born in the mortal world. This is the path of men of good conduct and activity. As a result of their avoidance of injury to living beings they are destined to live long. This has been declared by Brahmā.

CHAPTER ONE HUNDRED AND SEVENTEEN

Umā said :

1. What are those things which a man should regularly do in order to attain heaven? What should be his conduct and what holy rites should he perform ? What should he give in charity ?

Maheśvara said :

2-5. Any man coming under this category, O gentle lady, goes over to the world of gods : He should be a donor. He should honour Brahmins. The highly intelligent one should distribute edibles and foodstuffs, cooked food and drinks, clothes etc. among the poor, the distressed and the wretched. He should build places of rest and assembly chambers, sheds for giving water to travellers etc. He should dig lotus ponds. He should be pure in mind and body. He should perform daily routine of duties enjoined. He should make charitable gifts of seats, beds, vehicles, houses, jewels, money, plants, fertile fields, young women etc. always with a tranquil mind.

6-7. He spends a long time in heaven enjoying unsurpassed pleasures. He sports about in Nandana and other gardens rejoicing in the company of celestial damsels. O great goddess, O gentle lady, after coming down from heaven he is born among men in a highly blessed family endowed with wealth and grain.

8. There, he will be possessed of desirable qualities. He will be joyous. The man becomes rich. He enjoys great pleasures and accomplishes great deeds.

9. These highly blessed living beings of charitable disposition are those spoken of formerly by Brahmā as men of pleasing appearance liked by all.

10. Other men, O gentle lady, are the twice-born ones of miserly nature who do not give anything to anyone. Those thoughtless ones do not give foodstuffs even when they have them.

11. Even after seeing the poor, the blind and the wretched mendicants, even on being requested by them, they turn away because they are gluttonous and so covetous of palatable things.

12. They never give away money, garments, means of enjoyment, gold, cows or items of cooked food.

13. They are highly greedy and covetous, atheists, devoid of liberal-mindedness. Men of this nature, O gentle lady, are the thoughtless ones who go to hell.

14. After the lapse of some time when they take human birth those men of deficient intellect are born in some family devoid of wealth.

15. They are tormented by hunger and thirst. They are boycotted by the world. Devoid of any hope for the enjoyment of pleasure they keep on living their evil lives.

16. They are born of families of inferior worldly pleasures. Those men are engrossed in spurious pleasures. O gentle lady, it is by these activities that men become devoid of wealth.

17-22. There are other types of haughty people who are arrogant and engrossed in other activities (?). These narrow-minded people do not offer seat unto those who deserve one. These thoughtless people do not yield way unto those who deserve one. They do not honour those worthy of honour due to consecrated rites. Being thoughtless, they do not offer water for washing feet or drinking. They do not lovingly address their splendid and desirable elders in view of the fact that they are overwhelmed by greed that has increased due to their arrogance. They insult those who are worthy of honour. They slight elders. All men of this sort, O gentle lady, invariably fall into hell. If somehow those men come out of hell after many years, they take birth in the despicable family of Śvapākas, Pulkasas of thoughtless despicable nature. It is in these families that those people are born who slight and insult preceptors and elders.

23-27. A man of the following nature, O gentle lady, attains heaven: He is neither arrogant nor overwhelmed by false pride or prestige. He worships deities and guests. He is worthy of worship by the whole world. He performs obeisance. He speaks sweet words. He is pleasing to all due to his activities. He is fond of all living beings. He does not hate anyone. He has pleasing countenance. He speaks polished sweet words full of love. He offers words of welcome unto all living beings. He does not violently hit or injure anybody. He honours everyone as one deserves by good actions. He stands aside after offering the path unto one who deserves it. He worships his preceptor always. He takes pleasure in receiving guests. He worships honourable visitors.

28-30. After his sojourn in heaven he takes birth in the mortal world in an excellent family. There he enjoys all sorts of pleasures and possesses all jewels. He gives to the deserving ones charitable gifts in accordance with their merits. He is devoted to pious rites. He is honoured by all living beings. He is bowed to by all the world. He obtains the fruits of his actions. This is the means of virtue declared by the creator himself and I have described it.

31-33. A man of the following mode of habits and conduct falls into hell : He has a horrible habit. He is terrifying unto all animals. O splendid lady, he tortures and harasses living creatures with his hands and feet, with a rope or a stick and with clods of earth, columns or other means. His mind is bent on violence. He makes creatures suffer. He approaches living creatures making them tremble with fear.

34-35. After the lapse of some time, if he attains human form or birth he is born in a base family overwhelmed by many kinds of sufferings. He is hated by the world. He is the lowliest among men as a result of his actions. This, O gentle lady, should be understood in regard to human beings in the midst of their kith and kin.

36-41. The other sort of man looks at all living beings with kindness. He is like a father to them. His eyes are full of fondness and friendship. He is devoid of inimical feelings. He has perfect control over his sense-organs. Being merciful he does not cause fear in the living beings. He does not kill them. He earns the confidence of all living creatures. He does not injure any living being with his perfectly controlled hands and feet. He does not cause them any harm or frighten them by means of a rope, a stick, clods of earth or weapon. The actions of the man are always splendid. A man of such habits and conduct goes to heaven. There in a divine mansion where he lives joyously like gods. If after the end of his tenure in heaven he returns to the mortal world he enjoys increasing happiness. He has less stress and strain. He is devoid of terrifying grief. He enjoys pleasures. He has no strenuous labour to undertake. He is always free from mental agony. This, O gentle lady, is the path of the good where there is no affliction.

Umā said :

42-45. Some of these men are observed to be clever and mightily enthusiastic. They are richly endowed with wisdom and prescience. They are intelligent and experts on the subject of wealth. Others, O lord, are evil-minded and devoid of wisdom and prescience. What is that action as a result of which a man becomes intelligent ? How does a man become deficient in wisdom ? O Śiva, clear this doubt of mine, O lord, the most excellent one among the virtuous. Others are blind by birth. Still others, O lord, are distressed by sickness. Some men are observed to be impotent. Please tell me the reason thereof.

Maheśvara said :

46-48. Men of the following type attain heaven: They enquire after the welfare or otherwise of the brahmins well-versed in the Vedas, of the persons of accomplishment coversant with virtue. They avoid inauspicious activities and resort to splendid ones. In this world they attain happiness and they go to heaven later. If anyone among them takes human birth he is born with an extraordinary intellect. His learning is befitting the performance of sacrifices and is auspicious.

49. Those who cast their evil eye on other men's wives are born blind due to that evil conduct.

50. Men of sinful actions who look at a naked woman with a defiled mind become distressed due to sickness.

51. Foolish men of evil conduct who indulge in the sexual act with beasts become deficient and defiled in wisdom as well as impotent. They become eunuchs.

52. Men who bind animals or embrace them closely, men who defile their preceptor's bed and men who scatter their seminal discharge are born as eunuchs.

Umā said :

53. O the most excellent one among the gods, what is a despicable action ? What is it that is not despicable, by doing which a man attains prosperity and renown ?

Maheśvara said :

54. He who seeks the path of prosperity and asks brahmins about it, he who seeks virtue and he who yearns for good qualities attains heaven.

55. If at any time he takes up human birth, O gentle lady, he is born highly intelligent, wise and endowed with memory.

56. This, O gentle lady, is the path of virtue of the good. It should be followed. It is conducive to prosperity. This has been described by me for the perpetual benefit of men in the world.

Umā said :

57. There are other men of deficient wisdom who hate virtue. They do not wish to approach brahmins well-versed in the Vedas.

58. Some men observe holy rites. They have faith and they

closely adhere to the path of self-control (subjugation of sense-organs). Others are devoid of holy observances. They swerve from the path of discipline. They can be compared to the Rākṣasas.

59. Still others are regular performers of holy sacrifices. There are others devoid of delusion. Tell me how they become so. What is that action as a result of which they become so.

Maheśvara said :

60-63. The holy scriptures, composed formerly, prescribe the limits of pious activities of the world. There are holy men who obey them as their authority. They are seen to be men of steadfast holy rites. Those who are deluded call sin by the name of virtue. They do not observe holy rites. They do not observe rules of decorum and morality. They are said to be Brahmarākṣasas. If, due to the lapse of time or due to their endeavour (?) they are born as men they do become base men devoid of homas and vaṣaṭkāras. In order to clear your doubts, O gentle lady, the ocean of virtue has been expounded by me. Men may be efficient or inefficient in its observance.

CHAPTER ONE HUNDRED AND EIGHTEEN

Dialogue between Maheśvara and the Sages

Vyāsa said :

1-3. On hearing these words of her lord from the beginning, O brahmins, that holy mother of the universe became pleased, delighted and surprised. Near the lord, the destroyer of the three cities, there were certain excellent sages who had been to that mountain in the course of their pilgrimage. They worshipped the trident-bearing lord, bowed to him and asked him to clear their doubt, with desire for the welfare of the world.

The sages said :

4-6. Obeisance to thee, O Three-eyed one, O destroyer of

Dakṣa's sacrifice. O Lord of the universe, we shall ask you some questions to clear the doubts lurking in our hearts. In this extremely terrible world that causes hairs to stand on end and strikes terror, men of deficient intellect aimlessly wander for a long time. Tell us that means whereby they are released from the bondage of births and worldly existence. We wish to hear it. Our eagerness is great.

Maheśvara said :

7. O Brahmins, I do not see any means other than the son of Vasudeva for the liberation of men bound by the noose of action (and reactions) who undergo misery.

8. Those who worship well that lord who wields conch, discus and club, by word, deeds and thoughts attain the highest region.

9. Of what avail is their life and the beast-like activity of those people whose mind is not directed towards Vāsudeva who pervades the entire universe?

The sages said :

10. O Pināka-bearing Śaṅkara, O destroyer of the eyes of Bhaga, O lord adored by the worlds, we wish to hear the greatness of Vāsudeva.

Maheśvara said :

11. Hari the eternal Puruṣa is more excellent than Brahmā. He is Kṛṣṇa with golden splendour like the sun shining in a cloudless sky.

12. He has ten arms. He has great splendour. He is the destroyer of the enemies of gods. He is Hṛṣīkeśa marked by the scar Śrīvatsa. He is the leader of gods.

13. Brahmā is born of his belly. I am born of his head. The luminaries are born of his hair. Devas and Asuras are born of his bodily hairs.

14. The sages and the eternal worlds are born of his body. He is the abode of Brahmā himself and of Devas too.

15. That lord of the three worlds is the creator of the universe. He is also the annihilator of all living beings, mobile and immobile.

16. He is the most excellent among gods. He is the lord of Devas. He overcomes enemies. He is omniscient. He is the creator of all beings. He goes everywhere. He has faces all round.

17. In the three worlds there is no other living being greater than he. He is eternal. He is blessed. He is known as Govinda.

18. For the fulfilment of the task of gods he takes up human form. He bestows honour on others. He will be killing all kings in battle.

19. Without the help of Trivikrama, the hosts of Devas will be leaderless and they will be incapable of performing their divine functions.

20-21. He is the leader of all living beings. He is the leader of Devas. He is identical with the slightest created thing and the greatest as well. He is the supreme Brahman. He is the perpetual refuge of the brahminical sages. Brahmā is stationed in his umbilicus. I am stationed in his body.

22. The gods are comfortably stationed in his body. That lotus-eyed lord has goddess Lakṣmī in his belly. He stays in the company of Śrī.

23-25. His weapons are Śārṅga (bow), discus and sword. He has (Garuḍa) the enemy, of all Nāgas for his emblem in the flag. He is possessed of excellent good conduct, purity, self-control, valour, virility pleasing body, ever-increasing power, of straightforwardness, kindness, beauty of form and strength. He wields all kinds of divine miraculous weapons very wonderful to behold.

26. He is thousand-eyed and he operates the Yogic Māyā. He is Virūpākṣa. He is noble-minded. By gentle speech he praises friendly folk. He is fond of his kith and kin.

27. That lord has ample forbearance. He does not boast of himself. He bestows (the power to realise) Brahman. He removes the fear of those who are distressed by fear. He increases the delight of his friends.

28. He is the seat of refuge of all living beings. He is engaged in the protection of the poor. He is richly endowed with learning and wealth. He is honoured by all living beings.

29. He helps those who resort to him. He causes fear in the minds of his enemies. He is conversant with polity. He is richly

endowed with the quality of justice. He is the expounder of Brahman. He has conquered his sense-organs.

30-41. For the sustenance of Devas the lord who is possessed of the greatest intellect will be born in the family of Manu, in the splendid path of Manu, descended from Prajāpati and consecrated by piety. There is a son of Manu named Aṁśa. Antardhāman is his successor. (The son of) Antardhāman is the Prajāpati, Havirdhāman the uncensured. O brahmins, Prācīnabarhiṣ will be born as the son of Havirdhāman. Ten sons will be born to him with Pracetas as the eldest. Dakṣa the Prajāpati will be born as the son of Pracetas. Āditya will be the son of Dakṣa and (Vaivasvata) Manu will be born of Āditya. Ilā and Sudyumna will be born in the family of Manu. Purūravas will be born of Budha and Āyus will be born thereof. Nahuṣa will be born of him and his son will be Yayāti. Yadu of great prowess will be born of him and his son will be Kroṣṭṛ. The great son of Kroṣṭṛ will be called Vṛjinīvān. The unvanquished Uṣaṅgu will be born of Vrjinīvān. The heroic Citraratha will be born as the son of Uṣaṅgu. His younger (brother, the younger son of Uṣaṅgu) will be famous by the name of Śūra. O excellent brahmins, in the family of these kings of well-known prowess, possessed of good qualities and conduct and of purity and readiness to perform sacrifices, the well-known excellent Kṣatriya, Śūra of great vigour and prowess, will beget his famous son Vasudeva, Ānakadundubhi, who will expand his race and who will bestow honour on all. Vāsudeva of four arms will be born as his son. He will be liberal in gifts. He will honour brahmins. He will be fond of the twice-born. He will realise Brahman.

42-43. After killing king Jarāsandha, this scion of the family of Yadu will release the imprisoned kings. That powerful king will possess all earthly jewels of kings. He will be unhindered in the whole of the Earth due to his vigour and prowess.

44-47. He will be richly endowed with valour. He will become the Emperor of all kings. He will be staying in Dvārakā after he has slain the enemies. After conquering the wicked he will protect goddess Earth: Approaching him in the company of excellent deserving brahmins, all of you shall duly worship him like the eternal Brahmā. The powerful lord Vāsudeva of great prowess should be seen by anyone who wishes to see me and

Brahmā the grandfather. If he is seen I too am seen. I do not entertain any doubtful thought in this regard.

48-50. O ascetics, know that (Brahmā) is Vāsudeva. The hosts of Devas beginning with Brahmā will become pleased with that person of whom the lotus-eyed lord is fond. If any man in the world seeks refuge in Keśava he will attain fame and renown and go to heaven. He will become righteous and also the instructor in virtuous activities.

51. Acyuta, that lord of Devas, should be worshipped by a person conversant with virtue. When this lord is worshipped he will always possess virtue.

52. With a desire to do whatever is conducive to the benefit of all subjects, that lord of great splendour, the tiger among men created crores of sages for spreading Dharma (virtue).

53. They, beginning with Sanatkumāra, duly created by him, stay on the Gandhamādana mountain, performing austerities.

54. Hence, O leading twice-born, that eloquent lord conversant with Dharma should be bowed to. He shall salute on being saluted; he shall honour, on being honoured.

55. O excellent brahmins, that lord shall see on being seen; he shall offer refuge everyday, on being sought refuge in; On being worshipped regularly he shall accept worship.

56. Such is the great vow of the great primordial lord Viṣṇu the undespicable. It is always followed by good people.

57. The eternal lord is always worshipped by Devas in the universe. They follow him by resorting to a befitting fearlessness.

58. That son of Devakī should always be bowed to, by thought, by speech and by deeds by brahmins exerting themselves. He should necessarily be seen.

59. O excellent sages, this is the pathway laid down by me. If that lord of Devas is seen, the excellent Devas shall be seen.

60. I too always worship and bow to that lord, the grandfather of the worlds, the great Boar, lord of the universe.

61. All the three deities will undoubtedly be seen in him. All of us, all the gods, stay in his body.

62. The ploughshare-wielding lord, well-known as Bala,

having the lustre of a number of white mountains put together will be born as his elder brother. He will hold the Earth aloft.

63-67. He has a three-hooded head. He is one whose end is not seen. Suparṇa, the powerful son of Kaśyapa, was not capable of seeing the end of that noble lord, in spite of his prowess. He is Śeṣa who joyously moves about. He stays within embracing the Earth by means of his body. Viṣṇu is the lord who bears the earth. He who is Rāma is Hṛṣīkeśa, Acyuta, the lord who bears aloft the entire Earth. Both of them are divine, tigers among men with divine exploits. They wield discus and ploughshare. They are worthy of honour. They should be seen, O ascetics, this is a favour shown to you. Hence, all of you shall strenuously worship the most excellent one among the descendents of Yadu.

CHAPTER ONE HUNDRED AND NINETEEN

Goal of the devotees of Viṣṇu

The sages said :

1. Oh, the wonderful greatness of Kṛṣṇa has been heard by us. It is holy. It dispels sins. It is conducive to wealth. It destroys the round of births and deaths.

2. O great sage, after worshipping Vāsudeva, duly and with devotion what goal do the men who are engaged in the worship of Vāsudeva attain ?

3. Do they attain liberation or heaven, O great sage ? Or, O excellent sage, do they obtain both the fruits ?

4. O omniscient one, it behoves you to dispel this doubt lurking in our hearts. O excellent sage, excepting you there is noone else in this world who can dispel it.

Vyāsa said :

5. Well done, well-done, O excellent sages! What has been uttered by you is quite pertinent. Now listen to all those things

in order which bring about the happiness of the devotees of Viṣṇu.

6. By the mere initiation (into the fold) of Kṛṣṇa, men attain salvation. What then, in regard to those who devotedly worship Viṣṇu always !

7. O excellent sages, neither heaven nor salvation is inaccessible to them. Devotees of Viṣṇu obtain even the rarest things, would they desire them.

8. Just as after climbing the mountain of jewels one can take away any number as one pleases, so also O leading sages, one can obtain the cherished things from Kṛṣṇa.

9. Just as, after reaching the wish-yielding Kalpa tree, O brahmins, a person plucks the fruits as he pleases, so also one can take one's cherished things from Kṛṣṇa.

10. By duly and faithfully worshipping Vāsudeva, the preceptor of the universe, men attain the fruit of virtue, wealth, love and salvation.

11. By propitiating that lord of the universe with a purified inner soul men obtain desirable things difficult of access even unto Devas.

12. To those who devotedly worship the Imperishable lord Vāsudeva there is nothing inaccessible in the three worlds.

13. Blessed are those persons in the world who worship Lord Hari who dispels all sins and who bestows the desired benefits.

14. By worshipping the most excellent lord of Devas, brahmins, Kṣatriyas, Vaiśyas, women, Śudras and men of low castes attain the greatest goal.

15. Hence, O sinless sages, listen. I shall expound what you ask. I shall succinctly narrate the goal of those noble souls.

16-19. They eschew this human body which is the abode of ailments, which is unsteady, which is transient as the bubbles of water and which is subject to old age and death. They eschew the body which emits the foul smell of flesh and blood, which is full of urine and faeces and other foul substances, which has the bones as the supporting pole, which is impure and which has sinews, vessels and skin. They go to the several abodes of the guardians of quarters of the worlds by means of an aerial chariot that can go to any place as desired, that reverberates due to the divine Gandharva music, that has the colour (and lustre) of the mid-day sun and that is bedecked with series of stringed tinkling bells.

The Gandharvas will be singing songs of praise. They will be embellished by the celestial damsels.

20-28. They enjoy the pleasures of those several worlds for a period equal to a Manvantara. They enjoy all kinds of pleasures.

Thereafter, they go to the heavenly abode that bestows happiness. O brahmins, there they enjoy excellent pleasures for a period equal to ten Manvantaras.

O Brahmins, from there the devotees of Viṣṇu go to the Gandharvaloka. There they enjoy pleasures delightful to the mind for a period equal to twenty Manvantaras.

They are well honoured there and from there they go to the Solar region where they enjoys super-divine pleasures for a period equal to thirty Manvantaras.

From there, O Brahmins, they go to the Lunar region that bestows all pleasures. For a period equal to forty Manvantaras they enjoy splendid pleasures there. They are devoid of old age and death.

From there, O excellent sages, they go to the Stellar region bedecked with lofty mansions. They are embellished by all good qualities. For a period equal to fifty Manvantaras they enjoy all pleasures as they please.

From there, O Brahmins, they go to the region of Devas which is very difficult of access.

O Brahmins, for a period equal to sixty Manvantaras they enjoy rare pleasures along with the eightfold Siddhis. They are worshipped by Devas and from there they proceed to the region of Indra.

29-31. For a period equal to seventy Manvantaras they enjoy higher and nobler divine pleasures that heighten their mental happiness. From there they proceed to the excellent region of Prajāpati.

For a period equal to eighty Manvantaras they enjoy there all types of pleasures. From there, O brahmins, the devotees of Viṣṇu proceed to the region of Brahmā.

32-37. For a period equal to ninety Manvantaras they joyously sport there. Thereafter they return to the Earth and are born as brahmins of Yogic power in the excellent families of brahmins. They master the Vedas and scriptures and comprehend their meanings.

Thus they enjoy pleasures of all the worlds, come back to this Earth and go higher and higher.

In the course of every birth, O excellent brahmins, they enjoy all desired pleasures for a hundred years and thereafter proceed to the next world.

When a set of ten births is thus completed duly they proceed to the divine world of Hari from the region of Brahmā. After going there and enjoying inexhaustible pleasures full of good qualities for a period equal to a hundred Manvantaras, O excellent brahmins, they proceed to the World of Brahmā. They are devoid of births and deaths.

38. They take up divine bodies of great strength bedecked by earrings. Huge bodies, O excellent brahmins, they assume with a four-armed form, and sport there.

39. O excellent brahmins, in their eternal state they remain for ten thousand crores of years and are bowed to by all Devas.

40. Thereafter, O brahmins, those magnificent self-possessed men go to the abode of Narasiṁha. There they rejoice and sport for about ten thousand crores of years.

41. At the end of that period they go to the abode of Viṣṇu, resorted to by the Siddhas. There they play happily for ten thousand years.

42-44. Then O brahmins, those excellent aspirants go to the region of Brahmā. They stay there for a long time, for many hundred crores of years and then go to the city of Nārāyaṇa. The lordly aspirants enjoy the pleasures for millions of crores of years. Thereafter the excellent aspirants of divine form and great strength go to the city of Aniruddha. They are eulogised by Devas and Asuras.

45. Devoid of death and old age those devotees of Viṣṇu stay there for fourteen thousand crores of years.

46. Thereafter they go to the city of Pradyumna. Free of

ailments, O brahmins, they stay there for three hundred lakhs of crores of years.

47. They are delighted. They are endowed with strength and power. They can go anywhere as they please. Thereafter those Yogins go to the place where lord Saṅkarṣaṇa rules.

48-50. After staying there for a long time and enjoying thousands of pleasures they enter the unsullied Vāsudeva devoid of form and name. In that supreme entity devoid of death and old age they become free. There is no doubt that after going there they become liberated.

Thus, O excellent sages, the intelligent men engaged in the worship of Vāsudeva attain worldly pleasures and salvation.

CHAPTER ONE HUNDRED AND TWENTY

The benefits of singing devotional songs of Viṣṇu while keeping awake at night

Vyāsa said :

1-5. There is no doubt about this that a man who fasts on the eleventh day of either fortnight and carries out the following observances, goes to the greatest region of Viṣṇu. With mental and physical purity he should duly take bath and wear a neatly washed cloth. He should conquer his sense organs. With faith and mental purity he should worship Viṣṇu by fragrant flowers, scents, lamps, incense, cooked foods, different offerings, repetition of holy names and mantras, homas, circumambulations, hymns of various kinds, divine and pleasing vocal and instrumental music, prostration and excellent utterances of Jaya (Be victorious). After duly worshipping thus he should keep awake for the whole of the night narrating the stories of Viṣṇu or singing his songs of prayer. He should be devoted to Viṣṇu.

The sages said :

6. O great sage, describe to us the benefit of the chorus song of Viṣṇu while keeping awake. Great is our eagerness to hear the same.

Vyāsa said :

7. Listen, O excellent sages, I shall describe duly the benefit of the chorus song of Viṣṇu while keeping awake, as mentioned before.

8. The city of Avantī is well-known in the world. Lord Viṣṇu wielding conch, discus and iron club occupies it.

9. At the outskirts of that city there was a Cāṇḍāla who was an expert in singing. He earned much wealth by legitimate means. He duly maintained his servants.

10. That Cāṇḍāla was a devotee of Viṣṇu and he strictly adhered to the observances of holy rites. On the Ekādaśī day be used to come (to the temple), observe fast and sing songs of prayer.

11. His songs in praise of Viṣṇu were sung in various notes such as Gāndhāra, Ṣaḍja, Niṣāda, Pañcama, Dhaivata etc.

12-13. He used to keep awake at night and to sing songs in praise of Viṣṇu. At dawn on the Dvādaśī day he used to worship the lord and return home. O excellent brahmins, after feeding his daughter's sons-in-law and nephews he used to take food along with his attendants.

14. Many years of his life were thus spent by him in propitiating Viṣṇu by means of different types of songs (of prayer).

15. Once, on the eleventh day in the dark half of the month of Caitra he went to the excellent forest for the purpose of serving Viṣṇu.

16. Engrossed in devotion, he wanted to gather flowers from the forest. He reached the foot of a Vibhītaka tree in the great forest on the banks of Kṣiprā.

17. There he was seized by a Rākṣasa in order to devour him. The Cāṇḍāla then said to him— "I should not be devoured by you today.

18. "O good Sir, you shall devour me (tomorrow) in the morning. In truth I will come back again. O Rākṣasa, I have a great task to be performed today. So release me.

19. "In truth, I will come tomorrow. You will then eat me. For the purpose of serving Viṣṇu I have to keep awake in the

night. It does not behove you, O Rākṣasa, to cause any obstacle in the observance of the holy rite by me."

Vyāsa said :

20. The Rākṣasa said in reply : "O Cāṇḍala, I have not taken food for the last ten days and today you have come across me.

21. I shall not set you free. I shall devour you. I am overwhelmed by hunger".

On hearing the words of the Rākṣasa, the Cāṇḍāla said to him, consoling him by uttering gentle words which were firm and truthful:

The Cāṇḍāla said:

22. O Brahmarākṣasa, the entire world has its root in truth. Hence, listen, on truth I promise my return.

23. All these know each and every action of men, viz. the sun, moon, fire, wind, earth, firmament, water, mind, day, night, the two junctions (i.e. dawn and dusk) and Yama.

24-38. O Rākṣasa, I promise you that if I do not come again to you let me be infested by the sins which the following persons acquire in the circumstances mentioned, viz. the sin of one who indulges in dalliance with other men's wives; the sin of those who take wealth of others; the sin of a brahmin murderer; of one who drinks liquor; of one who defiles the preceptor's bed; the sin of the husband of a barren woman; the sin of the husband of a Śūdra woman; the sin of a temple priest who misappropriates temple funds; the sin of one who takes fish and meat; the sin of one who habitually eats the flesh of pig and tortoise; the sin of one who regularly takes the flesh of the backbone; the sin of one who takes meat without offering the same to gods; the sin of one who kills his friend; the sin of an ungrateful fellow and the paramour of a widow (who marries again); the sin of a pollution due to death of a relative; the sin of a man of ruthless actions; the sin of a miser; the sin of one who sends away guests without entertaining them; the sin that befalls one who indulges in sexual intercourse on the new moon day or the sixth, eighth or fourteenth day of a lunar fortnight whether dark or bright; the sin of a brahmin who cohabits with a woman in her monthly course; the sin of a person who indulges in sexual intercourse after performing Śrāddha; the sin of those who take food on Parvan days without taking bath; the sin that befalls one on eating filthy matter; the sin of those who cohabit with the wife of a friend; the sin of a back-biter; the sin of one who is fond of arrogance and deception; the sin of one who destroys honey; the sin that befalls one who promises to give something to a brahmin but does not give it; the sin due to a falsehood in regard to a virgin; the sin due to a falsehood in regard to cows and mules; the sin of a man who kills women and children; the sin of one who utters a lie; the sin of those who are disrespectful to Devas, Vedas, brahmins, kings, sons and friends and to chaste ladies; the sin of those who go to sleep after uttering a lie to or after being disrespectful to the teacher(?); the sin of those who commit arson; the sin of those who burn down forests; the sin due to the non-performance of domestic sacrifice of a householder; the sin of a slayer of cows; the sin of a base brahmin; the sin of a Parivitta and a Parivedin (i.e. the elder and the younger brothers of whom the younger marries before the elder); the sin of those who contract matrimonial alliance with them; the sin of a person who destorys a foetus. (Let all these sins befall me.) O Rākṣasa, of what avail are these different kinds of vows and pledges? Let a terrific vow be heard. It is being uttered though it is vey difficult to utter it. Let these sins befall me if I do not approach you, viz. the sin of one who sustains himself through the sinful activities of his own virgin daughter; the sin of a perjuror and that of a false witness; the sin of one who performs a sacrifice on behalf of a person unworthy of it; the sin of a Ṣaṇḍha (eunuch?); the sin of a Sramaṇa; the sin of one who returns to a householder's life after having renounced the world once; and the sin of a lecherous religious student.

Vyāsa said :

39. On hearing the words of the Cāṇḍāla the Brahmarākṣasa became surprised. He said : "Oh, go, keep your promise".

40. On being told thus by the Rākṣasa, the Cāṇḍāla gathered flowers and went to the temple of Viṣṇu.

41. He handed over flowers to a brahmin who washed them with water, worshipped Viṣṇu and went to his abode, O ascetics.

42. The Cāṇḍāla observed fast and kept awake during the night staying in the outer ground and singing songs of prayer.

43. As the night dawned into day he eulogised and made obeisance to the lord and set off to the place where the demon was waiting in order to keep his promise.

44. As he was going along the path a certain man asked him: "O gentle Sir, where are you going"? He told everything and the man said again :

45. "Since the body is the means of acquiring virtue, wealth, love and liberation, an intelligent man should maintain his body with great care.

46-48. It is the man who remains alive that obtains virtue, wealth, happiness and salvation. The living man obtains renown. A dead man has no place in the world. No one speaks about him."

On hearing these words, the Cāṇḍāla replied indicating the reason :

"O gentle sir, it is because of my promise that I am going. I have taken vows."

Vyāsa said :

49. The man said again unto him: "Don't be a fool. O my good man, haven't you heard what has been uttered by Manu?

50. (Learned men) say that the following five untruths are not sinful, viz. the lie that has been uttered for affording protection to cows, women and brahmins; the lie uttered while celebrating a marriage; the lie that has been uttered for the sake of friends; the lie uttered when one is faced with death; and the lie uttered when one is being robbed of all riches.

51. (?) Injunctions regarding righteousness are not applicable in the case of untrue statements to women, and enemies or those uttered when one is faced with death or destruction of wealth or when one is being deceived".

On hearing his words thus, the Cāṇḍāla replied :

The Cāṇḍāla said :

52. Do not say thus. Welfare unto you. Truth is honoured in the worlds. Whatever happiness is in the world is acquired by truth.

53. It is due to truth that the sun blazes; it is due to truth that waters are juicy; it is due to truth that fire burns; and it is due to truth that the wind blows.

54. The achievement of virtue, wealth and love and the rare acquisition of liberation becomes possible due to the truth of men. Hence one shall never forsake truth.

55. Truth is the supreme Brahman in the world. Truth is the most excellent among sacrifices. Truth descends from heaven. Hence one shall never forsake Truth.

Vyāsa said :

56. Saying this, the Cāṇḍāla ignored that excellent man and went to the place where the Brahmarākṣasa, the slayer of living beings, was waiting.

57. On seeing that the Cāṇḍāla had come, his eyes beamed with wonder. Shaking his head (approvingly) he told him:

The Brahmarākṣasa said :

58. Well done, well done, O highly blessed one. You have kept your promise. I do not consider you a mere Cāṇḍāla since you have distinguished yourself due to your truthfulness.

59. Due to this action I think that you are a brahmin pure and not fit to be disposed of. I shall tell you, gentle sir, something based on righteousness. Tell me what was done by you there in the abode of Viṣṇu on that night?

The Cāṇḍāla said:

60. Listen. I shall tell you exactly what has been performed by me on that night in that abode of Viṣṇu.

61. I knelt down beneath that shrine of Viṣṇu. I kept awake for the whole of the night singing songs of praise of Viṣṇu.

The Brahmarākṣasa said :

62. Tell me. How long have you been observing this rite of keeping awake devotedly in the abode of Viṣṇu?

63. He replied smilingly, "O Rākṣasa, I have been observing this rite of keeping awake every month on Ekādaśī day, for twenty years" On hearing the words of the Cāṇḍāla, the Brahmarākṣasa said:

The Brahmarākṣasa said:

64. It behoves you to carry out what I am going to tell you. O good man, give unto me the benefit of keeping awake for one single night.

65. In that case I shall set you free. I shall not leave you otherwise, O highly blessed one. I have vowed thrice.

After saying this he stopped.

Vyāsa said :

66. The Cāṇḍāla said to him : "O night-prowler, my own self has been surrendered to you. What is the use of talking much? Eat me up as you please".

67. The Rākṣasa said to him again: "Give me (the benefit of) keeping awake for two yāmas (six hours) along with the songs sung by you. It behoves you to take pity on me."

The Cāṇḍāla said :

68. Why this irrelevant talk? Eat me up as you please. I will not give you the benefit of keeping awake.

On hearing the words of the Cāṇḍāla the Brahmarākṣasa said to him:

The Brahmarākṣasa said :

69-71. Who is foolish and evil-minded enough to dare to look at you in order to harass you and inflict pain on you since you have been guarded by your own righteous activities?

Good men should be merciful towards a wretched fellow who has been overwhelmed by sins, who has been deluded by worldly pleasures and who has been distressed by the throes of hell.

Hence, O highly blessed one, take pity on me. Give me the benefit of keeping awake for a single yāma (three hours) and go back to your own abode.

Vyāsa said :

72-73. The Cāṇḍāla said to him again : "I will not go home nor will I give the benefit of keeping awake even for a single yāma". The Brahmarākṣasa then smilingly said to the Cāṇḍāla:

The Brahmarākṣasa said :

Give unto me the benefit of the song enthusiastically sung by you at the end of the night. Save me. Lift me up from (the mire of) sin.

Vyāsa said :

74-75. When this was uttered by him, the Cāṇḍāla said to him :

The Cāṇḍāla said :

What evil action has been committed by you formerly due to the fault of which you have become a Brahmarākṣasa?

Vyāsa said :

76. On hearing his words the Brahmarākṣasa remembered the evil actions committed by himself and became extremely distressed. He then said to the Cāṇḍāla :

The Brahmarākṣasa said :

77. Who was I before, what had I committed as a result of which I had to be born in an evil womb as a Rākṣasa—let it be heard.

78. Formerly, I was a brahmin well-known as Somaśarmā. I was the son of Devaśarman who used to perform sacrifices and regularly study the Vedas.

79. (faulty text) There was a certain king on whose behalf, I performed sacrifice though he had been ostracised and forbidden to use the mantras. Since I was interested in the holy rite I was engaged in the rites near the sacrificial post.

80. Afflicted by greed and delusion I performed the duty of Agnīdhra in the sacrifice. When it was concluded I performed an arrogant rite due to my folly.

81. (In my arrogance) I began to perform a sacrifice intended to last for twelve days. As it was being performed I had a stomach pain.

82-84. Ten days elapsed in full. But the sacrifice had not been concluded. As the offering was being offered to Śiva in a moment pertaining to Rākṣasa I died and due to that fault I became a Brahmarākṣasa. I was not conversant with the technique of sacrifice and I performed the sacrifice reciting the taxts without proper accents and notes. Due to this faulty performance I became a Brahmarākṣasa.

85. I am therefore immersed in the great ocean of sin. Lift me up therefrom. It behoves you to give me the benefit of the last song of prayer at the holy rite of keeping awake.

Vyāsa said :

86. The Cāṇḍāla said to him: "If you desist from killing living beings I shall offer unto you the benefit of the last song of prayer".

87. "Yes, of course", said he and the Cāṇḍāla invoked by means of Mantras the holy rite of keeping awake for half of a Muhūrta and offered the benefit of the last song of prayer.

88. After the benefit of the song of prayer had been given the Brahmarākṣasa became delighted. He bowed down to the Cāṇḍāla and went to the holiest of pilgrim-spots named Pṛthūdaka.

89-90. He decided on a fast unto death there, O brahmins, and died. Invigorated by the benefit of song of prayer he became freed of his Rākṣasahood. As a result of the great power of the holy centre he attained the region of Brahmā which is difficult of access. Freed of all agony he stayed there for ten thousand years.

91. At the end of that period he was born as a brahmin endowed with the faculty of memory and control over his sense-organs. O brahmins, I shall tell you his story later on.

92-93. Even as I narrate listen to the rest of the story of the Cāṇḍāla. When the Rākṣasa departed that self-possessed

(Cāṇḍāla) of good control over himself returned to his house. Remembering the incidents in the story of that brahmin this pure man became disinterested in worldly pleasures. He entrusted his wife to the care of his sons and began the circumambulation of the Earth.

94. Beginning with Kokāmukha (holy centre) he went up to the holy shrine of Skanda. After visiting Skanda he performed the rite of circumambulation in Dhārācakra.

95. O brahmins, he then came to the lofty rocky top of the excellent mountain Vindhya and reached the holy spot Pāpapramocana.

96. That scion of a Cāṇḍāla family performed the holy dip that dispelled his sins. Freed from sins he remembered many of his previous births.

97. In a previous birth he had been a mendicant who had restrained his body and controlled his speech and mind. He was intelligent and he mastered the Vedas.

98. Once while cows were being taken away by thieves the alms became defiled by dust and they were discarded by the mendicant.

99-102. Due to that fault and sin he was born as a Cāṇḍāla. He took his holy dip in the Pāpapramocana and passed away on the banks of the Narmadā river. O brahmins, he was reborn as an excellent brahmin though foolish. After he had completed his stay there for thirty years, a man of great spiritual attainment who was endowed with Yogic Māyā and Śakti was wandering here and there assuming an ugly form. On seeing him the foolish brahmin mockingly saluted him and said: "Welfare O Siddha, whence are you coming ?"

Vyāsa said :

103. On being addressed thus, the venerable one thought that he had been recognized and replied: "I have come from heavenly region."

104. The foolish one said to the Sīddha : "In the heaven do you know Urvaśī the most excellent celestial damsel born of the thighs of Nārāyaṇa ?"

105. The Siddha said: "I know that Urvaśī who is the

chief ornament of heaven, whose birth and parentage is very noble and who bears the Cāmara for Indra."

106-108. The brahmin bereft of straightforward ways said to the Siddha: "O my friend, my message should be conveyed to Urvaśī by you, with great respect. You will please tell me what she says in reply". The Siddha said: "Of course". The brahmin was pleased at that. The Siddha went to heaven at the top of Meru and met Urvaśī. He told her what had been said by the brahmin.

109. She said to that excellent Siddha: "I do not know the brahmin who is the ruler of Kāśī. The truth has been mentioned to you. The fact is not retained in my mind."

110. On being told thus the Siddha returned. After some time he went to Varāṇasī and was again met by the foolish brahmin.

111. On seeing him he asked again: "What did the lady born of the thighs, say to you ?" The Siddha said: "Urvaśī spoke to me thus, 'I do not know' ".

112. On hearing the words of the Siddha he said again with a gentle smile separating his lips: "Urvaśī should be told thus by you—'How will you know ?' "

113. "Of course I will do this." After saying this the Siddha went to heaven and saw Urvaśī coming out of Indra's abode.

114-119. The excellent Siddha said (everything) to her. She replied : "Let the excellent brahmin perform some holy rite whereby Siddha, I can know him. Not otherwise". Approaching the foolish brahmin again, the Siddha told what was said by Urvaśī. The brahmin thereupon pledged the following holy rite: "O Siddha man, this holy observance has been taken up by me in front of you. From today onwards I will not eat mixture. The truth has been uttered by me."

On being told thus, the Siddha went to heaven, met Urvaśī and said: "The man has said thus : 'From today onwards I will not eat Saktu at all' ".

Urvaśī spoke to him again : "Now I have come to know him. The manner of taking up such a vow indicates he is foolish and ridiculous." After saying this Urvaśī went to her abode.

120-122. The Siddha roamed over the Earth as he pleased. The excellent lady Urvaśī went to Vārāṇasī and took her bath in the waters of Matsyodarī assuming her divine form. This foolish brahmin too had gone to the river Matsyodarī. On seeing Urvaśī bathing there he was overwhelmed by passionate love that agitated him too much.

123. He showed many gestures and pranks befitting a foolish person. Urvaśī understood him. Coming to know that he was the selfsame fool as mentioned by Siddha she smilingly spoke:

Urvaśī said :

124. O highly blessed one, what do you desire from me? Let it be mentioned quickly. I shall carry out your injunctions. Rest assured.

The foolish brahmin said:

125. O lady of pure smiles, save my life by surrendering yourself.

Vyāsa said :

126. Then Urvaśī said to the brahmin: "I am now in the midst of a holy observance. Stay here for a while. Await my arrival".

127-130. The brahmin said: "I am staying (here). She then went to heaven. The celestial damsel returned after a month and saw that brahmin lean and emaciated as he had been staying on the banks observing the fast. Seeing him steadfast in his decision she assumed the body of an old woman. She then went to Matsyodarī and prepared a mixture of sugar, honey and ghee. After taking her bath the lady of nice eyes stood on the bank with a meaningful intention. She then called the brahmin and said :

Urvaśī said :

131. For the purpose of prosperity and well-being, O brahmin, a holy vow has been undertaken by me. At the conclusion of observance I am making this charitable offering. O brahmin, please accept it.

Vyāsa said :

132. He said : "What is this that is being offered ? It is sugar-coated. O gentle lady, my throat is being parched due to hunger. Hence I am asking. Please tell me".

133. She said: "O brahmin, it is a mixture prepared from flour mixed with sugar. Take this and please yourself. Do not delay".

134-135. On hearing that the brahmin remembered what had happened before. Although he was afflicted by hunger he said: "O gentle lady, I cannot accept this. In front of the excellent Siddha, the holy vow that I will not eat the mixture had been undertaken by me in order that Urvaśī might recollect me. Give this to someone else."

136. She said : "O gentle Sir, the observance undertaken by you refers to the wooden one. This is not made of wood. You have been extremely afflicted by hunger. Eat this".

137. The brahmin replied to her: "O gentle lady, the statement had not been qualified by me. A general vow had been undertaken by me."

138. That lady then said again: "O brahmin, if you do not want to eat take this home. Your family shall partake of it."

139-141. He said to her: "O lady of bright teeth, I am not going home. The excellent lady who surpasses everyone in the three worlds (Urvaśī) by her qualities had been here. Afflicted by love I had requested her and I had been consoled by her saying: 'Stay here for a while' and I had said: 'I shall stay'. O gentle lady, a month has elapsed after she had gone and I have been staying here. O one who has undertaken a vow, I have been steadfast in my love for truth and I am eager to have a union (with her)."

142. On hearing his words, Urvaśī resumed her excellent form. Smiling with a majestic grandeur she said to the brahmin:

Urvaśī said :

143-145. Well done, O brahmin. Desirous of seeing me you have observed the holy rite with fully concentrated mind.

I am Urvaśī, O brahmin, and I have come here with a desire to know you. You have been tested (and found to be) firm in your decision. You are saintly and truthful in your austerity. Go to the place Sūkarava well known as Rūpatīrtha.

O great brahmin, you will achieve a great Siddhi. Then you will attain me.

Vyāsa said :

146. O brahmins, after saying this Urvaśī flew up to heaven. That brahmin of truthful austerity went to Rūpatīrtha.

147. There he was devoted to peaceful enterprises. He was pure and he undertook holy observances. After casting off his physical body he went to the excellent Gandharvaloka.

148. For a period of one hundred Manvantaras he experienced all pleasures and then was born as a king in an excellent dynasty. He was eager in delighting and encouraging his subjects.

149. He performed various sacrifices, concluding them with excellent monetary gifts. After entrusting his sons with the work of ruling the realm he went again to Śaukarava.

150. He died in the holy spot Rūpatīrtha and again went to the region of Indra. After enjoying pleasures there for a period of hundred Manvantaras he came off.

151-152. O sages, for the union with Urvaśī he became Purūravas, the son of Budha in the excellent city Pratiṣṭhāna. Thus any brahmin of truthful austerity can attain salvation after enjoying pleasures if he propitiates Viṣṇu in the holy spot Rūpatīrtha in this birth.

CHAPTER ONE HUNDRED AND TWENTYONE

Manifestation of Māyā

The sages said :

1-2. The benefit of the song of prayer at the time of keeping awake in propitiation of Viṣṇu has been listened to by us. By virtue of it the Cāṇḍāla attained the greatest goal. O extremely intelligent one, tell us how devotion to Viṣṇu can be effected. Now we wish to hear about the holy rite or penance whereby that becomes possible.

Vyāsa said :

3. Listen, O leading sages. I shall mention in due order how a person shall attain devotion to Viṣṇu with great benefit.

4-5. The worldly existence is extremely terrible. It strikes terror into all living beings. It causes sorrows to men. Hundreds of miseries abound in it. A soul is born again and again in thousands of species of lower living organisms, O brahmins, and with great difficulty it attains human birth.

6. After human birth he attains brahminhood, power of discrimination, sense of piety and happiness in successive births.

7. Until the ultimate destruction of all sins of men accumulated in different births, devotion to Vāsudeva identical with the universe, is not possible.

8-9. Hence, O brahmins, I shall tell you how devotion to Viṣṇu is effected.

A person may be devoted to other Devas mentally, verbally and physically. His soul is directed to those gods. Thereby, O excellent sages, he may become inclined to perform sacrifices.

10. Then, O brahmins, with great concentration and purity of mind be begins to love the fire-god. When the fire-god is propitiated he becomes a devotee of sun.

11. O brahmins, he worships sun-god regularly. When that god is pleased he becomes devoted to Śaṅkara.

12. He performs the worship of Śambhu duly and strenuously. When the three-eyed god is satisfied he becomes devoted to Keśava.

13. By worshipping the imperishable lord of the universe named Vāsudeva, O excellent brahmins, he attains worldly pleasures and salvation.

The sages said :

14. O great sage, some men are averse to devotion of Viṣṇu. O brahmin, tell us why they do not worship Viṣṇu.

Vyāsa said :

15. In this world, O excellent sages, two types of created beings are well-known, viz. Āsura (demonic) and Daiva (divine). They are created formerly by the self-born lord.

16. By attaining the divine nature men worship Acyuta. Those who have attained the demonic nature slander Hari.

17. The wisdom of those base men is obliterated by Māyā of Viṣṇu. Without attaining Hari, O brahmins, they attain lowest states.

18. His Māyā is deep and incomprehensible to Devas and Asuras. It causes great delusion to men. It cannot be surmounted by persons who are not self-possessed.

The sages said :

19. We all wish to comprehend that insurmountable Māyā of Viṣṇu. O sage conversant with details of virtue, it behoves you to narrate. Our eagerness is great.

Vyāsa said :

20. That Māyā is like a dream or the jugglery of a conjuror. It pulls and stretches the world, excepting the lord himself who is competent to comprehend Hari's Māyā.

21. Even as I narrate, O brahmins, listen to the confounded states of a brahmin and Nārada due to this Māyā.

22. Formerly, in a city there was a glorious king well known as Āgnīdhra. His son was a pure soul named Kāmadamana.

23. He was Dharmārāma (who sported in piety). He practised forbearance. He was engaged in devotedly serving his parents. He was skilful in delighting his subjects. He exerted himself much in the Vedas and scriptures.

24. The father endeavoured to celebrate his marriage but he did not like it. So the father asked him: "Why don't you like to take a wife unto you ?.

25. Indeed all men desire it for pleasure. A wife is the root of all happiness. Hence take one unto you".

26. Even after hearing the words of his father he maintained silence with solemnity. O brahmins, the father urged him frequently.

27. Then he said to his father : "O dear father, I have resorted to an attitude befitting my name (i.e. Kāmadamana). This is clearly a devoted service to Viṣṇu and it protects us".

28-29. Approaching him, the father said: "O my son, this is not a righteous thing. This should not be adopted by a learned man. Do as I direct you, my son. I am your father and hence your lord. Do not immerse my family in the slough of hell due to the (impending) extinction of the family.".

30. On hearing the behest of his father the son of perfect self-control was reminded of the old strange ways of the world. He said :

The son said:

31. Listen to my words, dear father. It is a statement of truth with cogent reasoning. O king, one should act in conformity with one's name. It is very truthful.

32. I have acquired thousands of births, hundreds of deaths and old age and acquisitions of and separation from wives in all of them.

33. Hundreds of different states have been attained by me —like those of grass, shrubs, creepers, winding plants, reptiles, animals, birds, beasts, women, men etc.

34-35. I have been by turns a Gaṇa, a Kinnara, a Gandharva, a Vidyādhara, a great serpent, a Yakṣa, a Guhyaka, a Rākṣasa, a Dānava, an Apsaras, a divine being etc. Again and again I have attained a thousand oceans (?). I have been created many times during creation. I have been killed many times during annihilation.

36. In view of my being united with a wife I had been the victim of deception. Listen to what happened in the third preceding birth. I shall briefly mention it together with the greatness of a holy spot.

37. After passing through many births as man, god, Gandharva, Nāga, Vidyādhara, birds and Kinnaras, dear father, I was born in a family where I became a sage given to penance.

38. Then my devotion to Viṣṇu, the slayer of Madhu and the lord of worlds, was very steady. By means of devotion and different holy rites and fasts, the wielder of discus, club and other miraculous weapons was propitiated by me.

39. The delighted noble Viṣṇu came there riding on the lord of birds (Garuḍa) (with the intention of) granting me boons. He said in a loud voice: "O twice-born one, let any boon be prayed for. I shall give you whatever you desire."

40. Then I said to lord Hari: "O Keśava, if you are pleased I shall choose a boon. O Janārdana, I wish to know that great Māyā belonging to you".

41. The enemy of Madhu and Kaiṭabha then said to me: "O brahmin, of what avail is that Māyā to you ? I shall give unto you virtue, wealth and love, prominent sons and freedom from sickness.

42. Then I said again to the enemy of Mura: "This is my desire to conquer wealth and virtue. I wish to know your Māyā, O Puṣkarākṣa (Lotus-eyed one). Show that unto me".

43. Then lord Viṣṇu, the prominent Man-Lion, the lord of goddess of wealth said these words to me: "No one knows my Māyā nor will any one ever know it.

44-45. O brahmin, formerly the celestial sage Nārada, son of Brahmā, was a great devotee of mine. With great devotion, like you, he propitiated me formerly. I went unto him in order to grant him a boon. He too chose this very boon. Although he was prevented by me, he chose the same boon like you now, due to his excessive foolishness.

46. Then I said: "O Nārada, sink unto the water and you will know my Māyā". Thereupon Nārada dipped himself under water. He was transformed into the daughter of the king of Kāśī named Suśīlā.

47. When she reached the prime of youth (the king of Kāśī) gave her in marriage to Sudharmā of fine virtue, the son of the king of Vidarbha. O great sage, in her company he indulged in unsurpassed pleasures.

48. When his father passed away, the kingdom duly passed on to him. Sudharmā of great valour became delighted and ruled over the Vidarbha kingdom. He was surrounded by sons and grandsons.

49. Then a great battle ensued between king Sudharmā and the king of Kāśī. In that battle were both the king of Vidarbha and the king of Kāśī together with their sons and grandsons.

50. (Defective text) Suśilā came to know that her father and her husband were killed along with sons and grandsons. She set off from the city and went to the battlefield. On seeing her dead father and husband along with their sons and grandsons Suśīlā grieved much.

51-54. The distressed lady lamented for a long time in the midst of the armies of her husband and father. Grief-stricken she rushed to her mother. She then took the dead bodies of her husband, father, brothers, sons and grandsons to the great cremation ground and prepared the funeral pyre. She herself lit the fire. When the fire blazed forth, Suśilā rushed into it crying loudly "Alas ! my son, Alas! my son". She was then transformed again into the sage Nārada. The fire too assumed the pure lustre of cool crystal. The full lake appeared and he came out of it. Lord Keśava stood in front of him with conch, iron club, sword (etc.) in his four hands. Laughingly he said to Nārada the celestial sage:

55. "Who is your son ? Tell me, O great sage. With your senses gone whom do you bevail ?"

Thereupon, Nārada was ashamed. Then I said to him:

56. O Nārada, such is my Māyā. It is full of pain and misery. It cannot be understood by the lotus-seated lord, Indra, Rudra, and others. How will you comprehend this incomprehensible Māyā ?

57. On hearing my words the great sage said : "O Lord Viṣṇu, grant me (the boon of) devotion to you. Whenever opportunity arrives let me remember you. Let me have your perpetual vision.

58. O Acyuta, let the place where, in my grief, I had stepped on to the funeral pyre become a holy spot. Let it be presided over by you, O Keśava, together with the lotus-born lord Brahmā."

59. Then, O brahmin, Nārada was told by me thus "Let your funeral pyre be in the holy spot Śītoda. I, as Viṣṇu, shall stay here always. Maheśvara will stay on the northern side.

60. After cutting off that head of Brahmā which uttered harsh words, the three-eyed lord will come to this holy spot of thine for casting off the skull.

61. When the destroyer of the three cities, Śiva, takes his holy dip in this Tīrtha, the skull will drop down on the ground. Thereafter, this holy spot will become well known all over the Earth as Kapālamocana."

62. Ever since then the cloud-vehicled Lord Indra has never forsaken this holy spot. O brahmin, say that the sin of the slaughter of a brahmin ceased to become fierce in him (defective verse).

63. As long as the slayer of the enemies of Indra does not forsake that holy spot it will continue to be great and sacred. This secret holy spot has been eulogised by Devas as Avimukta. It is called Imperishable. It bestows merit.

64. Even after committing sins, if a man enters that Tīrtha he becomes pure and free from lapses. When he meditates on me he becomes pure and attains salvation due to the grace of the Lord.

65. In another birth he is born as one called Rudrapiśāca and experiences some misery. After many years he is freed from sins and he takes birth in the abode of a brahmin.

66. He will be pure and one having self-control. At the time of his death Rudra will repeat the beneficial Tāraka Mantra to him. After saying this to Nārada, an excellent brahmin, I went to the ocean of milk, my abode.

67-68. That brahmin (i.e. Nārada) went to heaven and is being honoured by the king of Gandharvas.

"Thus everything has been told to you to enlighten you. My Māyā cannot be understood. If you wish to know enter this water and you will come to know."

That brahmin, thus enlightened by Hari merged himself under water by the force of the inevitable future.

69-70. O father, that brahmin merged himself under the water in the Tīrtha Kokāmukha and then he was transformed into a girl in the abode of a Cāṇḍāla. She was endowed with beauty, good conduct and excellent qualities. She attained youthful age. She was married to Subāhu, son of a Cāṇḍāla, who was devoid of handsome features. She did not like her husband but he liked her much.

71. She gave birth to two sons bereft of eyesight and a

daughter who was deaf. The husband was very poor and so the helpless girl used to go to the river bank everyday and cry.

72. Once she went to the river taking the water pot with her. In order to take her bath she entered the water but was immediately transformed into her original form of a brahmin of good conduct engaged in holy rites and yogic practice.

73. As a long time passed by after her departure, her husband came to the holy river in search of her. He saw the water pot but not her on the bank. Thereupon in his excess of grief he lamented loudly.

74. Then the two blind sons and the deaf daughter came there. They too were distressed and on perceiving their crying father they wept bitterly.

75-76. Then he asked some brahmins who were on the river bank : "Tell me. Was a woman seen by you coming this way for water ?"

They said : "She entered the river but never came up. Only this much are we aware of."

On hearing their terrible words he began to cry again. Tears flooded his eyes.

77. On seeing him cry along with his daughter and sons I too became distressed. Grief reminded me, O King, that I was myself the Cāṇḍāla maiden.

78. Then, O King, I said to that Cāṇḍāla : "Why do you cry in distress ? You are not going to get her back by your foolish cries. It is in vain. Of what avail to you is this lamentation ?"

79. He said to me : "Both these sons are blind. The only girl is deaf. How can I, O brahmin, console these and bring them up ?"

80. After saying this he cried all the more loudly along with his children. The longer I watched the Cāṇḍāla crying the more I pitied him.

81. Preventing him from crying further in his grief, I narrated to him the incidents of my life. Thereupon the distressed man entered the waters of Kokāmukha.

82. Immediately after his entry into the water the Cāṇḍāla became free from sins by the efficacy of the Tīrtha. Even

as I stood watching, he entered an aerial chariot bright as the moon, O father, and went to heaven.

83. After his entering the water and passing away my grief increased causing me great delusion. Then, O excellent king, I dived into the sacred waters of the Kokā and went to heaven.

84. Again I was born, this time in the family of a Vaiśya. Here also I was distressed due to pain. I was endowed with the faculty of remembering my previous births due to the grace of the excellent Tīrtha. With a dejected mind I went to Kokāmukha putting sufficient restraint on my mind and utterances.

85. I observed holy rites and made my body emaciated. Then I went to heaven. Coming down therefrom I am now born in your abode. O father, I can remember my previous births by the grace of Hari.

86-87. I propitiated the lord in Kokāmukha. I have discarded my desire for both auspicious and inauspicious things.

After saying this he bowed to his father and went to Kokāmukha. He propitiated Viṣṇu in the form of Boar. The excellent man attained Siddhi.

Thus Kāmadamana forsook his defective physical body in the Kokāmukha, the extremely sacred and excellent Tīrtha. He went to heaven by aerial chariots resembling the sun, along with his sons and grandsons.

88. Thus O brahmins, the Māyā of the great lord, has been described by me. Even Devas are not able to think about it. It is like a dream or the jugglery of a conjuror. The whole universe is deluded by it.

CHAPTER ONE HUNDRED AND TWENTYTWO

Foretelling future

The sages said:

1. What has been narrated by you, O Vyāsa, regarding the inscrutable Māyā of Viṣṇu, has been heard by us.

2. From you, O great sage, we wish to hear the precise process of annihilation at the end of a Kalpa, called Mahāpralaya.

Vyāsa said :

3. Let it be heard precisely, O excellent sages, how the process of annihilation takes place at the end of a Kalpa as well as at the time of Prākṛta Pralaya.

4. O excellent brahmins, the human month is a day unto the Pitṛs (Manes), the human year is a day unto the heaven-dwellers and a thousand sets of four Yugas constitute a day of Brahmā.

5. Kṛta, Tretā, Dvāpara and Kali constitute a set of four Yugas containing twelve thousand Divine years.

6. The four Yugas are similar in form. Kṛta is the Yuga first. O sages, Kaliyuga is the last.

7. That is because creation is carried out by Brahmā in the first Kṛta yuga and similarly annihilation is carried out in the end in the Kaliyuga.

The sages said:

8. O holy Sir, it beloves you to describe in detail the nature of Kaliyuga when the four-footed sacred Dharma undergoes deficiency.

Vyāsa said:

9. Understand the form of Kali, O sinless brahmins, about which you have asked me. It is extensive but understand it briefly.

10. In the age of Kali the actions of men are not based on the conduct prescribed for Varṇas and Āśramas. Nor do they follow the specific injunctions of the Sāma, Ṛk and Yajus Vedas as their guide.

11. In Kaliyuga marriages are not sacred ties, students are not under the control of preceptors, sons are not righteous, there are no orderly holy rites in the sacred fire.

12. In Kaliyuga the strongest man, whoever he may be and in whichever family he is born, becomes the lord of all. Man maintains himself through girls taken from all the castes.

13. A brahmin is initiated in the Kali age by any expedient and, O leading brahmins, anything can be considered a mode of atonement.

14. Everything is considered a sacred text in the Kali age, O brahmins. Whoever utters whatever thing is taken to be a holy scripture. Deities are on the same footing in the Kali age. Everything is everyone's Āśrama (stage in life).

15. Fast, exertion and charity constitute pious activities in Kali age and rites are performed as one pleases.

16. In Kali age men become haughty and arrogant even with a little wealth. Pride of beauty in women will be on the basis of their tresses of hair.

17. As gold, jewels, diamonds as well as garments dwindle in the Kali age, women will be embellished by their tresses.

18. Women will forsake their husbands having no wealth. In Kali age it is the moneyed man who becomes the lord of damsels.

19. Whoever gives the maximum amount is considered their lord. Nobility in men is based on this lordship.

20. Hoarded wealth is exhausted in the maintenance of a home; intellect has the one end of hoarding wealth; riches come to an end in the enjoyment of pleasures in Kali age.

21. Women in Kali age will be harlots desirous of luxury. They covet men who have earned much by illegal means.

22. At that time, O brahmins, no man will brook a loss to his vested interest even to the extent of a fourth of a Paṇa (the smallest coin) even when he is entreated by his own friend.

23. O brahmins, in the Kali age, the mind will always be manly and courageous. Cows will be solemnly honoured as long as they yield milk.

24. Fearing a drought the subjects will be afraid of hunger. They will then have their eyes riveted to the sky.

25. Like the sages of yore men will have roots, leaves and fruits for their food. They will think of killing themselves in their misery due to the absence of rain.

26. They will have perpetual famine and pain. They will be incapable of mastering things. By virtue of their lapses their happiness will be spoiled.

27. At the advent of Kali age people will take food without taking bath. They will not honour and worship fire, gods, and guests. They will not offer libations and oblations with water and balls of rice.

28. In Kali age women will be greedy and lecherous. They will have puny bodies but they will be gluttonous. They will have little good fortune but plenty of offsprings.

29. Scratching their heads with hands, women will disobey their elders and husbands. They will be unrestrained.

30. Women will be furious. They will be more interested in sustaining themselves; they will be wanting in the purity of bodies. They will habitually speak harsh and untruthful words.

31. Even the women of noble families will be ill-behaved. They will yearn for men of bad conduct. They will be unchaste and disloyal to their husbands.

32. Men of no holy rites will study the Vedas. Householders will not perform homas nor will they give appropriate things in charity.

33. Forest-dwellers will take to the diet pertaining to the villagers. Mendicants will be influenced by filial affection and other contacts towards sons.

34. At the advent of Kali age kings will no longer protect their subjects. They will take the wealth of common man under the pretext of taxes and fees.

35. Whoever happens to possess horses, chariots and elephants will become the king. In the Kali age, those who happen to be weak will be servants.

36. Vaiśyas will forsake their traditional duty such as agriculture, trade etc., and take to the Śūdra activities. They will sustain themselves by means of crafts etc.

37. Śūdras will take up the holy rite of begging for alms. Base men will display their signs of renunciation. Unconsecrated men will resort to heretic activities.

38. Harassed by the burden of taxes and famine, people will become miserable. They will migrate to those lands where wheat and barley abound.

39. As the Vedic path falls into disuse, as the people become more and more heretic, sins will increase and the span of life of the people will shrink.

40. When men begin to undertake austerities not prescribed by sacred texts there will be infantile mortalily due to the fault of kings.

41. Girls will give birth to children at the ages of five, six and seven years begotten by men of the ages of eight, nine and ten.

42. Hairs will begin to turn grey at the twelfth year. No one will live upto the twentieth year.

43. Men will be destroyed in a short time because their wisdom and intelligence will be mediocre and their kings will be wicked. They will wear false marks.

44. The increase in the severity of the Kali age should be inferred by wise persons as the heretic activities are observed more and more.

45. Whenever there is destruction and loss of good people following the Vedic path the increase in the severity of Kali age should be inferred by wise persons.

46. When the undertakings of men of virtuous activities do not flourish, O brahmins, the prominence of Kali age should be inferred by wise persons.

47. When persons cease to perform sacrifices in the worship of Puruṣottama, lord of sacrifices, the influence of Kali age should be inferred.

48. The increase in the severity of Kali should be inferred by wise and intelligent persons when there is no interest in Vedic discussions and heretical doctrines are entertained.

49. In the Kali age, O brahmins, men overpowered by heresy will never worship Viṣṇu, the lord of the Universe, the Supreme lord, the Creator of everything.

50. Men influenced by heresy will prattle thus : of what avail are Devas ? Of what use are the brahmins and the Vedas ? Of what avail is the purificatory wash with water ?".

51. At the advent of Kali age, O brahmins, clouds will shower less rain, plants will produce less, and fruits will have less nutritional value.

52. In Kali age clothes will come down only upto the knees, the trees will be like the Śamī tree, the castes will exhibit the characteristics of Śūdras.

53. When the Kali age approaches and advances foodgrains will turn into atoms; cow milk will be mostly that got from goats and the unguent will be Uśita grass.

54. In the Kali age, O excellent sages, mothers- and fathers-in-law will be mainly considered elders. Men and women shall take food in open buildings (Eating Houses) along with their friends (?).

55. Men following their fathers-in-law will say : "Whose mother ? Whose father ? A man is the product of his own Karman."

56. Men of insignificant intellect will be afflicted again and again by verbal, mental and physical faults and they will commit sins everyday.

57. O brahmins, everything that is conducive to misery in respect of persons without truth, cleanliness and honourable shyness will take place in the Kali age.

58. At that time when there is no self-study of the Vedas, when there is no utterance of the Mantra Vaṣaṭ, when there is no utterance of Svadhā and Svāhā, there will rarely be a brahmin in the world.

59. In a short time he will perform an excellent meritorious rite which in the Kṛta yuga is done by hard penance.

The sages said :

60. At what time does a simple act of piety yield a great benefit? It behoves you to mention it entirely. We have a keen desire to hear.

Vyāsa said :

61. In the blessed Kali age, O brahmins, there shall be a great benefit through less strain. Women and Śūdras shall become blessed. Understand one thing more.

62-63. In regard to penance, practice of celibacy, performance of Japa, O brahmins, what is achieved in the Kṛtayuga in ten years is achieved in a year in the Tretāyuga. It is achieved in a month in the Dvāparayuga and in a day and night in the Kaliyuga. Hence we can say a person achieves good things in the Kali age easily.

64. By singing songs in praise of Keśava in the Kali age one obtains what one obtains in the Kṛta yuga by meditation, in the Tretā yuga by performing sacrifices and in the Dvāpara by conducting worship.

65. In the Kali age, a person attains increased virtue by means of a simple effort. People become well-versed in piety with a little strain. Hence I am pleased with Kali age.

66-69. Formerly, the twice-born grasped the Vedas by observing the holy rites. Thereafter, they performed sacrifices by means of wealth acquired by pious means. Meaningless talk, eating unconsecrated food (Vrata Bhojana) and aimless squandering of money (Vrata Svam) shall lead to the downfall of the twice-born along with their attendants. Improper performance of everything leads to faults. O brahmins, the twice-born cannot take in food and drink as they wish because they are bound by certain conventions in every activity. They are endowed with humility and they attain other worlds with great stress and strain.

70. But a Śūdra achieves salvation merely by serving the twice-born. He is authorized in Pākayajña (mere cooking of his food is no less than a Yajña). Hence a Śūdra is more blessed.

71. In the Kaliyuga, there is no restriction on what should be eaten or what should not be eaten. There is no restraining law in regard to sins. O leading sages, hence this has been mentioned as something good.

72. Wealth should be acquired by men without a conflict with their duties; wealth should be distributed among deserving persons; sacrifices should be duly performed.

73. In its acquisition and maintenance there is great strain and pain, O excellent brahmins. Similarly, in the matter of utilising it properly too there is great effort; wealth should be known as something very difficult to deal with.

74. By means of these and other strenuous efforts, O excellent brahmins, people attain Prājāpatya and other worlds in due order.

75. A women attains other worlds by duly serving her husband by thoughts, words and deeds. That is because, O brahmins, she attains the same world as he.

76. Thus she attains those worlds without much effort like the man.

For the third time it has been mentioned by me that women are good.

77. Thus has been mentioned, O brahmins, what you have come here for. Hence, ask as you please. I shall explain everything clearly to you.

78-80. In the Kali age, virtue is achieved with very little effort by men who wash off their sins by means of water in the form of qualities of the soul. O excellent sages, the same is achieved by Śūdras devoted to the service of the twice-born. Similarly, it is achieved by women without strain merely by serving their husbands. Hence, all these three are considered by me highly blessed.

In the Kṛta and other yugas the twice-born have to undergo great strain in accomplishing piety.

81-82. But O excellent sages, in Kaliyuga, men attain Siddhi (spiritual achievement) by means of simple austerities. Blessed people act virtually. O sages, conversant with virtue, what has been desired by you has been described by me even without being asked. What else shall be done, O brahmins?

CHAPTER ONE HUNDRED AND TWENTYTHREE

Foretelling Future (contd.)

The sages said :

1-3. We do not know whether the advent of Kali is imminent or far off. Therefore, we wish for final Yuga and the end of Dvāpara age. For the present we have come here for the acquisition of Dharma. We shall take up the greatest virtue and happiness with the smallest effort. The final Yuga that causes terror and heartburn has approached. It has destroyed Dharma. O sage, conversant with Dharma ! it beloves you to describe it along with the symptoms in detail.

Vyāsa said :

4. In the final Yuga will come up those kings who will cease to be protectors and take away the portion of oblations. They will be interested only in saving themselves.

5. In the final Yuga, non-Kṣatriyas will become kings, brahmins will resort to Śūdras for sustenance and Śūdras will maintain the conduct and way of life of the brahmins.

6. In the final Yuga, O excellent sages, brahmins well-versed in the Vedas as well as fallen evil ones will take food sitting in the same row. Havis offerings will be devoid of usual holy rites.

7. Men will become ill-mannered. They will be devoted to the hoarding of wealth. They will be fond of liquor and meat. Base men will carnally approach the wives of their friends.

8. In the final Yuga, thieves will carry out the activities of kings. Kings will practise thieving, servants will take food and enjoy without taking permission first.

9. In the final Yuga, wealth and assets will become important. The conduct and activities of the good will not be honoured. The fallen ones will not be rebuked and treated with contempt.

10. Men will be ugly with the noses missing and the hairs in disarray. Girls less than sixteen in age will give birth to children.

11. In the final yuga, cooked food will be sold in the open places; brahmins will sell the Vedas; women will sell their honour.

12. Everyone will discuss and expound the supreme Brahman and the Vedas. Brahmins will follow the Vājasaneya texts. The propounders will resemble the Śūdras and the brahmins will become the disciples (of Śūdras).

13. Śūdras will begin to expound Dharma. Their teeth will be white. They will conquer their sense-organs. They will wear ocher robes. They will sustain themselves with knavishness and crooked intellect.

14. In the final Yuga beasts of prey will increase in number and cows will dwindle in number. Good men will decrease.

15. The base ones will stay in the end. The subjects will lose bashfulness. They are doomed in that final age.

16. Even the excellent brahmins sell fruits of their austerities and sacrifices. The seasons will become adverse during that ultimate age.

17. Similarly, steers under training will be yoked to the plough even when they are two years old. When the yuga comes to a close, the clouds will begin to shower in a quaint way.

18. Those who are born in the family of heroes will become kings as the lower subjects become baser and baser at the close of the age.

19. Charitable gifts will be obligatory on the parts of parents while the sons will never perform sacred rites as the age comes to a close.

20. When the age comes to a close, the Earth will be mostly barren arid soil; the highways will be infested with robbers; almost all the people will become merchants.

21. Sons will eagerly share the hereditary assets and charitable gifts. Urged by greed and other bad qualities they will be antagonistic to one another and will even attempt to take away other's shares.

22. At the close of the Yuga when tenderness, beauty and jewellery cease to exist women will be decked by means of their tresses.

23. A householder devoid of stamina and virility will attempt to have sexual pleasure. When the Yuga comes to a close no sexual indulgence will be on a par with that with one's own wife.

24. The following is the characteristic feature of the close of the Yuga. Most of the men will be base in character and ignoble; their handsomeness will be futile; men will be in a minority; there will be more women.

25. Population will consist mostly of beggars; people will never give anything to one another. They will perish on being harassed by kings and robbers or destroyed by fire or fighting.

26. When the Yuga comes to a close, plants will cease to bear fruits; young men will exhibit the characteristics of old men and men of no good conduct will be happy in the world.

27. When the Yuga comes to a close rough and low winds showering hailstone will begin to blow in the rainy seasons; the other world will become of doubtful existence.

28. Kings like the Vaiśyas will maintain themselves with wealth and foodgrains. When the Yuga passes off, no one will behave like kinsman to anyone.

29. Agreements and promises will cease to function. When the Yuga comes to a close a debt will lose itself along with a sense of propriety and decorum.

30. Delight of men will be fruitless and the anger of men will be fruitful. When the Yuga comes to a close people will begin to rear goats for getting milk.

31. Similarly, sacrifices will be performed not in accordance with the sacred texts. Men who profess to be scholars will be acting in an unauthorized manner.

32-36. There is no doubt that there will not be anyone to expound what is mentioned in the scriptures. Without resorting to elderly persons everyone will come to know everything; when the close of the Yuga is imminent there will be no one who is not a poet; all the stars will be devoid of Yogas; the twice-born people will not abide by their holy rites. When the close of the Yuga is imminent, the kings will be robbers. Bastards, dishonest men and liquor addicts will begin to expound Brahman. At the close of the Yuga, excellent brahmins will perform horse sacrifice. Brahmins will eat forbidden food. They will perform sacrifices on behalf of those who do not deserve them. When the close of the Yuga is imminent brahmins will become greedy of wealth. They will utter the word "Bhoḥ". No one will learn (the Vedas).

37. Women will have a single conch shell (tied round their necks) which they will tie up with a rope. Stars will be devoid of lustre. The ten quarters will become adverse.

38. At the close of the Yuga the red lustre of twilight will be of a burnt hue. Sons will employ their fathers in their own jobs and the daughters-in-law their mothers-in-law.

39. In the ultimate Yugas women as well as men will live like this. They will take food and enjoy without conducting holy rites. Brahmins will not perform sacrifices in the sacred fires.

40. Without offering alms and oblations men will partake of their meals. Deceiving their husbands who are asleep women will go elsewhere.

41. The husbands may not be sick, nor devoid of handsomeness; they may not be weak, they may not be jealous too. (Still the women are disloyal to them.) When the Yuga comes to a close no one will be grateful for helps rendered.

The sages said :

42-43. When virtue is held in abeyance and suspense thus, in which country will those men who are harassed by taxes reside? What will be their diet? What will be their pastimes? What will be their rites? What will be their likes? What will be their magnitude? What will be their span of life? What quarter will they resort to before they reach once again the Kṛta Age?

Vyāsa said :

44. After this, when the virtue falls down the subjects will become devoid of good qualities. After attaining loss of good conduct they will attain deficiency in their longevity.

45. They will incur decline in strength due to deficiency in longevity; pallor and discolouration due to decline in strength, sickness and pain due to pallor; and despondency due to pain of sickness.

46. Due to despondency self-knowledge will be aroused in them; due to self-knowledge inclination towards piety (will be acquired by them). By attaining the highest point thus they will reach the Kṛta Yuga.

47. Some will be practising piety to a certain extent; some will attain a neutral state; some will follow misconceived piety; some will attain jolly temperament.

48. Some will come to the conclusion that only perception and inference constitute true testimony; others will say that nothing can be true testimony.

49. Some will be addicted to atheism and ruin piety; some will become deluded. Brahmins will profess to be great scholars.

50. People will be excluded from the knowledge of scriptures. They will retain faith only in what is current for the nonce. Men devoid of knowledge will become arrogant.

51. When piety becomes unsteady and disarranged, there will still be people honoured by the noble ones who will practise auspicious rites and resort to charitable deeds.

52. When people begin to eat indiscriminately, when they think that they are protected by themselves, when they conceal themselves, when they become devoid of mercy, when they are shameless in their character, these are the signs of Kali age.

53. During the period of the onslaught of Kali that destroys strict adherence to wisdom, even unprepared persons will attain Siddhi in a short while.

54. O brahmins, if the people of lower castes resort to the perpetual course of conduct of the brahmins, it is a feature of Kali.

55. When the Yuga comes to a close there will be great wars, heavy downpour, strong gusts of wind and scorching heat. It is the characteristic feature of Kali.

56. When the close of Yuga is imminent, Rākṣasas and beings who know through the spies enjoy the Earth in the guise of brahmins.

57-60. The following types of evil men will abound in the world : Persons devoid of self-study of the Vedas; persons who do not utter Vaṣaṭ mantras; evil leaders; arrogant ones; those who eat flesh; those who eat indiscriminately; those with futile holy rites; foolish ones greedy of wealth; petty ones; those with insignificant paraphernalia; those who are surrounded by diverse dealings (?) ; those who have fallen down from perpetual piety; those who take away other's jewels; those who harass other men's wives; passionate men; wicked men; deceitful persons; and men fond of risky adventures. When these persons abound there will be sages of many forms. They will be men of want and privation (?)

61. Men will honour and worship by means of discourse all those important persons who are born in the Kali Age.

62. There will be persons stealing vegetables, garments, foodstuffs and small baskets and boxes.

63. There will be thieves outwitting other thieves, there will be slayers of murderers. When the thieves are destroyed by other thieves, there will be peace everywhere.

64. When a time characterized by worthlessness and full of disturbances comes and there are no holy rites, men who are afflicted by the burden of taxes, will resort to the forest.

65. When the holy rites of sacrifices cease to be performed, demons, beasts of prey, worms, mice and serpents will attack men.

66. At the close of the Age some excellent men in certain places will enjoy prosperity, abundance of food, of good healt and self-sufficiency in the kinsmen.

67. In the different regions there will be separate groups of persons equipped with rafts and requisites. They will be protected by themselves as well as robbed by themselves.

68. As time passes on, men will be dislodged from their countries; they will lose valuable things along with their kinsmen.

69. They will be afflicted by starvation and they will run away in great fright taking their children with them. They will cross the river Kauśikī.

70. They will resort to the lands of Aṅga, Vaṅga, Kaliṅga, Kāśmīra and Kośala. They will occupy valleys and chasms between the mountains abounding in sages.

71-72. They will occupy the entire ridge of the Himālayas and the coasts of the briny sea. They will use rotting leaves, barks of trees and skins of deer and stay there when the Age comes to a close. The men will stay in the forests along with the alien barbarous groups of Mlecchas.

73. The Earth will be neither void nor full of forests. Kings will be both protectors and non-protectors.

74. Men will sustain themselves by means of deer, fish, birds, beasts of prey, serpents, insects, worms, honey, vegetables, green fruits and roots.

75. Like sages men will use barks of trees, skins of deer and will have for their food the rotting and decaying leaves and fruits.

76. The people will not be able to extract oil from seeds. They will be assailed and struck by darts fixed to wooden pieces. They will always rear goats, sheep, asses, mules and camels.

77. They will resort to the banks of rivers and for the sake of diverting the course of water they will restrain the flow of currents. They will be engaged in mutual petty trade and deal in cooked food.

78-79. The hairs growing from their bodies will remain so and dirt will get accumulated in between. Some of them will have many children, and others will be devoid of progeny. They will be devoid of nobility of birth and good conduct. Some will sustain themselves by evil means. The base and vile subjects will follow a base moral code.

80-82. The maximum expectation of life of those men will be thirty. The people will be weak and emaciated due to the enjoyment of worldly pleasures. They will be overwhelmed by the sadness of old age. Due to sickness their virility becomes reduced. Since the reliance on life expectation is restrained people desist from indulgence. They are desirous of meeting and serving pious men. As business dealings become rarer, they will resort to truthfulness.

83. Due to the non-fulfilment of their desires they will be pious in their conduct. Themselves afflicted by destruction they will perform consecratory rites.

84. Thus the people, desirous of serving, will adhere to the good practice of charitable gifts, truthfulness and protection of living beings. Then Dharma (virtue) will function to the extent of one-fourth and the people will attain welfare.

85. As people gradually change for the better and their capacity to infer improves they will enquire, "What is the tasty thing?" They will see that it is Dharma (virtue).

86. The people, who had incurred loss and damage once, will attain prosperity when they take to virtue. They will then see the Kṛta Yuga.

87-88. People are of good conduct in the Kṛta Yuga and it is said that there is loss in the Kali Age. The time "is but one even as the moon is but one. When the moon is enveloped in darkness it does not shine. It is then like the Kali Age. When the moon is released by darkness, it shines. It is then like the Kṛta Yuga.

89-93. This classification of Ages is mere secondary assertion. But the supreme Brahman is the real meaning of the

Vedas. It is non-disjointed, it is not realized; it is held as hereditary legacy.

Penance is assertion of what is desired. It is made fixed and steady. Holy rites are achieved by means of good qualities and good qualities are purified by means of holy rites.

Benediction is in consonance with place and time on viewing the person (who is the recipient of the same). In every Age it has been cited by sages at the proper time.

The auspicious and meritorious benedictions are but the reaction of virtue, wealth, love, salvation and gods. So also is longevity in the different ages.

The changes of the Ages have begun to function long since due to the nature of the creator. The world of living beings is always undergoing change by fall and rise. It does not remain still even for a moment.

CHAPTER ONE HUNDRED AND TWENTYFOUR

Description of Annihilation

Vyāsa said :

1. The reabsorption of all living beings is of three kinds. (1) Naimittika (conditional) (2) Prākṛtika (natural) and Ātyantika (the ultimate one).

2. The conditional re-absorption is Brāhma (pertaining to Brahmā). It is the re-absorption at the end of a Kalpa (set of four Yugas). The ultimate one is salvation and the Prākṛta (natural one) is (delimited) by the Parārdhas.

The sages said :

3. O holy sage, explain the number of Parārdha as it has been mentioned before, and by doubling which the natural re-absorption has to be realized.

Vyāsa said :

4. O brahmins, each one of the digits is considered ten

times as much in value as the previous one on the right. Therefore at the eighteenth place it is called Parārdha (i.e. one followed by seventeen zeros).

5. Double the Parārdha is considered, O brahmins, as Prākṛta Laya (natural reabsorption). At that time everything manifest merges and dissolves into the unmanifest which is the cause of all.

6. Human Nimeṣa (i.e. winking time) is called a Mātrā and it is the basic unit of time. Fifteen Mātrās constitute one Kāṣṭhā and thirty Kāṣṭhās one Kalā.

7. Fifteen Kalās make a Nāḍikā. In the calculation of time by means of the measurement of water it is equivalent to half of thirteen Palas ($6\frac{1}{2}$ Palas of water trickling down through a hole may take a Nāḍikā of time i.e. 24 minutes to flow out completely).

8. According to Māgadha calculation it is time for the full trickling down of a Prastha of water through four holes four Aṅgulas from one another, pricked by means of golden pulses (?) (? Each hole is of the size of a pulse grain).

9. O excellent brahmins, two Nāḍikās make one Muhūrta (48 minutes). A day of twentyfour hours consists of thirty Muhūrtas and thirty days make a month.

10. Twelve months make a year and this constitutes a period of a day and a night in the heaven. Three hundred and sixty human years make one divine year.

11. Twelve thousand divine years make a set of four Yugas. A thousand sets of four Yugas are considered to be one day of Brahmā.

12. It is called a Kalpa. O excellent brahmins, fourteen Manus reign over that period of time. At the end of that period is the Naimittika Laya (conditional re-absorption) of Brahmā.

13. O leading brahmins, its nature is very terrible. Listen to it even as I narrate. I shall explain the Prākṛta Laya (natural re-absorption) afterwards.

14. At the end of a set of four Yugas when the surface of the Earth is almost worn off there will be a very severe drought extending over a period of a hundred years.

15. Then, O excellent sages, almost all of those earthly

things that are of poor strength are destroyed due to the excessive pressure.

16. Then the imperishable lord Kṛṣṇa assumes the form of Rudra and endeavours to keep the subjects within himself for the purpose of annihilation.

17. Then, O excellent sages, lord Viṣṇu is stationed in the seven rays of the sun and sucks up the water.

18. After drinking up the water present in the elements and living beings, O brahmins, he makes the entire surface of the Earth dried up and withered.

19. He dries up oceans, rivers, mountains and mountain springs. He sucks up the water that is present in the nether worlds too.

20. As every particle of water vanishes there will be seven suns, each of a thousand rays and they become increased in size due to their watery diet.

21. Blazing from beneath and above, O brahmins, those seven suns burn up the three worlds along with the nether worlds.

22. On being burnt by those blazing suns, the three worlds, along with the extensive area of mountains, trees and oceans, become devoid of viscidity.

23. Then the entire area of the three worlds, O brahmins, has all the trees and watery parts dried up. The Earth attains the shape of the back of a tortoise.

24. Thereafter lord Hara, the annihilator of all created beings, terrible like black fire, burns the nether worlds from below by means of the hot breath of the serpent Śeṣa.

25-26. After burning the nether worlds that huge fire reaches the Earth. It burns the entire surface of the Earth. Then the terrible fire burns the Bhuvaḥ world and the Svarga world. With the clusters of flames whirling and curling the fire revolves there itself.

27-28. At that time the entire area of the three worlds appears like a frying pan. It is surrounded by whirling clusters of flames. At that time, O brahmins, the residents of the two worlds lose their strength. They are enveloped by the scorching heat. When their abodes are taken away (i.e. consumed by fire), they go to the Maharloka.

29. From there also people proceed ahead to Janaloka on being scorched by the great sunshine ten times more powerful. They are desirous of a supreme abode.

30. After burning the entire universe, O excellent sages, the lord in the guise of Rudra, produces clouds by means of breath expelled from his mouth.

31. Thereafter, rise up in the sky the Saṃvartaka clouds that are terribly destructive. They are as huge as big herds of elephants. They contain fierce lightning streaks and they rumble.

32. Some of these clouds are like a collyrium mountain; some are like the elephant Kumuda. Some are smoky in colour. Some are yellow.

33. Some are turmeric; some resemble the exudation of lac juice; some appear like lapis lazuli; and some are like sapphire.

34. Some resemble a conch shell and others the turner's lathe; some are like Jāti flower (white jasmine) and some are like Kunda. Some are scarlet coloured like the tiny insect Indragopa (glow-worm) and some are like Manaḥśita (?)

35. Some of the terrible clouds rise up like the petals of a lotus; some have the shape of an excellent city; some are like big mountains.

36. Others resemble the apartments on the tops of houses; some are like the dry tracts of ground. They are huge in body and loud in their sound; they cover the sky completely.

37. Making heavy downpours, O brahmins, they subdue the extremely terrible fire that has spread over the entire area of the three worlds.

38. Even after the fire has been extinguished, O excellent sages, those clouds shower down water for more than a hundred years flooding the entire Universe.

39. After flooding the entire Earth by means of heavy downpours with the torrents, O brahmins, they flood the Bhuvarloka and the heaven above.

40. With the whole universe enveloped in darkness, with all beings mobile and immobile destroyed, those great clouds shower for more than a hundred years.

CHAPTER ONE HUNDRED AND TWENTYFIVE

The natural re-absorption

Vyāsa said :

1. O excellent brahmins, when the water encroaches upon the abode of seven sages (Great Bear) the entire area of the three worlds becomes a vast sheet of water.

2. Then, O brahmins, the wind arising out of the expiration of Viṣṇu destroys those clouds in the course of hundred years and more.

3-4. Lord Hari, identical with all living beings, the creator of all living beings, the lord without beginning, the primordial cause of the univese who cannot even be contemplated upon, drinks up the whole of the wind. The lord then assumes the form of Brahman, Hari the cause of (everything) lies on the bed of the body of Śeṣa in that vast sheet of water.

5. He is (then) eulogised by Sanaka and other Siddhas abiding in the Janaloka. He is meditated upon by the aspirants of liberation abiding in Brahmaloka.

6. He then employs the divine Yoganidrā (yogic slumber) consisting of Māyā of the Ātman (soul). He is the Supreme lord pondering over himself with the appellation of Vāsudeva.

7. O excellent brahmins, this is called the Naimittika (conditional) Pratisañcara (re-absorption). The Nimitta or condition there is the fact that Hari lies down there after assuming the form of Brahmā.

8. When Sarvātman (the soul of all) is awake, the universe is active. When Acyuta lies down on the bed of Māyā (Illusion) this visible universe vanishes.

9. A thousand sets of four Yugas constitute a day of the lotus-born Brahmā. When the whole universe becomes a vast sheet of water, a period of as much duration is said to be his night.

10. Waking up at the close of the night, Brahmā continues the work of creation. As mentioned to you before, it is Viṣṇu who assumes this form of Brahmā and continues the work of creation.

11. This is annihilation at the end of a Kalpa (or) Intervening annihilation, brahmins. The Naimittika (conditional) annihilation has been described to you. Listen to the other one, the Prākṛta (natural) annihilation.

12-14. O brahmins, a series of annihilations is achieved by means of fire, absence of rain etc. in upper and lower regions. The created ones, Mahat etc. are particularly dissolved. When the process of reabsorption is thus brought about by Kṛṣṇa's will, the waters at the outset, grasp and destroy smell and other characteristic features of the Earth element. The Earth thus deprived of its smell is then ready for its reabsorption.

15-16. When the Gandhatanmātra (the suble primary element of smell) is destroyed the Earth dissolves into the Water. The waters fill everything. They move about everywhere with great velocity and loud report. The Lokāloka (? the mountain of that name) is surrounded by water alone, the water with surging waves.

17. The (special) quality of the waters (i.e. taste) is drunk (consumed and destroyed) by the Fire element. When the Rasatanmātra (the subtle primary element of taste) is destroyed, the heated waters perish.

18-19. Then the waters with their taste element dead and destroyed attain the state of fiery element. When the water element has attained the state of fiery element and is enveloped by the fiery element all round, that fire spreads everywhere and takes up the water. Then the fire gradually fills the entire universe.

20. It spreads everywhere, at the sides, above and below along with its rays. The fire-element has its great quality, rūpa (colour), that causes lustre, that is destroyed by Vāyu.

21-23. When the fire element is dissolved, when everything has assumed the form of the wind element, then the rūpatanmātra (the subtle primary element of colour) is destroyed. The fiery element, bereft of its colour subsides and the great wind element begins to blow. When splendour is dissolved in the wind element and the whole world is deprived of light since it has been dissolved in the wind, the wind begins to blow in the ten directions, upwards and sideways.

24-26. Then Ether consumes and destroys the quality of touch, the quality of the wind element. Then the wind-element subsides. The Ether remains uncovered. It is devoid of colour, taste, touch and smell. It has no tangible form. It fills everything. Characterised by the quality of sound it stands enveloping everything.

27-28. Then the Supreme spirit of Ahaṃkāra (Ego) consumes and destroys its quality of sound. The elements and the Indriyas (sense organs) get simultaneously merged in Bhūtādi. This Bhūtādi (Ego) is of the nature of Abhimāna (referring all objects to self). It is Tāmasa (constituted of darkness). The Great Principle, the Cosmic Intellect consumes and destroys Bhūtādi.

29-30. The earth element and the Great Principle are at the extremities of the universe within and without. Thus there are seven Prakṛtis (causes) beginning with the supreme principle, the Cosmic Intellect. All of them get merged among themselves in the reverse order. Similarly this cosmic egg gets merged in water by which it has been enveloped.

31. (The cosmic egg) consisting of seven worlds along with the mountains, the seven continents and oceans is enveloped by water and it is drunk (i.e. destroyed) by the fiery element.

32-34. The Jyoti or fiery layer merges into the gaseous layer; the gaseous layer merges into the Ether; the Bhūtādi or Ego consumes the Ether and the Great Principle or Cosmic Intellect consumes it. O brahmins, the Prakṛti (Nature) consumes the Cosmic Intellect accompanied by all these. O excellent brahmins, that entity wherein there is the equilibrium of all the attributes (guṇas), none of them being enlarged or rendered deficient is called Prakṛti (Nature), Hetu (cause), Pradhāna (the Chief) and Param Kāraṇam (greatest cause). This is the Prakṛti, the whole of which is of the nature of (partly) manifest and (partly) unmanifest.

35-36. The form that is manifest merges, O brahmins, into the unmanifest. That imperishable one is pure and single, eternal and omnipresent. And that is the part, O excellent brahmins, of the supreme soul identical with living beings. It is here that the conceptions of names, classes etc. perish.

37. It is worth knowing. It is of the pure form of existence. It is of the nature of knowledge. It is greater than (the embodied) soul. It is Brahman. It is the greatest abode. It is the greatest soul. It is the greatest lord.

38-39. That Viṣṇu is identical with this (visible world), from whom no one returns. Prakṛti has already been mentioned by me as one of manifest and unmanifest forms. Prakṛti and Puruṣa (i.e. Individual Soul) merge into the supreme Ātman; and the supreme Ātman is the support of all. He is the great Lord.

40-42. He is sung about in the Vedas and the Vedāntas by the name of Viṣṇu.

The Vedic rites are twofold : 1 the Pravṛtta (the active), 2 the Nivṛtta (the refraining one). By means of both of these the lord is worshipped in the form of sacrifice. This lord of sacrifices, the best among Puruṣas, is worshiped by persons by means of (active paths) in Ṛk, Yajus and Sāman.

The lord, with (knowledge) as his soul and form, is worshipped by means of Jñānayoga as well as Nivṛtti Mārgas. Viṣṇu who is worshipped thus bestows the fruit of liberation.

43-45. Whatever thing exists and is mentioned by short, long and prolated vowels, and what is beyond the pale of words—all these are identical with Viṣṇu the unchanging. He is both manifest and unmanifest. He is the unchanging Puruṣa. He is the supreme Ātman. He is the universal soul. He is Hari who assumes the universal form.

Prakṛti which is of manifest and unmanifest forms merges into him.

46-49. Puruṣa, O brahmins, merges into the undistorted soul.

O brahmins, the time unit in the form of two parārdhas has been mentioned by me. O great brahmins, it is the day time of Viṣṇu the lord.

When Prakṛti merges into the manifest and when Prakṛti and Puruṣa remain firm therein—it is his night of an equal duration.

Really there is neither day nor night in regard to the eternal supreme soul. It is only figuratively mentioned thus in regard to that lord.

Thus O great sages, the Prākṛta Laya (re-absorption) has been mentioned to you.

CHAPTER ONE HUNDRED AND TWENTYSIX

The Ultimate Re-absorption

Vyāsa said:

1. After understanding the three types of suffering, O brahmins, beginning with the Ādhyātmika (i.e. the organic), a learned man realises perfect knowledge and has Vairāgya (detachment). He then attains the ultimate re-absorption.

2. The organic (suffering) is of two types, viz. the physical and the mental. The physical suffering is of various types. Let it be heard.

3-4. The physical suffering and ailment is of various types such as headache, cold, fever, fistula, enlargement of the spleen, piles, intumescence, asthma, nausea, ailment of the eyes, diarrhoea, leprosy, ailment of the limbs and many others. It behoves you to listen to the mental (suffering).

5-6. The suffering arising from love, anger, fear, hatred, greed, delusion and despondency, the attack of misery, jealousy, insult, envious impatience and spiteful malice—these are mental sufferings. O excellent brahmins, the mental suffering too is of various kinds. O excellent sages, they are different in these ways.

7. The Ādhibhautika (extraneous and material) suffering occurs to men from animals, birds, men, evil spirits, serpents, ogres, reptiles and other beings.

8. O excellent brahmins, the suffering arising from coldness, heat, winds, rains, water, lightning etc. is called Ādhidaivika.

9. O excellent sages, misery is of thousands of varieties arising from birth in the womb, old age, ignorance, death and (falling into) hell.

10. The creature in the womb is enveloped by faeces in plenty. Its back, neck and clusters of bones are broken.

11. It is excessively tormented by the scorching foodstuffs of its mother, of extremely pungent, sour, hot, bitter and saline taste. It suffers excessive pain.

12. It is unable to stretch or bend its limbs. It lies in the slough of faeces and urine. It is afflicted everywhere.

13. It gets suffocated. It is conscious. It remembers hundreds of births it has had. It stays in the womb in great misery as a result of its own actions.

14-15. At the time of delivery the child in the womb whose face is defiled by faeces, blood, urine and semen is excessively tormented by the wind Prājāpatya. His bones and joints are crushed. He is made to face down the powerful organic winds at the time of delivery. The child that is harassed thus manages to come out with difficulty from the womb of the mother.

16. On being touched by the external wind he attains an extremely senseless state. On being born, O excellent sages, he attains the loss of special knowledge (of the previous births).

17. His limbs are afflicted as it were by thorns. He is pierced and split as it were by saws. He is just like a worm that has fallen on the ground from a pus-discharging foul ulcer.

18. He is unable even to scratch himself. He is unable to turn on his sides. It is at the desire of others that he gets his food such as the milk from the mother's breasts.

19. He is dirty. While he sleeps on his bed he is bitten by flies and worms, still he is unable to remove them.

20. (Thus) the miseries at the time of birth are many. Similarly those Ādhibhautika (extraneous and material) miseries too that he undergoes after his birth in the course of his childhood, are many.

21. As a man he is enveloped by the darkness of ignorance. His mind is deluded. He does not know: "Where have I come from?" "Who am I?" "Where will I go?" "Of what nature am I?"

22. "By what bonds am I fettered?" "What is its cause?" "Is it without any cause?" "What should be done?" "What

should not be done ?" "What should be spoken ?" "What should not be spoken ?"

23. "What is good ?" "What is evil ?" "In what does it consist and how ?" "What is our duty ?" "What is it that we should refrain from ?" "What is it that is meritorious ?" "What is it that is faulty ?"

24. Thus foolish men who like animals are given to sex and eating suffer great pain resulting from ignorance.

25. Ignorance is a Tāmasika trait. In the case of ignorant persons, although there is a predilection for the commencement of what should be done, yet there is the omission of duty, O brahmins.

26. Sages say that the result of omission of duty is (falling into) hell. Hence ignorant people experience excessive misery both here and hereafter.

27. Then, during old age man undergoes many miseries as follows : His body is shattered by old age. His limbs are enfeebled and flaccid. His teeth are broken and loose. He is covered by wrinkles and protruding sinews and neves and veins.

28. His eyes are incapable of seeing far off. His pupils are fixed to the sky. Clusters of hair come out of his nostrils. The whole of his body shakes and shivers.

29. His bones are laid bare. The bones at his back are bent. Since his gastric fire does not function, he takes but little food. He is capable of only a few movements.

30. He experiences difficulties in rising up, in moving about, in lying down, in sitting and in his movements. His eyes and ears become less keen. Saliva exudes from his mouth and defiles his face.

31. With his sense organs intractable he looks up to his early death. He is not capable of remembering anything experienced at the very same moment.

32. In uttering a sentence even once he has to put in great effort. He spends sleepless nights due to the strain of ailments such as asthma, bronchitis (cough) etc.

33. The old man has to be lifted up or laid to rest with the help of another man. He is disdained and insulted by his servants, sons and wife.

34. He is slack in maintaining cleanliness. He continues to have a great zeal in eating and sporting to the great derisive merriment of even servants. All his relatives are disgusted with him.

35. Remembering the activities of his own youth as though they were experienced in another birth he is all the more distressed. He then heaves deep sighs.

36. These and similar ones are the miseries he experiences in the old age. Now listen to those miseries which he experiences at the time of death.

37. His neck, legs and hands become loose. He is overwhelmed by (physical) trembling. Again and again he becomes despondent. Again and again he gains the support of his knowledge.

38. He is distressed due to his excessive fondness for gold, grain, sons, wife, servants, house etc. He becomes worried with the thought "What will befall to these ?"

39. His bones and joints are torn and shorn as it were by great and terrible ailments like the saws that appear to be the arrows of the god of death. They pierce the vulnerable spots of his body.

40. The puplis of his eyes roll. He begins to beat and kick with his hands and feet. His palate, lips and throat become parched and he begins to snort and grumble.

41. The organic Udāna wind afflicts him by choking his throat. An excessive heat spreads over him. He becomes distressed due to thirst and hunger.

42. It is with great distress that the soul leaves the body. He is then afflicted by the servants of Yama. Thereafter with great distress and pain be adopts a Yātanādeha (the body for suffering the torture).

43. These and other similar ones are the miseries of men at the time of death. Now listen to those miseries which are experienced in hell by the persons who die.

44. The dead undergoes tortures in various ways. The servants of Yama catch him by means of noose etc. They strike him with sticks. The very sight of Yama is terrible. It is terrible to behold even the path (leading to Yama's place).

45. O exellecnt brahmins, the tortures in different hells are different. They are terrible and the means employed are mud, sand, fire, mechanical devices, weapons etc.

46-49. The tortures of men in hell are as follows: They are tormented by saws. They are flown in the crucible. They are split by daggers. They are buried under the ground. They are impaled on pikes. They are cast into the jaws of a tiger. They are devoured by vultures and eaten by panthers. They are boiled in oil. They are drenched in slushy corrosive acid. They are cast down from a great height. They are thrown obliquely by mechanical discharging devices. The tortures experienced by sinners in hell are numerous, O brahmins.

50. It is not in hell alone, O excellent brahmins, that there is range of miseries. Even in heaven one has no peace of mind because one is afraid of a fall therefrom due to the decrease of meritorious deeds.

51. Again he becomes a foetus in the womb. The man is born again. Again he gets merged into the womb on being born. He then perishes.

52-53. Sometimes the child is still-born, sometimes the child dies (later) in childhood (or) in youth.

Whatever is pleasing to men, O brahmins, that alone becomes the seed of the tree of misery.

The pleasure brought about by wives, sons, friends etc., house, fields, wealth etc. is not so much as the unhappiness that they bring unto men.

54-57. Thus, men are mentally distressed by the fiery heat of the sun of worldly miseries. Excepting the shade of the tree of liberation where else can those men get happiness ? The mass of misery is thus threefold and they afflict one in the womb, during conception, birth, old age etc. Learned men consider the ultimate attainment of the lord alone as the cure for these ills. This attainment of the lord is characterised by the feeling of happiness. There is no other source of delight higher than this.

Hence effort to attain it should be made by learned men.

58. O excellent brahmins, the means of attaining the same is said to be knowledge as well as holy rites. Knowledge is mentioned as twofold : 1) arising from scriptural texts and 2) arising from discrimination.

59-61. The Śabda Brahman (Brahman exemplified in words) is that arising from scriptural text. The Para Brahman (supreme Brahman) is that arising from discrimination.

Ignorance is like the pitch darkness. Knowledge arising from sense organs is like a lamp. Knowledge arising from discrimination, O brahmins, is like the sun.

O excellent sages, what Manu too has said after remembering the meaning of the Vedic Texts, let that be heard even as I say in this context.

"Two Brahmans are to be comprehended i.e. Śabda Brahman and Para Brahman.

62. One who is well-conversant with the Śabda Brahman attains the Para Brahman. The Atharva Veda says: "Two types of learning are to be undrstood".

63-64. The attainment of the Akṣara (Imperishable) is by means of Parā Vidyā (the superior knowledge). The Aparā Vidyā (the subsidiary type of learning) is the mastery of Ṛgveda etc.

Know ye all that omnipresent eternal material cause of all beings, which is unmanifest, which has no old age, which is difficult to ponder over, which is unborn, which is devoid of change, which cannot be pointed out, which has no form, which does not possess hands, legs etc. and which has no other cause.

65. Everything worthy of being pervaded is pervaded by it and poets see it. That is Brahman. That is the greatest abode. That should be meditated upon by those who desire liberation.

66-68. It is mentioned in the statements of the Vedas. It is subtle. It is the greatest region of Viṣṇu. He is called Bhagavān (Lord), who knows the origin and dissolution of living beings, the advent and departure of living beings as well as the Vidyā (Learning) and Avidyā (Ignorance).

The following are denoted by the word Bhagavān: knowledge, power, potentiality, ability to rule, vigour and all types of splendour except those qualities etc. that are to be despised and discarded.

All the living beings reside in the supreme soul.

69-70. Hence Vāsudeva is named Sarvātman, the soul of all. Prajāpati (Brahmā) mentioned this formerly to the sages when he was asked to comment upon the names of Vāsudeva, the endless, truthfully. Since the lord abides in the living beings and the living beings abide in him, he, Vāsudeva, is the creator and dispenser of the worlds. He is the supreme lord.

71. He is Saguṇa (having attributes) and transcends all beings, Prakṛti, Guṇas and Doṣas (merits and demerits). Since the entire inside of the universe is enveloped by him, he is Akhilātman (soul of all). He transcends all other coverings.

72. He is possessed of all splendid qualities. With a small portion of his power be maintains the creation of all living beings. Voluntarily he assumes a large physical body of his choice. He accomplishes everything that is conducive to the welfare of the world.

73. He is the sole receptacle of his power, vigour and other qualities. He is greater than the greatest. There is no great obstacle unto his splendour, power and ability to rule. In the great lord than whom there is no greater lord there are no pains etc.

74. He is the lord named Parameśvara. He has both the individual and cosmic collective forms. His form is both manifest and unmanifest. He is the lord of all. He is the eye of all. He knows everything. He has all powers.

75. That whereby this pure, supreme single form (that is free from impurity and devoid of all defects) is comprehended, perceived or attained is Jñāna (knowledge). That which is other than this is Ajñāna (ignorance).

CHAPTER ONE HUNDRED AND TWENTYSEVEN

Practice of Yoga

The sages said :

1. Now tell us the Yoga which is an antidote for the contact with miseries. On understanding it we shall come in unison with the unchanging Puruṣottama.

Sūta said :

2. On hearing their words, the highly delighted Kṛṣṇa-Dvaipāyana, the Yogin, the most excellent among those who understand Yoga, said thus:

Vyāsa said :

3. O brahmins, listen. I shall recount Yoga that destroys worldly existence. By practising it, a Yogin shall attain liberation which is extremely difficult of access.

4-5. At the outset the devotee shall propitiate the preceptor devoutly and listen to the Yogic scriptural texts. He must then eifficiently master Itihāsa, Purāṇa and Vedas. The intelligent one shall fully understand the diet (of a Yogin), the pitfalls during the practice of Yoga, and the proper time and place for the same. He shall be free from the mutually opposed pairs. He shall desist from hoarding possessions and then practise Yoga.

6-9. The following diet is conducive to the steady practice of Yoga : flour of fried grains, rice gruel, butter milk, roots, fruits, milk, barley food, ears of corn and oil cakes.

One shall never practise Yoga when the mind is unhappy, when one is (excited) weary or hungry, when the mutually conflicting pairs are present, when it is very chilly, when it is too hot, when there is too much of wind.

One shall not practise Yoga in a place which is too noisy, too close to water or too near fire. One shall not practise it in a dilapidated cowpen, in a cross-road, in a place infested by reptiles, in a cremation ground, nor on the banks of a river. Yoga shall not be practised in a monastery, in an anthill, in a dangerous place or near a well. One should not practise it on a heap of dry leaves.

10. If out of foolishness, anyone were to practise Yoga without taking into consideration these restrictions as to places, certain defects are produced and they cause obstacles. I shall describe them.

11. Deafness, sluggishness, loss of memory, dumbness, blindness and fever are produced immediately. Similarly ignorance is caused.

12. Hence (arrangement for) safety should always be made by every means by a person conversant with Yoga, since the physical body is the means of achievement of virtue, wealth, love and liberation.

13-20. Places for the practice of Yoga shall be as follows : a lonely hermitage, a secret (one with privacy) place, a place free from noise, fear and (unnecessary) movements, a clean vacant house and a beautiful secluded temple.

The time for practice of Yoga shall be as follows : the first or last Yāma (a period of three hours) of the night or in the forenoon or at midday.

A devotee shall keep his mind pure and well-concentrated. His diet shall be proper. He shall control his sense-organs.

He shall be seated facing east on a beautiful seat that is comfortable and steady. It shall be neither too raised up nor too much depressed.

The devotee shall be pure, truthful in speech and devoid of desire. He shall observe moderate periods of sleep. He shall subdue anger. He shall be engaged in what is conducive to the welfare of living beings. He shall put up with the inconvenience of suffering the mutually opposed pairs (i.e. excessive heat and chill etc.). He shall be self-possessed. He shall keep his body, legs and head in a steady posture.

He shall place both the hands on the navel. He shall be calm. He shall be seated in the lotus posture. The eyes should be fixed on the tip of the nose. He shall control his vital airs and speech. All the sense organs with the mind shall be withdrawn into the heart. Otherwise silent, he shall utter the Praṇava (Oṁkāra), continuously with the mouth well-covered. He shall be steady.

He shall subdue the activities of Tamas by means of Rajas and those of Rajas by means of Sattva. He shall maintain a pure and quiet posture with the eyes closed. (Thus) the Yogin shall always be in unison with Puruṣottama who is the bestower of salvation, who dwells in the cavity of his lotus-like heart, who is omnipresent and who is unsullied.

21. At the outset he shall fix the sense organs, the organs of action and the elements in his soul. He should unite his soul

with the supreme soul. It is then that the devotee performs Yoga.

22. The supreme region is characterized by the hundredth part of the tip of a hair (i.e. it is very subtle). The Yogins who are devoted to meditation see it by the lamp of their mind. The devotee conversant with Yoga is capable of withdrawing the sense organs like a turtle that withdraws its limbs.

23. If the mind of a person is able to find its ultimate end in the supreme soul after abandoning all sensuous objects, his success in Yoga is assured.

24. When the mind is free from sensuous objects as the Yogin is in communion with the supreme Brahman in the course of his ecstatic experience and the mind gets dissolved in the supreme Brahman, he attains the highest place.

25. When the mind of the Yogin is disengaged from every sort of activity after attaining the highest bliss, he attains salvation.

26. By the power of Yoga the Yogin attains the pure Puruṣottama who is termed the "fourth" and who transcends the three states (viz. wakeful, dreaming and slumbering). There is no doubt in this that he is liberated.

27. A Yogin who is free from desires for any object of lust, who is pleasing to look at in any posture whatsoever (or who sees pleasant things everywhere), and who is aware of transience of everything, shall be liberated and not otherwise.

28. He who is conversant with Yoga shall not indulge in the objects of sense. He shall undoubtedly be liberated by absence of attachment and regular practice of Yoga.

29. Yoga is not achieved merely by resorting to the Lotus posture, nor by concentrating on the tip of the nose. The unison of the mind and the sense organs with the soul is called Yoga.

30. Thus, O excellent sages, the Yoga that bestows liberation, that is the cause of release from worldly bondage, has been recounted by me. What else do you wish to hear?

Lomaharṣaṇa said :

31. On hearing his words they said: "Well done, Well done". After praising and honouring Vyāsa they began to ask him once again.

CHAPTER ONE HUNDRED AND TWENTYEIGHT

Review of Sāṁkhya and Yoga

The sages said :

1. O sage, O excellent brahmin, no satiety is observed by us in imbibing the verbal nectar coming out of the ocean of your mouth.

2. Hence, O sage, describe in detail the Yoga that bestows salvation. O most excellent one among the bipeds, we wish to hear about Sāṁkhya too.

3. O brahmin, how does an intelligent brahmin, well versed in the Vedas, one who is the performer of sacrifices, an intelligent devotee devoid of jealousy, one whose mind dwells on truth and virtue, attain Brahman?

4. Does he attain it by performing austerities, or by living a celibate life, or by renouncing everything, or by means of his intellect, or by resorting to thought propounded by Sāṁkhya or Yoga? On being asked this, please tell us.

5. By what means does a man attain concentration of mind and control over senses? It behoves you to explain this.

Vyāsa said :

6. No one achieves (spiritual attainment) without knowledge and austerity, without subduing the sense organs or without renouncing everything.

7. All the major elements are the earlier creation of the self-born lord. They are fixed into the bodies of all living beings.

8. The physical body is from the Earth element. The viscidity is due to the Water element. The eyes are from the Fiery element. The Air element is the support of Prāṇa and Apāna (i.e. the organic gases). The Ether element is the inner cavity of the embodied beings such as the bowels etc.

9. The deities presiding over the various parts of the body are: Viṣṇu at the time of departure, Indra over the physical strength, the Fire-god in the bowels, the interstices of quarters over the ears, Sarasvatī, goddess of speech, over the ears and the tongue.

10-11. Ears, skin, eyes, tongue, nose together with the five organs of action are the ten indriyas. They are the means of getting food and apprehending sound, touch, colour, taste and smell. One shall always know these sense-objects as separate from the sense-organs.

12. The mind is in unison with the sense organs just as the non-poisonous snake is in conjunction with (animals) beyond its control. The individual soul stationed in the heart is always in unison with the mind.

13. The mind is competent to rule over the sense organs. The individual soul is competent to control and discharge the mind.

14. The following are eternally present in the physical bodies of the embodied beings : sense-organs, objects of senses, intrinsic nature, consciousness, mind, vital airs namely Prāṇa and Apāna and Jīva (the individual soul).

15. (?) There is no support unto the Sattva; what is termed by the word Guṇa is not the conscious ones. The splendour creates Sattva and by no means the Guṇas.

16. Thus the physical body consists of seventeen entities and it is enveloped by sixteen qualities. O brahmins, the wise sage sees by means of his mind the soul within the soul.

17. It cannot be perceived by the eye nor by the sense-organs. It is by means of the illuminated mind that the higher soul is revealed.

18. The Ātman is devoid of sound, touch, and colour; it is free from taste and smell; it has neither body nor the sense-organs. One shall see it in one's own body.

19. He who sees that which is unmanifest in all the physical bodies and that which is excessively honoured among mortals is capable of becoming Brahman after his demise.

20. Wise sages view the Ātman equally in a Brahmin richly endowed with learning and humility, in cow, in elephant, dog or in an outcaste.

21. The single soul abides in all living beings, mobile and immobile. The visible worlds are pervaded by it.

22. When one sees the soul in all living beings and all living beings in the soul, the individual soul becomes identical with Brahman.

23. The soul is in the supreme soul to the extent to which the soul sees and understands in the soul. He who knows this is capable of immortality.

24. The soul has no region. Even Devas seeking the region of the soul that is the inner soul of all living beings and is devoted to the welfare of all living beings, become deluded on the way.

25. Just as the movement of birds in the sky or that of the fishes in the water is imperceptible, so also the movement of those who have achieved knowledge.

26. Kāla (Time, God of Death) cooks all living beings in the soul by means of the soul. But nobody knows that wherein Kāla itself is cooked.

27. It is neither above, nor at the sides, neither below, nor in front, nor in the middle. No one seizes it.

28-29. The worlds are stationed in it. There is nothing extraneous to these. Even if one has the speed of the wind and one goes forth ahead like an arrow discharged from the bowstring one shall never reach the end of the ultimate cause.

There is nothing that is subtler than it; there is nothing that is grosser than it.

30. It has hands and feet all around; it has eyes, head and face all around; it has ears all around; it stands up enveloping everything in the world.

31. It is minuter than the minutest atom; it is greater than all great things; though it abides steadfastly within all living beings yet it is not perceived.

32. There are two states of the Ātman, viz. the imperishable and the perishable. The perishable one is in all living beings; the imperishable is divine and immortal.

33. The Haṁsa (swan, here the soul) builds for itself a city with nine gates (i.e. the body with nine doors, viz. eyes etc.). He controls it invariably. He is like this in regard to all living beings, whether mobile or immobile.

34. Super-seers say that the swan-like property of the unborn soul comes from the fact that it discards doubtful alternatives and gathers bodies (?)

35. What is termed by the word Haṁsa is perishable individual. What is Imperishable is the unchangeable one. He

who knows this attains the Imperishable and discards vital airs and with that his very birth.

Vyāsa said :

36. You had asked me, O brahmins, and so Sāṁkhya which is combined with perfect knowledge has been duly and truthfully recounted by me.

37-39. Henceforth, O brahmins, I shall recount Yoga. The unity of intellect and mind as well as of all the sense-organs (should be understood). This knowledge is the highest one. It is the knowledge of the all-pervading soul.

It should be understood after eradicating the defects of Yoga, which (seers) know to be five in number. It can be understood (only) by one who is tranquil, one who has controlled his senses, one who practises spiritual exercises, one who takes delight in the soul, one who is enlightened and one whose activities are pure.

40-43. The five defects are : lust, anger, greed, fear, and slumber.

One conquers anger by practising mental tranquillity, and lust by avoiding lustful thoughts.

A self-possessed man is fit to eradicate slumber by resorting to Sattva (activities).

By the practice of mental fortitude one shall guard oneself against sexual lust and gluttony.

One shall guard hands and feet by means of the eye.

One shall guard eyes and ears by means of the mind.

One shall guard one's mind and speech by means of good activity.

One shall eschew fear by means of vigilance and attention. One shall eradicate arrogance by resorting to intelligent men.

One shall be watchfully alert and conquer these defects of Yoga.

He shall bow down to the sacred fires, Brahmins and deities.

44-46. One shall avoid arrogant speech coupled with violence. One shall speak words pleasing and favourable to the mind. He who has splendour consisting of brahmanical brilliance perceives the entire universe consisting of mobile and immobile beings. He has become identical with the living beings.

By means of the following one's splendour increases and sin decreases : meditation, self-study of the Vedas, charitable gifts, truthfulness, shyness, straightforwardness, forgiveness, cleanliness, purity of the soul, and the control of senses.

47-48. The devotee practising Yoga shall be impartial to all living beings. He shall sustain himself with things available; he shall shed his sins; he shall conquer the sense-organs; he shall take limited diet. He shall then become brilliant. After subduing lust and anger he shall resort to the region of Brahman. He shall maintain purity of the body and mind. He shall concentrate his sense-organs and the mind. Early in the night as well as early in the morning he shall fix the mind in the soul.

49-51. A creature has five sense organs. Even if one of them is moistened, his intellect begins to flow out like water from the foot of a mountain.

Just as the killer of fishes takes turtles, so he shall take the essence of the mind at the outset. The devotee who is conversant with Yoga shall then control ear, eye, tongue and nose. Thereafter if he controls them and fixes them in the mind he shall discharge all conceptions (mental fancies) and retain the mind in the soul.

52-54. If and when he fixes the five sense organs in the mind and the heart, when these sense-organs with the mind as the sixth abide in the Ātman and are pleased in that situation—he attains the Brahman then. They see Ātman in the Ātman. It is like the flame that shines free from smoke; it is like the brilliant sun; it is like the fire of lightning in the sky.

55-56. Everything is seen there. Since it is all-pervading it is seen everywhere. Noble-souled brahmins, who are wise, who are bold, who have great intelligence and who are engaged in the welfare of all living beings see it.

The devotee shall practise thus for a limited period. Keen in the practice of the holy rites he shall seat himself in a secluded spot and attain similarity with the Imperishable one.

57-59. (Defective) There are some pitfalls in the achievement of Yogic power. The devotee shall avoid them. They are delusion, error, deliberation; miraculous results in regard to smelling hearing, seeing and touching; abilāity to bear chilliness and heat, gaseous shape; presence of mind and obstacles (?) By Yogic practice he should control all these. The devotee who understands reality shall ignore them. By means of his equanimity he shall cause them to recede. The devotee like a sage practising silence, shall practice Yoga with perfect mental purity in all the three worlds.

60-64. He shall practise on the top of a mountain, in a monastery or under a tree.

Just as a merchant who is worried over his articles of trade puts them into a safe, so the aspirant after Yoga shall restrain his sense-organs and concentrate his mind. His mind shall never get fed up with the Yogic practice.

He shall adopt means whereby the unsteady mind can be put under control. He shall never swerve therefrom. He shall steadily resort to the Yogic practice. He shall take up vacant rooms for residence and maintain concentration. Neither mentally nor verbally nor physically should he proceed out of bounds. He shall be indifferent to everything worldly. He shall maintain restrictions on his diet. He shall be impartial to everything whether obtained or not obtained.

Whether anyone congratulates him and wishes him or not he shall be impartial to them. He shall not wish for either welfare or disaster.

65. He shall not be too delighted for a gain nor be worried for a loss. He shall be impartial to all living beings. He shall thus be one having properties similar to those of the wind.

66. Within six months, Brahman approaches that devotee whose soul has become healthy and normal, who views everything impartially, who has become virtuous and perfect and who is perpetually engaged in Yogic practice.

67. (Thus) the Yogin is in a position to view a clod of earth, a piece of rock and an ingot of gold impartially. On seeing others distressed due to pain he shall not be deluded nor shall he swerve from his path.

68. Even a man of very low caste or a woman desirous of virtue shall attain the supreme goal through this path.

69. On seeing this unborn, ancient, unageing, eternal

(Lord) who is imperceptible and who is beyond the ken of sense organs, O Brahmins, intelligent men attain equality with Brahman, a goal from which there is no return.

CHAPTER ONE HUNDRED AND TWENTYNINE

Review of Sāṁkhya and Yoga

The sages said :

1. Should the Vedic injunction be "Perform rites and renounce them"? Whither do they go by means of Vidyā (learning), and what do they attain by means of holy rites ?

2. We wish to hear this. Your Holiness may be pleased to explain it to us. There is a mutual inconsistency in this (injunction) because both are opposed to each other.

Vyāsa said :

3. Listen, O leading sages, I shall briefly explain the Kṣara (perishable) and Akṣara (imperishable) in the form of holy rites and (knowledge) about which you have asked me.

4. Listen now, O brahmins, to the quarter whither they go by means of learning and what they attain by means of holy rites. The reply to this (question) is intricate and complex.

5. It is but proper to say that Dharma (virtue) exists. In the same context if anyone were to say that it does not exist, then this shall be tantamount to saying that this resembles a Yakṣa and that there is no Yakṣa.

6. There are the two paths wherein the Vedas are well-founded. Dharma is characterised by Pravṛtti (Activity, taking active part in worldly life). The other alternative is Nivṛtti (cessation of active participation).

7. A creature is bound by activity. He is liberated by means of Vidyā. Hence ascetics, the wise ones, do not engage themselves in activity.

8. On account of activity (i.e. by performing various rites) one is reborn after death into an embodied form consist-

ing of sixteen constituents, i.e. sense-organs etc. On account of learning one is transformed into the eternal unmanifest Brahman, the Akṣara or Imperishable one.

9. Those possessed of inferior intellect praise Karman (performance of holy rites). Thereby they attain a series of bodies to indulge themselves in. They then perform worship.

10. Those who have acquired the highest intellect, those who perceive the efficiency of Dharma do not praise Karman, like one who drinks the river water and so does not praise the well.

11. One attains happiness and misery, birth and non-birth as a result of Karmans. By learning one attains that after reaching which one never feels sorry.

12. After going there one does not die; after going there one is not reborn, after going there one does not become old; after going there one does not increase.

13. It is the (place) where the supreme Brahman is. It is unmanifest, unmoving and fixed. It is not split and analysed. It has no extension. It is immortal. The devotee who understands the esoteric doctrine the Yoga, (attains it).

14. Those who are impartial to all, those who are friendly to all, those who are engaged in everything conducive to the welfare of all living beings are not affected by mutually opposed pairs nor by mental activities.

15. The Puruṣa possessed of learning is different, Brahmins, from the Puruṣa possessed of Karman. O brahmins, the moon that stands with its full complement of subtle digits is different from the sense of touch it has.

16. This has been mentioned by the sage and it is sung in detail. It cannot be seen or recounted like a piece of thread in a wheel in the sky.

17. The embodied form has the full complement of all digits. It has eleven created things within itself. O brahmins, understand it to be of the nature of Karmans and Guṇas.

18. The splendid ātman that has resorted to the body like the moon in the sky should be known as Kṣetrajña. It is eternal. It has realized Brahman by means of Yoga.

19. Tamas, Rajas and Sattva should be known as the qualities of Jīva (Individual Soul). The Jīva has all the qualities of the supreme soul.

20. They say that consciousness is a quality of the Jīva. It activates the qualities of the Jīva. Thereafter those who allow importance to the physical body say they can create seven worlds.

Vyāsa said :

21. The creatures of Prakṛti are known as (individual soul). They do not comprehend him nor does he know them.

22. The individual soul performs his activities through the sense organs, with the mind as the sixth among them, just as the sober charioteer manages his chariot by means of superb well-controlled horses.

23-24. The sense-objects are greater than the sense-organs; the mind is greater than the sense-objects; the intellect is greater than the mind; the Great principle known as Ātman is greater than intellect; the unmanifest one is greater than all these. The Immortal one is greater than the unmanifest. There is nothing greater than the Immortal. That is the climax. That is the supreme goal.

25. Thus the Ātman that is hidden in all living beings is not easily revealed. It is perceived by persons of subtle vision by means of perfect, subtle intellect.

26-27. (Defective) The Yogin shall cause his sense-organs including the mind to dissolve in the inner soul by means of his intellect. He shall not ponder over the sense-objects through (the activities of) the sense-organs. He shall not think much by means of his mind. He shall train it by means of Vidyā and make it perfect in meditation. He shall attain tranquility of the soul. He shall not have anyone else to rule over him. He shall go to the supreme region.

28-29. One who slavishly submits to his sense organs, one whose faculty of memory is shaken, becomes a victim of death by yielding himself. But one should subdue all (wishful) thoughts and direct the mind towards Sattva. After stabilising the mind in the Sattva one shall become victorious over death.

30. By means of clearness of his mind the ascetic eschews the auspicious and inauspicious. One whose soul is pleased abides in the Ātman and attains everlasting bliss.

31-32. The clearness of the mind has the following characteristics : It is like happiness during slumber. It is like the lamp that shines unflickeringly in a windless place. Similarly one who practises Yoga early in the night or early in the morning by uniting the Ātman (Individual Soul) with the Ātman (Supreme Soul) sees the Ātman in the Ātman. He shall limit his diet and purify his senses.

33-35. This is the secret of the Vedas : it is unparalleled, it is free from ailments : it convinces one about the existence of the Ātman. This sacred doctrine shall be imparted to one's son. The wealth of all virtuous discourses and truthful narratives has been churned for ten thousand years and this nectar has been taken out.

Just as butter is produced out of the curds or fire is produced from the sacrificial twig, so also this knowledge has been acquired for the salvation of wise scholars.

36-39. This knowledge should be imparted to souls who have concluded their religious student-stage. This should never be mentioned to one who is not tranquil, who has no control over his sense-organs, who does not perform austerities, who has not mastered the Vedas, who is not obedient, who is not straightforward, who is jealous, who does not act according to directions, who is given to argumentation or who is a backbiter.

This secret knowledge should be imparted of one who is praiseworthy, who is tranquil, who is austere and who is obedient. It should by no means be imparted to anyone else.

40. Even if the whole of the earth filled with all jewels were offered against this, a man who knows reality shall consider this (knowledge) better than that.

41-42. The Adhyātma (spiritual) doctrine that is superhuman contains greater secrets than the Yogic knowledge. It has been perceived by great sages. It is sung about in the Vedāntas.

O good and noble ones, I shall give unto you what you ask me, whatever is in my mind. Whatever doubt you have in your heart has been cleared by what has been heard by you all. What else shall I tell you ?

The sages said :

43. Describe once again to us the Adhyātma doctrine in detail, O holy one, the most excellent of all sages, so that we can fully understand it.

Vyāsa said :

44. What is recounted as Adhyātma in regard to a person I shall explain to you all. Let its explanation be understood properly.

45. The great elements are the Earth, Water, Fire (light) Air and Ether. He who is the creator of these elements is within all the living beings.

The sages said :

46-47. The Ether etc. have no shape. No one sees anybody in them. How can one then explain their presence in the physical bodies ? There are certain qualities in the sense-organs. How can one comprehend them ?

Vyāsa said :

I shall explain this precisely in accordance with what is seen (in the scriptures). Listen attentively and comprehend them according to reality.

48. Sound, ear, void space—these there are the traits of Ether. Vital airs, movement and touch are the qualities of Vāyu (Air).

49. Colour, eye and gastric action (digestion)—the fiery element is threefold thus. Taste, tongue, sweet—are the qualities of Water.

50. What is smelt, nose and the physical body—are the qualities of Earth. This is the group of sense organs evolved out of the five elements.

51. The quality of touch belongs to the Wind ; the quality of taste to Water ; the quality of colour to Fiery element ; the quality of sound to Ether and the quality of smell is that of the Earth.

52. The mind, intellect and intrinsic nature—are born of their origins. They transcend Guṇas ; they are greater than Guṇas.

53. Just as the turtle stretches and withdraws the limbs, so also he who has excellent intellect controls his set of sense-organs.

54. The fact that one sees upwards, sideways as well as below the soles of feet indicates that the excellent intellect abides by this duty alone.

55. The intellect is led by the Guṇas. It is the intellect that leads the sense-organs. Should the intellect be absent whence can there be the Guṇas ?

56. There are five sense-organs in man ; the sixth is mind; the seventh is intellect; the soul is the eighth.

57. The eye perceives; the mind entertains doubt; the intellect determines; the soul is the witness.

58. Rajas, Tamas and Sattva are born of their respective causes. They are common to all beings. They are Guṇas.

59. That which one sees within the soul—something which is pleasant and delightful is Sattva. It is something quiescent and calm.

60. That predilection, which is attended by distress either in the body or in the mind is Rajas. One shall see that Rajas has become active.

61. That predilection which is attended by delusion is Tamas. It is vague, incomprehensible and incapable of being explained.

62. They call the following Sāttvika qualities: Extreme delight, pleasure, bliss, mastery over oneself, and normal restful nature of the mind, with or without reasons thereof.

63. The following are the symptoms of Rajas : conceit, untruthfulness, covetousness, delusion and impatience.

64. Similarly, the following are Tāmasa qualities : Deluded state, blunders, languor, slumber, inability to be awake. (The people under their influence) live somehow. They do not live a full useful life.

65. The external prompting for action is threefold. The mind indulges in fanciful creations of conceptions. The intellect is the factor of energetic determination. The heart dwells only on what is endearing.

66. The objects are indeed greater than the sense-organs; the mind is greater than the objects; the intellect is greater than the mind; and the soul is greater than the intellect.

67. The intellect is indeed the soul; the intellect is the leader of the soul. When the intellect undergoes aberration and change in regard to emotion it becomes the mind.

68. Inasmuch as the sense-organs are separate it is the intellect that undergoes aberration. In the act of hearing it becomes the ear and as the organ that touches it is called the sense of touch.

69. In the act of seeing it shall be the eye and in the act of tasting, the tongue; in the act of smelling the nose; the intellect undergoes changes.

70. They call them the sense-organs. The intellect becomes diffused in those forms. Remaining steady in the state of intellect in a man it is called intellect.

71-72. (?) Sometimes it gets pleasure : sometimes it bewails; sometimes it loses sense. (But really it is) not affected by pleasure and pain. Just as the ocean, lord of the rivers, surges towards the great shore with its billows, so also the intellect that is intrinsically emotional surges towards the three emotions (viz. pleasure, pain and delusion).

73. When the intellect yearns for and seeks something it becomes the mind. One shall see them intellectually as separate in their basis.

74. The sense-organs are based on the intellect. They must be collected entirely (?) in the order in which each is evolved.

75. When the mind is undivided it is the intellect. Emotion exists in the mind. When Rajas begins to function it transcends Sattva also.

76. Those that abide emotionally in all these three, function after the objects like the spokes in regard to the rim.

77. (?)One shall make use of the mind for the purpose of illumination even as the sense-organs are perfected by the intellect (either) moving befittingly or remaining indiffernt.

78. If only one understands this as natural one does not become deluded. He does not bewail and he is delighted. He is always free from hostility.

79. Indeed the soul cannot be perceived by the sense-organs that are subject to lust, that function in diverse ways, that cannot be controlled and that are ignorant and foolish.

80. When one holds their reins firmly by means of the mind and controls them, the soul reveals itself like a figure illuminated by a lamp.

81. When darkness is repelled the living beings are brought to light. This should also be considered in the same manner.

82. Just as an aquatic bird is not affected by the water even as it moves through water, so also the Yogin of liberated soul is not affected by the faults of Guṇas.

83. Similarly one who has realized the soul is not affected by the defects (of worldly existence) even when he continues to live in the world. He does not cling to anything. He is by no means contaminated.

84-85. Since he abandons the Karmans done previously he is not affected by them. One who has love towards the great Ātman, one who has become the soul of all living beings but one who gets stuck up due to the contact of Guṇas—in regard to such a one, the soul takes up birth. He gets entangled in the Guṇas. The Guṇas do not understand the soul. But the soul knows the Guṇas.

86. He shall contemplate the Guṇas. He is the seer of everything in the manner it exists. A man shall perceive the difference between Sattva (Guṇa) and the Kṣetrajña (Individual Soul).

87-89. One of them creates the Guṇas and the other does not create. The two are naturally separated and joined together. Just as gold and pebbles are found existing together (though separate), just as the mosquito and Udumbara are found together though separate, just as the Iṣikā (shoot of a grass) exists together with the Muñja grass and is also separate, so also the two remain together and are separate from each other.

CHAPTER ONE HUNDRED AND THIRTY

Review of Sāṁkhya and Yoga

Vyāsa said :

1. Sattva creates Guṇas and the Kṣetrajña presides over them. As though indifferent, the lord presides over them.

2. It is all but natural, that it creates these Guṇas. Just as the spider weaves its web so also it creates Guṇas.

3. Some are of this firm opinion : Those who have started functioning do not stop the same; (the fact is) the functioning is not perceptible. But others accept cessation of activity.

4. One should ponder over these two and come to a decision in accordance with one's intellect. Of course, in this manner a great doubt may occur.

5. Indeed the Ātman has neither birth nor death. A man shall sport about after realizing it. He should never be angry nor too delighted. He shall be free from enmity and jealousy.

6-9. (Defective) Thus everyone should reflect on (the supreme Being) by means of intellect and heart. He should consider that the worldly pleasures are evanescent. He should be free from doubts. He shall cross the earth that has fallen down in the same manner as scholarly men cross the swollen river by diving and swimming in it.

O brahmins, this (earthly existence) is fickle and unsteady. A scholar does not feel distressed. Knowing the reality he walks on firm ground after pondering over the Ātman and the knowledge of Ātman.

After understanding the creation of living beings, their advent as well as departure, and observing (everything) well, a man obtains excellent quiescence and tranquillity.

10-11. This is the entire (aim) of the twice-born and especially of the Brahmin. It is the knowledge of Ātman. It is the ultimate resort. It is confined to impartiality and love towards all. One shall become enlightened after understanding the reality. What else is the characteristic of an enlightened one ? After comprehending this, learned men become liberated and contented.

12. The enlightened ones do not have to face the great fear that the unenlightened ones have to after death in the other world. No one has a greater status than the eternal one which the enlightened one has.

13. Man is detracted from the inner world. On not seeing the lord there, he bewails. If there is efficiency in that respect, those who comprehend both—the done as well as the undone—do not bewail.

14. If one performs Karmans without yearning for benefit, it burns away sins. If actions are performed with pleasure or hatred as motives the same is the result of his actions.

The sages said :

15. May Your Holiness be pleased to tell us that most excellent virtue than which there is no greater virtue and that which is greater than all valuable things.

Vyāsa said :

16. I shall recount the ancient virtue eulogised by the sages, which is the most excellent of all virtues. Listen to it, O excellent sages.

17-18. The sense-organs agitate us. One shall intelligently control them like a father who controls his sons during their formative childhood years. The concentration of the mind and that of sense-organs is the greatest austerity. That is the most excellent of all virtues. It is mentioned as the greatest virtue.

19. By means of perfect knowledge one shall control those (sense-organs) including the mind as the sixth and shall be self-contented. He shall not ponder over the multifarious objects of thought.

20. When these (sense-organs) refrain from their respective objects and remain in their abodes, you will all see the supreme Ātman, the eternal one, by means of the self.

21. The intelligent Brahmins see the great Ātman, the soul of all like the smokeless fire.

22-23. Just as great tree with many branches having flowers and fruits does not know specifically "Where is my flower? Where is my fruit?", so also the (individual) soul does not know "Whence have I come? Whither will I go?" It has another inner soul that sees everything.

24. One sees Ātman by Ātman through the mind that is illuminated by perfect knowledge. O brahmins, you all shall be free from passionate attachment on seeing Ātman.

25. Even in this world you will attain great intellect and become liberated from all sins like serpents that shed off their slough. You will be devoid of anxieties and free from ailments.

26-30. The river of worldly existence is terrible. It has currents everywhere. The five sense organs are its crocodiles. The conceptions of the mind are its banks. Greed and delusion are the grasses that cover them up. Lust and anger are the reptiles that are there. Truthfulness constitutes holy waters and falsehood the turbulent eddies. That excellent river of worldly existence has anger for its marshy bed. Its source is the Unmanifest one. It is a rapid river agitated by lust and anger. Those who are not self-possessed cannot cross it. O brahmins, cross that river by means of your intellect. If flows into the ocean of worldly existence. It is impassable as it falls into the nether regions of the vaginal passage. It starts with one's own birth. It is difficult of access due to the whirlpool of tongues. Intelligent persons of great courage and steadfast intellect cross it. One who has crossed it is liberated from everywhere. His soul is purified. He is pure and self-possessed.

31-32. He is capable of becoming Brahman by adopting excellent intellect. He crosses great distresses. He is devoid of sins and his soul is clean and pleasant. From all places he sees all living beings (?) He becomes neither angry nor elated. He is also not wicked in his mind.

33. Thereafter, you will see the birth and annihilation of all living beings. Wise men have considered this as the most excellent of all virtues.

34. O most excellent ones, among persons upholding virtue, the wise sages of truthful speech consider this as the most excellent virtue. O Brahmins, the souls are all-pervading. This principle should be imparted to one's sons.

35. This great secret doctrine of the soul is the highest

of all esoteric doctrines. This should be imparted to a pure and devoted follower.

36-37. What I have recounted is a highly secret doctrine with the soul as witness thereof. The Ātman is neither a female nor a male, nor is it a neuter one. Brahman is devoid of misery and happiness. It is identical with the past, present and future. After realizing this, no man or woman shall have to undergo rebirth.

38. All these facts have been described, O brahmins, by me.

39. (Defective) A person of delighted mind, whose son possesses good qualities and who is compassionate towards good sons will think about the welfare of those sons.

The sages said :

40. It has been said by Brahmā that liberation is to be acquired through a certain means and not without means. O sage, we wish to hear that means.

Vyāsa said :

41. In regard to this, O extremely intelligent ones, a close scrutiny is proper. O sinless ones, always seek all objects through that means.

42. The intellect is the means of finding a pot. But it is not the cause of the pot. The same formula applies to the means of virtue. It is not the cause of other Dharmas.

43. The path that leads to the eastern sea does not go to the western sea. Indeed there is only one path unto liberation. O sinless ones, listen to that.

44. One shall dispel anger by patience and forbearance; lust by avoiding mental conceptions. A bold man (a self-possessed one) deserves to dispel slumber by resorting to Sattva quality.

45. One shall guard against fear by avoiding errors. One shall protect (one's soul) and its knowledge. One shall courageously cause wish, hatred and lust to recede.

46. He who knows reality shall win over slumber and intellect by means of knowledge. The Yogin shall subdue

ailments by taking wholesome food in limited quantities after the previous intake has been digested.

47. One shall conquer greed and delusion by contentment; sensual object by means of the vision of reality; the evil by tenderness and compassion; and virtue by indifference (?)

48. The learned man shall conquer hope and ambition by restraining his mind; competence (?) by avoiding close contact. He shall conquer affection by the thought of (?) non-eternity and hunger by Yogic practice.

49. One shall conquer self by means of self by merciful compassion; excessive greed by means of contentment; languor by early rise. One shall conquer fanciful doubt by means of decision.

50. One shall conquer variety of languages by means of silence, fear by heroism. One shall control speech and mind by his intellect. One shall conquer intellect by the eye of knowledge.

51. The great Ātman shall control knowledge. The tranquillity of the Ātman shall control the Ātman. These things shall be understood by a tranquil person of pure activities.

52-54. The seers know that the defects of Yogic practice are five, viz. lust, anger, greed, fear and slumber. The devotee shall dispel these defects and resort to the Yogic means duly. (They are) meditation, self-study of the Vedas, charitable gifts, truthfulness, shyness, straight-forwardness. forbearance, clealiness, pious conduct and control over the sense-organs. One's splendour increases by means of these. One dispels sin by means of these.

55-57. Everything that he wishes for is achieved. His perfect knowledge begins to function. He shakes off his sins and becomes brilliant. He shall have limited diet. He shall conquer sense-organs. He shall keep lust and anger under his control. He shall thus enter the region of Brahman.

This is the clean, pure and vivid path of liberation : The state of being not deluded, the state of being unattached, avoidance of lust and anger, the state of not being puffed up, absence of excited anxiety and the state of being steady. Similarly the control of speech, body and mind can become imperishable (in their consequence) as one pleases.

CHAPTER ONE HUNDRED AND THIRTYONE

Review of injunctions regarding Yogic practice

The sages said :

1. O brahmin, O excellent sage, it behoves you to relate to us the respective peculiarity of Sāṁkhya and Yoga, O sage, conversant with virtue, everything is known to you.

Vyāsa said :

2. The followers of Sāṁkhya praise Sāṁkhya. The followers of Yoga praise Yoga. In order to exalt one's side they give cogent reasons.

3. O excellent sages, "How can one who is not competent be liberated?" Thus, saying with good reasons, learned men mention Yoga to be more excellent.

4-5. The brahmins give reasons to justify Sāṁkhya. "He who is unattached to the sensual objects shall be liberated from his body after understanding all movements and goals and not otherwise. Thus men of great intellect state that Sāṁkhya is a philosophy of liberation.

6. A reason competent to justify one's own side, words conducive to one's welfare, should be accepted. The opinion of excellent persons should be accepted by you all who are honoured by good men.

7-8. Yogic austerities are causes of spiritual attainment. The Sāṁkhyas adhere to the decision of scriptural texts. O excellent brahmins, Sāṁkhya and Yoga are based on reality. Both these systems are known to the sages as systems approved by good men. If they are practised in accordance with the scriptural texts they are sure to lead to the supreme goal.

9. O sinless ones, proper means of clealiness has been mentioned in both of them equally. Compassionate mercy to all living beings is also mentioned. The observance of holy rites is also similar, but spiritual vision is not the same in both (?)

The sages said :

10. If the observance of holy rites, purity, and merciful-

ness are similar, O great sage, how is the spiritual vision not equal. Tell us kindly, O excellent brahmin.

Vyāsa said :

11. Defaulters in Yogic practice attain the following five defects mentioned in the Yogic path : passion, delusion, affection, lust and anger.

12. Just as the big fish cut off the net and escape into the water once again, so also the persons devoid of sins attain that region by taking recourse to Yoga.

13-14. Similarly, just as the strong deer break loose, cut the net and attain freedom being liberated from all bondages, so also the brahmins equipped with strength break their bonds of covetousness. After cutting them off by means of Yoga they attain auspicious path devoid of impurities.

15-16. The persons equipped with strength are firm and steadfast. On the other hand, those without the strength of Yoga perish, just as the birds devoid of strength, O leading brahmins, fall into net. Sinless ones do not get involved in bondage. Such are the powers of Yoga.

17-18. Just as on getting entangled in a fine net weaker birds fall into misfortune while stronger ones free themselves, so those who are possessed of strength are liberated, while the feeble ones perish. Similarly, the brahmins who are devoted to Yoga are bound by the fetters arising out of their past Karmans. The weaker ones perish and the strong ones get free.

19. O brahmins, the fire of very little magnitude is very weak and it calms down on being overwhelmed by huge (quantities of) fuel. The Yogic power too is similar.

20. The same fire, O brahmins, becomes stronger once again on being accompanied by the wind. It may then burn the entire earth instantly.

21. The extremely powerful Yogin whose strength is the perfect knowledge of reality and whose splendour is illuminated, is capable of drying up the entire universe like the sun at the time of dissolution.

22. Just as a weak man, O brahmins, is taken away by the force of a current, so also the Yogin, devoid of strength is carried away by the force of sensuous objects.

23. A powerful elephant is capable of obstructing the same water current. Similarly after attaining the Yogic strength no man is led astray by sensuous objects.

24. Those who are endowed with the power of Yoga, become masters of everything and enter the region of Prajāpatis, Manus and Bhūtas.

25. Neither Yama, nor the infuriated Antaka (The annihilator), nor Mṛtyu (i.e. god of Death) of terrible exploits enter, O brahmins, the path of Yoga of unlimited splendour.

26. O excellent brahmins, there are thousands of Ātmans (souls). By means of them one shall practice Yoga and after attaining the Yogic power, wander over the earth.

27. One may indulge in enjoying worldly pleasures and do severe penance thereafter. Again, O brahmins, he shall subdue them like the sun that subdues the qualities of brilliance.

28. O excellent sages, for infusing more strength into the Yoga that is based on strength, one shall undoubtedly resort to Viṣṇu, the source or origin of liberation.

29. These powers of Yoga have been mentioned by me, O excellent brahmins, by way of illustration. Again, O brahmins, I shall mention the subtle ones.

30. Listen to the illustration, O excellent sages, in regard to meditation upon the soul or in regard to concentration of mind.

31. Just as an archer who does not err and who has full concentration, hits his target so also the Yogin of perfect unison, attains salvation undoubtedly.

32-33. A person of good concentration can steadily fix up his mind to a pot filled with oil and climb a flight of stairs. In the same manner the liberated soul can make use of steady Yoga. He makes the soul free from impurities like a mirror in which the sun reflects.

34-35. Just as, O leading brahmins, the helmsmen who have perfect concentration row the ships in the high seas and take them to the port, so also, O brahmins, the knower of Yoga who has concentration on the soul attains the inaccessible region of bliss after leaving off this body.

36-37. Just as the charioteer, O brahmins, who has good concentration and capable horses takes the excellent man wielding the bow to the desired place immediately, so also, O brahmins, the Yogin with full concentration and Dhāraṇā, quickly attains the greatest region, like an arrow discharged at the target.

38. He who is engrossed and embedded in the soul is steady. He attains the unageing region as though by breaking the noose of the fish.

39-41. The following are the spots in the body where the Yogin should concentrate and meditate: navel, head, stomach, heart, chest, sides, eye, ear and nose. The Yogin of unlimited exploits, who practises great sacred rites with mental purity and concentration, meditates on these spots. O excellent brahmins, he unites his soul to the subtle Ātman (soul supreme). Adopting the excellent Yoga he burns, in a trice, all the Karmans both auspicious and inauspicious and, should he wish so, he is liberated.

The sages said :

42. It behoves you, O excellent one, to explain this. What is the diet of the Yogin ? What things does he conquer and subdue ? How does he gain in strength ?

Vyāsa said :

43. The Yogin who consumes coarse barley for a long time, O excellent brahmins, becomes a purified soul. With this single diet the Yogin attains great strength.

Extra verse

(43a.) O brahmins, the Yogin who is accustomed to eat bits of grain as well as Pinyaka (oil cake), and who avoids oily substances shall attain great strength.

44. Wandering through (and residing) in the caves for many fortnights, months and seasons of diverse incidents, and drinking water with milk added (now and then), the Yogin shall attain great strength.

45. After fasting incessantly for an unbroken period of a month, the Yogin becomes purified in soul and attains great strength.

46-48. Yogins of great intellect and devoid of passions illuminate the great and subtle soul by themselves, O excellent sages, by conquering and subduing lust, anger, chilliness, heat, rain, fear, sorrow, slumber, objects of sensuous pleasures, terrible allergies very difficult to be conquered, the sense of touch, drowsiness and the unconquerable lethargy. Meditation and studious habits are their assets.

49. This path of learned brahmins is very difficult to tread. Only a few pass happily through this path and quickly as well, O excellent sages.

50-52. Only a very few persons can comfortably pass through such a forest path as is terrible and abounds in serpents and reptiles. It contains many deep fissures and crevasses. It is devoid of water. It is impassable. It is full of thorns. It is dense and unbroken with thickly grown jungle trees. (In some places) the trees are burnt down by the forest fire. The whole path is infested by thieves and robbers. (Only a very few can pass through such a path.) In the same manner only a few brahmins can pass through the path of Yoga. It is admitted that a person of many faults shall desist from that path.

53. One should closely adhere to the path of Yoga as though that were as keen as the edge of a razor. This close adherence is the Dhāraṇā. It is difficult for persons devoid of self-possession to tread this path.

54. Dhāraṇā, O brahmins, is complex and complicated. Just as the boats of men devoid of helmsmen do not reach the auspicious goal, so also men devoid of Dhāraṇā do not attain their ends.

55. He who practises Yoga by adhering to Dhāraṇā duly, conquers death and the misery of frequent births. He excels others in happiness.

56. This great path of Yoga has been resorted to by a number of sages. This has been precisely (explained) in various scriptures. This is decisively (nurtured) by the twice-born people.

57-60. The path of Yoga, O leading sages, is in consonance with the path of the Vedas. It is approved of by Brahmā, Śiva and Viṣṇu, the bestower of boons. Bhava and Dharma (god of death) have attained dignity (due to the path of Yoga). The sons of Brahmā (i.e. Sanaka, Sanandana etc.) have also attained dignity (due to the path of Yoga). The Yogin passes through the various stages of Prakṛti, namely, the pure Sattva, the grand Rajas and Tamas full of pain. He attains divine power, and the goddess who is Varuṇa's consort. He achieves entire splendour and great courage. He attains the status of or identity with the moon in the sky who is pure by nature, Viśvedevas, serpents, Pitṛs (Manes), mountains, terrible oceans, rivers, elephants, along with the mountains, Sādhyas, Yakṣas, quarters, Gandharvas, Siddhas, men & women. The noble-souled Yogin then becomes liberated before long.

61. After attaining Yogas and experiencing them, those men attain Nārāyaṇa quickly. The story thereof, O excellent brahmins, is relevant in regard to divine beings as well as a splendid person of great virility and intellect.

CHAPTER ONE HUNDRED AND THIRTYTWO

Review of the principles of Sāṁkhya

The sages said :

1. This practice of Yoga, the path of Yoga, that has been approved of by dignified persons, O leading brahmin, has been well narrated to the pupil by you who wish his welfare.

2. Now please expound in essence the practice of virtue according to Sāṁkhya, for whatever is known in the three worlds has been understood by you.

Vyāsa said :

3. Listen ye, O sages, to the principles of Sāṁkhya, who have realised the souls. These principles have been laid down by the old men of yore, Kapila and others, who were not inferior to lords.

4. In that system, O excellent sages, a few complexities are seen. In it there are many good qualities and no defects.

5. That is achieved by practising the rites mentioned as under. By means of knowledge, O brahmins, all things are realised. All unconquerable human objects of pleasure and the entire objects of evil are also realized.

6. The objects of pleasure of Nāgas, Gandharvas, Pitṛs and lower creatures are known.

7. The objects of pleasure of Suparṇa (Garuḍa), Maruts, sages and royal sages are known.

8. The objects of pleasure of Asuras, Viśvedevas and divine sages are known. The great objects of Yogas are also understood.

9. The objects of pleasure of whatever is being eaten as well as the object of pleasure of Brahmā are known. The maximum period of life is understood in essence by the people.

10. The maximum duration of happiness is clearly understood, O excellent sages. The misery of persons indulging in worldly pleasures, coming at the due time, is understood.

11. The misery, O brahmins, of those souls that take birth among low creatures or fall into hell, is understood. The merits and demerits of heaven, O brahmins, are entirely understood.

12-14. The merits and demerits of the Vedic system are to be understood. The defects and merits of the path of knowledge should be understood. The merits and the demerits, brahmins, of the Sāṁkhya knowledge should be understood. The devotee shall understand Sattva of ten qualities and Rajas of nine qualities, Tamas of eight qualities, Buddhi of seven qualities, Tamas of three qualities, Nabhas of six qualities.

15-16. Rajas that has two qualities and Sattva of a single quality are also be understood. By knowing the path in essence and by seeing annihilation the devotees, richly endowed with perfect knowledge and wisdom, attain splendid salvation even as the subtle ones attain great Ether. Salvation is attained by purified souls.

17-23. The organ of vision is to be understood as combined with the quality of colour; the organ of smell is to be understood as combined with the quality of smell; the organ of hearing is to be understood through the quality of sound; the tongue is combined with the quality of taste. The quality of touch pertains to the skin. The wind that is dependent upon it can be touched and known. (Delusion) is to be understood as combined with tamas and covetousness is to be understood as combined with delusion. Viṣṇu is to be understood as combined with Krānta (that has taken three steps). Indra is to be understood as combined with power. Fire god is to be understood as attached to the belly. The goddess is to be understood as combined with water. Waters are to be understood as dependent on fiery element. The fiery element is combined with gaseous element. The gaseous element is to be understood as dependent on Ether. The Ether is combined with the principle of Mahat. The Tamas is stationed in Mahas (splendour); Rajas is attached to Sattva and Sattva is attached to the Ātman (soul); the Ātman is attached to Īśa as well as lord Nārāyaṇa. Lord is attached to liberation and liberation is not attached to any. The physical body with Sattva quality should be known as surrounded by sixteen qualities; the nature and imagination should be known as dependent on the physical body; the soul is as though stationed in the middle; there is no sin therein.

24. The Karman of the persons indulging in worldly pleasures, O leading brahmins, should be known as sinful; sense-organs and the objects of senses should be known as stationed in the Ātman.

25. The rarity of salvation should be known by means of the Vedic literature. The (vital airs such as) Prāṇa, Apāna, Samāna, Vyāna and Udāna should be known duly.

26. The primordial wind element should be known and then the resultant wind also should be known. They should be known as divided into seven. The remaining ones should also be known as sevenfold.

27-28. The following persons should be thought upon: Prajāpatis, sages, excellent creations, seven sages, royal sages who scorch the enemies, divine sages, Maruts, brahminical sages resplendent like the sun and persons who have slipped down from their gorgeous splendour in the course of a long period of time.

29. The destruction of the groups of elements, O brahmins, should be heard. The splendid movement of the words should be known. Those who deserve the worship of persons of sinful actions should be seen.

30. The misery of those who have fallen into the abode of Yama (in the river) Vaitaraṇī should be realised. The inauspicious movements of creatures in the variegated wombs should be observed.

31-32. Their residence in the inauspicious belly should be seen and understood, the belly in the city of nine entrances (i.e. the body with nine orifices, viz. two eyes, two ears, two nostrils, mouth, urethra and anus), which is the receptacle of blood and water, which is filled with phlegm, urine and faecal matter, which has a strong obnoxious odour, which is a mass of semen and blood, which is fixed up by means of marrow and sinews and which has a tangled web and woof of hundreds of nerves.

33-38. One shall thoroughly understand that the Ātman is conducive to one's own welfare. O brahmins, one shall completely comprehend the different sorts of Yogas. O excellent sages, one shall observe the despicable activities of creatures of Tāmasa quality and those of the creatures of Sāttvika quality with handsome but false Ātmans. (In the same manner) one shall observe the despicable activities of the Sāṁkhyas for the sake of great men despite the fact that the Sāṁkhyas are persons who have comprehended the soul. One shall observe the terrible harassments of the moon (and other) luminaries, the fall of stars and revolutions of other heavenly bodies. One shall observe the miserable separation of couples, O brahmins. One shall observe also the inauspicious tendency of various living beings to devour one another. One shall also realise (people's) delusion during childhood and the inauspicious nature of the wing body (?). In some places, even the Sattva quality depends on passion and delusion. By all these means one man among thousands resorts to salvation-consciousness. The rarity of liberation should be realised. The realisation is only through (Vedic Literature).

39. Respect for things not yet received, neutrality in regard

to what has been acquired and the viciousness of objects of worldly pleasures, shall be fully comprehended again, O brahmins.

40. One shall comprehend residence in the families of creatures intending death as well as the emergence of creatures that are dead after breaking the splendid bodies (?)

41. The misery of even the Sāttvika creatures, O brahmins, must be comprehended. The fate of the persons who had killed brahmins and hence had a downfall, must be comprehended.

42. The evil fate of vicious brahmins addicted to the drinking of liquor, as well as those who indulge in illegitimate union with the wife of the preceptor shall be comprehended.

43-44. By means of perfect knowledge, O excellent brahmins, men behave well towards their mothers. They behave in the same manner towards the people of the world including gods. With the same knowledge one shall comprehend the fate of persons of inauspicious activities. The fates of those beings that are born in the wombs of lower creatures should be comprehended separately.

45-49. One shall comprehend the following: the glorious arguments in the Vedas, the successive orderly changes of the seasons, the passing off of the years, months, fortnights and days. The waxing and waning of the moon shall be observed directly. The ebbing and the flowing of the tides in the seas shall be perceived. Riches are observed to decline and increase. Unions are observed to come to an end and an era too is replaced by another era. The feebleness and bewilderment that one experiences due to egotism shall be duly comprehended. All the defects stationed in the soul and all the inauspicious defects arising out of one's own body shall be perfectly understood.

The sages said :

50. What defects arising out of Utpātas (dangerous portents) do you see, O most excellent one among the knowers of Brahman ? It behoves you to clarify this doubt of ours completely.

Vyāsa said :

51. O brahmins, intelligent scholars speak of five defects in the body, the scholars who are the followers of Kapila and

his Sāṁkhya system. They are conversant with the path. Listen, O excellent sages.

52. Lust, anger, fear, slumber and breath—these defects are seen in the bodies of all embodied beings.

53. By means of patience they cut off anger; by avoiding close intimacy they remove lust; by resorting to Sāttvika substances they remove slumber; and they remove fear by means of avoidance of errors.

54. They cut off and remove breath, O brahmins, by means of reduced diet. Good qualities are known by means of hundreds of good qualities and defects by means of hundreds of defects.

55. Reasons must be known by means of hundreds of reasons; wonderful things should be known by means of wonderful things.

The world is like the foam of waters. It is created by means of hundreds of māyās by Viṣṇu.

56. It resembles the wall painted in a picture. It has as much strength as grass (i.e. it is flimsy and feeble). It is conducive to great harm. It wanders about in darkness. It must be seen as one resembling bubbles (of water) during rain.

57. It is almost ruinous though it appears to be pleasant. It instils fear even after its destruction. Just as an elephant that has got stuck up in mud becomes helpless, so also the world gets stuck up in the slough of Rajas and Tamas.

58-61. The Sāṁkhyas, O brahmins, are highly intelligent. They abandon all attachment towards their progeny by means of knowledge and the object of knowledge that is all-pervasive and great, O brahmins. With the weapon of knowledge of the Ātman, O excellent ones, and with the rod of penance, they sever off the inauspicious Rājasa odours, Tāmasa odours, meritorious Sāttvika odours and those odours based on the body arising due to the physical touch. Thereafter they cross the terrible watery expanse of misery wherein anxiety and grief are great eddies; it is extremely terrible due to sickness and death; great fear acts like great serpents. Tamas is like a tortoise. Rajas is like fish. They cross this terrible expanse by means of their intellect.

62-68. By the path of knowledge, the sinless persons, the sages of great achievement cross the ocean of worldly existence wherein affectionate attachment is mud; old age is the fort, and the sensation of touch is like an island, O excellent brahmins; Karman is the great depth; truth is the bank; holy rites are the places to stand by, O intelligent ones; violence is the quickness and rapidity of the current; it is turbid due to different Rasas; different gestures of love are great jewels; misery and fever are the winds; grief and thirst are the great whirlpools; it has great pain due to sickness; O excellent brahmins, the set of bones is the flight of steps with phlegm for joining them; liberal charity is the mine of pearls; the terrible outpourings of blood are the coral beads; laughter and lamentation are the loud reports; it is very difficult to cross on account of various acts of ignorance; the dirt accummulated by the tears of lamentation is the brine; contact and union are the goals; this world of birth is one that deceives with sons and relatives for their towns; this (ocean of worldly existence) is an ocean unto all living beings with nonviolence and truthfulness for its line of boundary; it is full of surging waves due to the (incessant) contacts of vital airs; milk flows in successive waves (?); the territory here is the rare salvation; it is an ocean with the submarine fire at its mouth. Sinless ascetics cross this ocean (of existence).

69. After crossing (the ocean of) births which is difficult to cross they enter the pure sky and thereafter on seeing them come, the sun carries them with its rays.

70. The rays enter them like fibres of lotus, O brahmins, as it blows over the territories. O sinless ones, the wind Pravaha takes them up there.

71. O brahmins, the subtle, sweet smelling, cool wind Pravaha with gentle touch receives those ascetics who are devoid of passion and the Siddhas whose asset is penance and who are endowed with virility.

72. That wind which is the most excellent of all the seven winds, and which goes to the splendid worlds leads them, O great brahmins, to the most excellent goal from the firmament.

73. The firmament carries the lords of the worlds to the

greatest goal from the Rajas. The Rajas carries, O great brahmins, to the greatest goal of Sattva.

74. The pure soul carries the Sattva to the great and splendid lord Nārāyaṇa. The lord of pure soul carries them to the supreme soul by himself.

7 . After attaining the supreme soul they become rid of all defects. They are always free from dirt. They become capable of immortality. O brahmins, they do not come back.

76. That is the greatest goal, O brahmins, of those noble souls who are free from the mutually clashing pairs, who are devotedly engaged in truthfulness and straight-forwardness and who have kindness and sympathy for all living beings.

The sages said:

77. After attaining the most excellent region of the lord, do those persons of steady holy rites sport about there, till their death and rebirth ?

78. It behoves you to describe accurately what exactly is the reality therein. Excepting you we cannot, O excellent one, afford to ask any other mortal.

79-80. This would be a great defect in salvation if other ascetics would also stay in the same place, perfect knowledge leading them to salvation, along with the sages who have attained spiritual achievement. Hence O brahmin, we consider Dharma characterised by Pravṛtti (i.e. life of pious activities as opposed to life of pursuit of knowledge) as the most supreme one. But on the other hand, there is likelihood of another misery in regard to a person completely engaged in the great knowledge.

Vyāsa said:

81. The question has been put most relevantly, O excellent sages. Your dilemma has been enunciated. O excellent sages, there is confusion and delusion even amongst scholars in regard to this problem.

82. Even here listen to my words in regard to the perfect truth where the great intellect of those noble souls, the followers of Kapila, finds a place.

83. The sense-organs too of the embodied beings, O brahmins, are aware of their body. They are Ātman's Karaṇas (organs

of activity and knowledge); the soul perceives all types of subtle entities through them.

84. (The sense-organs) devoid of Ātman as a result of sinful actions, perish like the waves in a great ocean.

85. While the embodied soul is asleep or agitated the subtle soul wanders about along with the sense-organs like the wind that blows everywhere.

86. It sees duly. O sinless ones, it touches after remembering (?). It becomes aware of all as before, O brahmins.

87. Since they are not masters, the sense-organs merge into their respective places like serpents which are killed.

88. The subtle soul encompasses the movements of sense-organs in their respective places and moves about.

89-91. The individual soul pervades different qualities of Sattva, Rajas and Tamas, the qualities of intellect, O excellent ones, the qualities of mind, the qualities of firmament, the qualities of wind, O omniscient ones, the qualities arising from affection, the qualities of waters, O brahmins, and all the qualities of earth. The Kṣetrajña pervades, O excellent brahmins, the qualities in these individual souls and moves about due to auspicious and inauspicious Karmans.

92-97. Sense-organs move along with the soul just as disciples go along with a great saint (preceptor). After going beyond Prakṛti they attain the subtle, Nārāyaṇa of great soul, the great ultimate resort, greater than the greatest and devoid of all aberrations. He is free from all sins. He has entered a state of freedom from all ailments. That supreme soul is devoid of all qualities. He is blissful, excellent ones. There, O brahmins, the excellent mind and the sense-organs come at the proper time taking up the message of the preceptor. It is possible to attain tranquility and good qualities in the course of a brief period by means of the above mentioned Sāṁkhya and Yoga. The highly intelligent Sāṁkhyas attain the highest goal. O great brahmins, there is no other knowledge equal to this one that brings about salvation.

98. May you be in no doubt in this matter. It is knowledge that is the great Sāṁkhya. The primordial and the eternal Brahman is imperishable and Dhruva (everlasting).

99. Persons of tranquility and calmness speak of it as that which has no beginning, middle or end; that which is free from mutually opposed pairs; the Agent, the eternal one and the Kūṭastha (firm and steady like the peak of a mountain).

100. It is from this that all the processes of creation and annihilation issue forth. So say the eloquent great sages in the sacred scriptures.

101-103. The brahmins, Vedas and persons who are conversant with the Sāman verses call him the greatest lord, the endless one, the greatest Acyuta (one who does not slip or swerve) and Brahmaṇya (favourable to the Brahman). Brahmins with their intellect turned towards Guṇas, the followers of Yoga who are united with the great one and the Sāṁkhyas with their vision directed towards the unmeasured one (praise him). He has no manifest form, O great brahmins. The Veda says that knowledge is (his form). O excellent sages, they speak about many means of recognizing it.

104. There are two types of living beings on the earth, O excellent brahmins, the stationary and the Gamya (the mobile ones). Of these two the mobile ones are better.

105. Jñāna (knowledge) is greater than all great things, O brahmins. O great sages, whatever is seen in the Vedas, in Sāṁkhya, in Yoga and in Purāṇa—everything has come from Sāṁkhya.

106. What is seen in the great Itihāsas (epics), what is particularly seen in truthful scriptures and whatever knowledge is there in the world, O great sages, has come from Sāṁkhya.

107. Everything that is seen in the world, the great strength, knowledge, salvation, penance—all these subtle things have been duly laid down in Sāṁkhya, O brahmins.

108. Sāṁkhyas attain their welfare easily even from the things opposed to it. After realising them they become content. They fall in the abodes of brahmins again.

109. After breaking their bodies they enter salvation. The followers of Yoga and Sāṁkhya reside in heaven. Hence they are more interested in Sāṁkhya, that is very valuable and resorted to by dignified persons, O brahmins.

110. O sages, in the case of those brahmins who are not devoted to this knowledge their oblique movement (i.e. their birth among lower creatures) is seen but not downfall into the abode of those who commit sins. Those brahmins are not important at all.

111. The Sāṁkhya system is vast, great, ancient and free from impurities. It is as vast as the great ocean. It is dignified and splendid. The followers of Sāṁkhya dedicate everything unto Nārāyaṇa.

112. This great truth that the ancient universe originates from Nārāyaṇa has been spoken by me. At the time of creation he creates and at the time of annihilation he annihilates them again.

CHAPTER ONE HUNDRED AND THIRTYTHREE

The perishable and the Imperishable

Sages said :

1-4. What is it that is called Imperishable from which one does not return again. O great sage, we ask you about the distinction between the perishable and the Imperishable in order to understand it correctly, O excellent sage, O leader of sages. Indeed, you are mentioned as the most excellent among those who are endowed with knowledge by sages of great fortune and ascetics of noble souls who have mastered the Vedas. We wish to hear everything regarding this, from you, O sage of great intellect. We are never satiated by hearing the excellent nectar-like speech of yours.

Vyāsa said :

5. In this connection I shall recount unto you the legend of yore, the dialogue between Vasiṣṭha and Karāla-Janaka.

6. Vasiṣṭha, the most excellent one among the sages, having the features of the sun, was sitting in his hermitage when king Janaka asked him about the perfect knowledge leading to salvation.

7-8. Formerly king Karāla-Janaka asked the excellent sage Vasiṣṭha who was seated, after paying him obeisance with joined palms. He asked him about those topics with particular relevance to the supreme soul, determining the ways and means of spiritual pursuit. He asked that sage who moved about as he pleased, who performed excellent deeds, who was sweet-tempered and who was never puffed up.

Janaka said :

9-10. O holy one, I wish to hear about the great eternal Brahman from whom men of intellect never return. What is it that is called Kṣara since this universe dissolves therein (i.e. in the Brahman)? What is it that is spoken of as Akṣara which is auspicious, conducive to happiness and free from ailment?

Vasiṣṭha said :

11. Let it be heard, O ruler of the Earth, how this universe dissolves and perishes, where it dissolves at first, and how long does it take.

12. A Yuga consists of twelve thousand years. Know that a Kalpa is made up of four Yugas. A cycle of four hundred Kalpas is called a day of Brahmā.

13-14. O king, the night is also of the same duration at the end of which he wakes up and creates the great element firmament and other creations without end. The self-born lord, devoid of form and benefactor of the world creates the universe that has form. It is in the lord that the universe is rooted and has its origin, O excellent king.

15-16. (The supreme soul) is Īśāna, the never-diminishing flame, with the powers of Aṇimā (minuteness), Laghimā (lightness) and Prāpti (accessibility). It has legs and hands all around. It has eyes, heads and mouths all around. It has ears all around. It stands enveloping everything in the world. He is Lord Hiraṇyagarbha and is known as Buddhi (Cosmic Intellect).

17. It is called by various names in Sāṁkhya. In the Yoga system it is called Mahat and Viriñci.

18. It has various forms. It is the soul of the universe. It is known as single and Imperishable. All the three worlds have been held by it as though they formed one unit.

19. In the same manner it is known as omniformed because of its multifarious forms undergoing some physical change it creates in itself.

20. Pradhāna is a very great city called so because it is the abode of elements etc. Ahaṁkāra (Great Ego) has great splendour and it is bowed to by Prajāpati.

21. They call the manifestation from the Unmanifest *Vidyāsarga*. Mahat and Ahaṁkāra constitute *Avidyāsarga*.

22-28. So also from the *Eka* (single one) the *Acara* (immobile) and the *Cara* (mobile) are born. They are known as *Vidyā* and *Avidyā* and proclaimed so by persons who ponder over Vedic passages and scriptures. Know that there is a third type of creation, O king, from Ahaṁkāra i.e. the creation of elements (*Bhūtasarga*), viz. wind, fire, firmament, water and earth. In Ahaṁkāra itself, O king, know the fourth creation as *Vaikṛta*(i.e. diverse manifestation). The five elements and their five particular qualities, viz. sound, touch, colour, taste and smell, are produced simultaneously. Know the fifth type of creation, O great king, to be *Bhautika Sarga* (the creation of the evolutes of the five elements). They are the organs of sense and action as well as the mind. Ear, skin, eye, tongue and nose—these five are sense organs. Speech, hands, feet, anus and penis—these five are *Karmendriyas* (organs of action). These organs arose simultaneously along with the mind. Thus there are twenty-four principles in action in the creation. By knowing this set of twenty-four principles the brahmins cease to be worried. They see the reality.

29-33. Thus the excellent set of the three worlds is produced. It should be known, O excellent one, among men. In the whole world in all the creations the Ātman that pervades is the same whether it is the ocean of hell, the abode of Yakṣas, Bhūtas and Gandharvas, Kinnaras, Nāgas, Cāraṇas, Piśācas, Devas, sages and demons; whether it is the creation of flies, worms, mosquitoes, worms in the putrid matter, mice, dogs, low caste people who cook dogs, Caṇḍālas, Pulkasas, Eṇeyas, hunters of deer, horses, elephants, donkeys, tigers, wolves and cows. We have already heard that there is the abode of embodied beings in water, land and air. Certainly nowhere else.

34-36. It is the soul of all living beings that is known as Imperishable (*Akṣara*). Everyday the entire universe drops off and perishes. It moves off from the *Avyakta* (the unmanifest one). Since the universe perishes it is called (Perishable). They say that the universe is conducive to delusion. It is called *vyakta* (manifest) and it arises from *Avyakta*. The *Akṣara* is great and eternal. It avoids *Kṣara* (the perishable). From this no one returns. Thus, O great king, the *Akṣara* has been explained unto you.

37. The twenty-fifth-principle is formless. It is eternal and it is real. Intelligent scholars call it *Tattva* because it depends on *Sattva*.

38. That which is devoid of form creates the (manifest) and presides thereupon. The manifest is the twenty-fourth principle and the formless is the twenty-fifth one.

39. It alone abides in the heart of all forms. It is equipped with soul (?). It is conscious and it instils consciousness in all objects. It has no form but it identifies itself with all forms.

40. It assumes forms of creation and annihilation through the peculiar characteristics of creation and annihilation. Although it is devoid of attributes it remains within the view.

41. Although this great soul undergoes certain changes due to millions of creations and annihilations it does not absolutely identify itself with them all (?)

42. Not being enlightened itself and due to the resorting of unenlightened persons it becomes enveloped with Tamas, Sattva and Rajas and is born in different wombs.

43. Due to the residence together it thinks like this—"I am not the other one", "I am this one and hence not the other one". Thus it follows the attributes.

44. Due to Tamas it takes up beings of Tāmasika nature; due to Rajas it takes up beings of Rājasika nature and by devoting to Sattva it takes up Sāttvika beings.

45. The colours are three, viz. white, red and black. Know that all these colours belong to Prakṛti.

46. The persons of Tāmasa nature fall into hell; persons of Rājasa nature become human beings. Persons of Sāttvika nature go to the heavenly world and enjoy happiness.

47. Due to the sins committed in this world one falls into the womb of the lower animals; if sins and merits both are practised one takes birth among men; and if merits alone are practised one takes birth among gods.

48. Thus the wise persons say that salvation is based on Avyakta. It is the twenty-fifth principle which functions due to knowledge.

CHAPTER ONE HUNDRED AND THIRTYFOUR

A dialogue between Vasiṣṭha and Janaka

Vasiṣṭha said :

1. Thus due to the state of being unenlightened, the soul devoid of knowledge and enlightenment proceeds from one physical body to thousands of bodies. Therefore it does not differ in the course of its transmigration.

2. On account of its acquisition of penance or decrease of good qualities the soul sometimes takes up bodies among gods or among lower creatures.

3. From human birth it proceeds to heaven and from god it becomes a human being. From the state of man it proceeds to hell.

4. Just as the silk worm wraps itself by its thread-like fibres so also this soul though devoid of Guṇas wraps itself by means of Guṇas.

5-8a. Though the soul is devoid of mutually opposed pairs it is affected by them in different births. At the time when a person suffers from ailments such as headache, eye-pain, toothache, sore throat, dropsy, diarrhoea, Gaṇḍamālā, Vicarcikā, leukoderma, burns, scalds, epileptic fits etc., the characteristic symptoms of diverse types appear in the bodies of these souls. The soul identifies itself with the bodies. As in the case of identification so also in regard to meritorious deeds.

8b-12. The persons perform meritorious deeds of various kinds with a desire for welfare. The various kinds of meritorious rites are as follows: some wear four clothes; some lie down on the ground; some are seated in the Vīrāsana. After Vīrāsana some take up the posture of Ākāśa Śayana (lying in the firmament); some lie on bricks and rocks; some on spherical rocks; some lie on ash rocks; some have the ground for their bed as well as unguent. Drinking and cooking are conducted in heroic abodes (?) Lying down is on planks or on beds equipped with fruits and articles of domestic use. A man lies down in gardens attached to barns (?) He wears leather pieces or silken clothes along with the hide of black deer. He may wear fur garments studded with jewels or wear tiger skin garment.

13. He may wear lion hide or silken garment. Plank may be his robe or he may be wearing a mat.

14. Mat alone may be his garment or he may be wearing bark garment. We may take pride in wearing other types of clothes.

15. He may have diverse types of food and different kinds of jewels. He may take food once a day or on different nights with intervals of a night in between.

16. The time for taking meals may be the fourth, sixth or eighth one (i.e. calculating at the rate of two meals per day he may take meals once in two, three or four days).

17. Some men may fast for a month; their diet may be confined to roots; a person may eat fruits or air alone or oil cake, curd and cowdung.

18. Some may take in cow's urine; some the Kāśa flower. Some may take in only water moss. Some may sustain themselves by other things.

19. Some may live upon scattered old leaves or scattered fruits. A devotee resorts to different kinds of very difficult austerities with a desire for spiritual achievement.

20. He may perform different kinds of Cāndrāyaṇa rites. There may be symbols pertaining to the four stages of life or to virtue and evil.

21. He resorts to various shelters. He may indulge in different heresies. He may resort to isolated shadows of rocky chiffs or to mountain streams.

22. He may resort to lonely river banks, different forests, or lonely mountain caves.

23. He may adopt different types of holy rites and observances and various kinds of austerities, sacrifices of various types and different kinds of scholarly arts.

24-25. He may resort to the path of merchants or to the four castes viz. brahmins, Kṣatriyas, Vaiśyas and Śūdras. He may distribute charitable gifts of various kinds among the wretched, the blind, the miserable ones. He may identify himself with different attributes, viz. Sattva, Rajas and Tamas, Dharma, Artha and Kāma.

26-28. After honouring the Ātman, the Ātman divides itself into various types of persons. The various items in the holy rites are Svāhākāra, Vaṣaṭkāra, Svadhākāra and Namaskāra (obeisance), sacrifice, study, presiding over sacrifices, teaching of Vedas and Śāstras. They say that this is both auspicious and inauspicious due to birth and death or destruction.

29. Divine Prakṛti causes fear and annihilation. At the end of the day, he passes beyond Guṇas and remains single.

30. Just as the sun controls at the proper time the cluster of his rays, so also the soul controls all these and identifies itself with them for the sake of sport.

31-32. It identifies itself with these various features and qualities of the soul pleasing to the heart. Carrying out the function of creation and annihilation it identifies itself with those activities. It is the master of attributes and it possesses the Guṇas. It is interested in the path of activities. It is equipped with the paths of activity as well as inactivity.

33. O great King, this entire universe is blinded by Prakṛti. Everything is pervaded in many ways by Rajas and Tamas.

34-40. The soul thinks like this: "The Dvandvas afflict me continually and pass beyond. They are born of me and they resort to me at the time of annihilation. All these are to be crossed". So thinks the soul, O king, since the intellect is partial (?). Similarly it thinks as follows : "I have to enjoy these merits when I go to the heavenly world. Here too I shall enjoy it even as it gives rise to auspiciousness or inauspiciousness. After I have performed this once it must yield happiness to me so that there shall be pleasure and happiness in every birth. Let there not be misery at any time. Human birth is miserable unto all and so also is the fall into the hell. From the hell I shall again go to the mortal world. From human birth I shall attain the status of gods and from godliness I shall attain human status again." And in due succession he attains hell from the status of human beings. This is the soul of the twice-born. It is surrounded by Guṇas.

41. Therefore the attainment of hell by gods and human beings is relevant. Being overwhelmed by the sense of "Myness" it always moves there round and round.

42-53. There are thousands of crores of creations in these forms that end in death.

He who performs the actions the fruit whereof is either auspicious or inauspicious, attains the particular fruit, taking up forms in all the three worlds.

It is Prakṛti that performs actions, the fruit whereof is either auspicious or inauspicious. And it is Prakṛti that can go as it pleases anywhere in all the three worlds and attains results.

One shall know of all these three regions as pertaining to Prakṛti, viz. 1) the birth as one of the low creatures, 2) the birth as a human being, 3) the birth in the heavenly world of gods.

Since it is unmanifest it can be inferred by means of symbols too.

In the same manner he considers the manly symbol only due to inference. Mingling with other symbols it becomes the unerring symbol of Prakṛti.

After presiding over the pores of vital airs the soul considers the actions to be in the Ātman itself.

All the sense organs such as the ear etc. and the five organs of action initiate passion etc. in the Guṇas along with the Guṇas.

The Ātman which is devoid of sense organs and organs of action thinks like this : "I am doing this. These are my organs".

One who is devoid of wounds thinks "I am wounded". One who is without a symbol thinks that it has a symbol. The

Ātman has no Kāla (Time) but he thinks it has a Kāla. Ātman is devoid of Sattva but thinks that it has Sattva. The Ātman is immortal but he thinks that it dies. He thinks that the Ātman is mobile while in reality it is immobile.

Ātman is really devoid of action but he thinks that it has action.

Ātman has no attachment but he thinks it has attachment. Ātman is different from a principle but he thinks it has principles. Ātman is devoid of birth but he thinks that it has birth.

Since he is not enlightened he considers the Ātman that is imperishable to be perishable.

Thus due to the state of not being enlightened and because unenlightened persons are resorted to, the soul attains thousands of crores of births ending with its downfall. It takes up thousands of births ending with its death, among the lower species of creatures or in the region of gods.

54-58. Due to the state of not being enlightened, the person of evil intellect is being taken away in a thousand ways like the moon in the current of water. Do also know that the moon is eternally possessed of sixteen parts but the ignorant one thinks it growing constantly. He is born again and again for ever.

The sixteenth digit is subtle. Let it be considered the real Moon. This digit is not consumed by Devas (gods). It remains for ever.

After destroying my-ness, O excellent king, he is born and joins Devas too. Since Prakṛti has three Guṇas, he is also Triguṇa (with three Guṇas).

CHAPTER ONE HUNDRED AND THIRTYFIVE

A dialogue between Vasiṣṭha and Janaka (contd.)

Janaka said:

1. The relationship between the two viz., the Imperishable and (Perishable) is to be wished for. It is essential that there

should be a relationship between the two. The relationship between a woman and a man (is described here).

2. Without a man no woman conceives. Without a woman no man is able to evolve a form.

3. In all types of living beings the couple (i.e. male and female) evolve a new form by means of mutual contact. The new form evolved will have the features of both—the male and female.

4-6. For the sake of pleasure, the two will have intimate contact during the prescribed period after menstruation and a new form having the characteristics of those two will be evolved. I shall explain what constitute the characteristic features of the man and what of the woman who becomes the mother. O brahmin, we know that the bone, sinews and the marrow are derived from the father. We have heard that the skin, flesh and blood are acquired from the mother. O excellent brahmin, it is thus that the matter is explained in the Vedas and scriptures.

7. What is mentioned in the Vedas is authoritative, so also what is mentioned in the scriptures. The Vedas and scriptures are the two eternal authorities.

8-10. In the same manner (i.e. as in regard to a man and a woman) Prakṛti and Puruṣa have perpetual contact and hence, O holy Sir, the function of salvation does not exist. Or, should salvation be explained as something that is performed later on ? Do mention this to me. You are always sought after by me directly. Desirous of salvation we wish for the soul that is free from ailment, that cannot be conquered, that is free from old age, that is eternal, that is beyond the purview of sense-organs and that has no other overlord.

Vasiṣṭha said :

11. What Your Highness said, quoting the example from the Vedas and scriptures is quite apt. I shall add that you are a person who understands the real principle.

12. The texts of both, viz. the Vedas and other scriptures are held by you, O king. Be the person who understands the essence of the texts correctly.

13. If a person is interested only in holding the texts of the Vedas and other scriptures and he is not conversant with

the real meaning and principles it is in vain that he holds those texts.

14. He who does not understand the meaning of those texts is merely a carrier of a burden. The acquisition of the texts is not in vain in regard to a person who is conversant with the meaning and principles of the texts.

15. On being asked, only a man like me is competent to state the meaning of a text. Due to a true understanding, he alone grasps the correct meaning.

16. If a person of imperfect intellect is not eager to understand the meaning of the texts, how can that person of imperfect knowledge explain the texts with cofindence ?

17. If a person who has not understood the basic principles of a scriptural text begins to explain it out of greed or arrogance, he is a sinner and he will fall into hell.

18. A person of loopholes (i.e. imperfect knowledge) will never explain the text truthfully and confidently since he is neither self-possessed nor conversant with the meaning and basic principles of the text.

19. Hence listen, O great king, how this is being viewed actually by the noble-souled followers of Sāṁkhya and Yoga systems.

20. Whatever the followers of the Yoga system see (and understand), the Sāṁkhyas too follow. He who sees the identity of the Sāṁkhya and Yoga systems is wise.

21. Skin, flesh, blood, bile, marrow, bone and sinew—O dear one, these can be perceived by the sense-organs, as Your Highness has already told me.

22. A substance is evolved out of another substance and a sense organ is produced from another sense organ. One attains a body from another body and a seed from another seed.

23. How will there be Guṇas in the great Ātman because it is devoid of Guṇas ? How can this embodied soul devoid of sense-organs have the Guṇas ? How can there be Guṇa in a seed that is not solid ?

24. Guṇas are produced from Guṇas and they cease to exist there itself. In the same manner the Guṇas arising out of Prakṛti are produced from Prakṛti but they end therein itself.

25-28. Skin, flesh, blood, fat, bile, bone-marrow and sinew—know them to be eight along with semen that is natural. The symbol of a woman is Prakṛti. It is male as well as female. This is called Vāyu (Wind), Pumān (Man) and Rasa (Juice). Prakṛti is devoid of symbol. It is perceived through the symbols born of itself in the same way at through flowers and fruits; the formless things are perceived among things with form. In the same manner the symbol is perceived through inference. Among the principles the twenty-fifth principle, O dear one, is of fixed nature.

29. It has neither beginning nor end; it is infinite; it observes everything; but it is isolated. It is due to the identification through the guṇas that it is called Guṇa.

30. The Guṇas exist in one with Guṇa. How can there be Guṇas in one without Guṇas? Hence those people who look at Guṇas know thus.

31. When this soul identifies itself with the Guṇas belonging to Prakṛti it is one with Guṇas and it observes the different Guṇas.

32-33. The fact that they call Sāṁkhya and Yoga as existing beyond Intellect explains that it is highly intelligent while knowing; and it is unenlightened while avoiding the enlightened. They call Īśvara when it is manifest through its Guṇas. They call Īśvara without Guṇa, the perpetual presiding deity.

34. Scholars who are experts in Śaṁkhya and Yoga and who seek the Supreme Soul understand the twenty-five principles consituted by Prakṛti and Guṇas.

35. The persons who are unenlightened, do not understand the enlightened and unmanifest one. They understand the manifest identical with the unmanifest.

36. This principle is perfect but their vision is imperfect. They do not understand the known as separate from the unknown.

37. This principle of perishable and Imperishable has been mentioned to you. They call Ekatva (unity) Akṣara (Imperishable) and Nānātva (diversity) is called Kṣara.

38. This is stationed in the twenty-five principles. They say that it is perfect. Its unity is perceived. So also its diversity.

39. There is a separate citation of the principle and one who is conversant with the principle. Learned scholars say that the principles are twenty-five in number.

40. The learned men state that the twenty-fifth principle is devoid of Tattva (? principle). It is the practice that what should be discarded should be discarded. A twenty-fifth is eternal because of its reality.

Janaka said :

41. What has been stated by you, O excellent brahmin, viz. diversity and unity (is not understood by me) even as I observe it. Their example is in doubt.

42. Undoubtedly, with the gross intellect I do not see the reality, O sinless one, of that which is being known through Buddha (that which is understood) and Prabuddha (the enlightened).

43. The explanation too of the perishable and the imperishable, given by you, O sinless one, has been missed by me due to the unsteadiness of intellect.

44. Therefore, I wish to hear this, viz. the philosophy of diversity and unity as well as the mutually opposite pairs that are to be understood essentially and unobstructedly.

45. O holy one, I wish to know separately the distinction between knowledge and ignorance, the Imperishable and the perishable, Śāṁkhya and Yoga entirely, as well as the enlightened and the unenlightened.

Vasiṣṭha said :

46. Oh, I shall narrate unto you what you ask me. O great king, listen separately from me the function of Yoga.

47. To the followers of Yoga, meditation is a great power. The learned ones say that meditation is of two types.

48. (1) The concentration of mind, and (2) the control of breath. Prāṇāyāma is of two types, viz. Saguṇa and Nirguṇa. The Nirguṇa is mental.

49. One should not practise Prāṇāyāma for two units of time,O ruler of men, after passing urine, evacuating bowels and taking food. After that he shall do so with eagerness.

50-53. The devotee observing silence shall mentally turn the sense-organs away from the objects. (The control of breath) may last for ten or twelve (Mātrās). The intelligent devotee shall not induce himself to retain breath for more than twenty-four Mātrās. It is mentioned by scholars that breath control should not be practised while standing. We have heard that the Ātman of the universe should be known always. Indeed yoga can be practised by a person whose mind is not shaky. The person who meditates should be free from all attachments. His diet should be light. He shall control and conquer his senses. He shall fix the mind to the heart either early in the night or in the later half of the night.

54-55. O king of Mithilā, he shall steady the sense-organs by his mind. He shall steady his mind by his intellect. He shall be still like a stone. He should not tremble. He shall be steady like a post and still like a tree. He shall control himself by means of intellect. He shall be conversant with the mode and process of breath control. They call him yukta i.e. one who is in the state of Yoga.

56-57. He does not hear. He does not smell. He does not see anything. He is not aware of touch. His mind does not think or imagine anything. Like a log he does not know anything. The learned scholars call him Yukta and one who has attained Prakṛti or the primordial state.

58. Just as even when the lamp is not seen the light is seen, so also the soul without Liṅga shall have the movements below, above and sideways.

59. Being equipped with that the soul is stationed in the heart. When it is seen thus, O dear one, it is called by people like me Immanent soul, that which should be known, the knower.

60. Like fire without smoke, like sun with all its rays, like lightning in the sky, he sees the Ātman in the Ātman.

61. It has no source of origin and it is immortal. Only the learned scholars possessing courage and Brahmins adhering to their dharma can see it.

62. They call it minuter than the atom, and greater than the greatest. Though it stands firm everywhere in all living beings it is not perceived.

63. It is the creator of universe by means of intellect that could be observed by the light of the mind. Standing beyond the great Tamas, O dear one, it is (Non-Tāmasa).

64. Persons who are conversant with truth and who are masters of the Vedic lore declare that it is far off from darkness. It has various appellations, viz. Vimala (Devoid of impurities), Vimata (One who is particularly honoured), Nirliṅga (That which is beyond symbols) and Aliṅga (That which has no symbols).

65. Yoga alone is the substance of the worlds. What else can be the characteristic feature of Yoga? One who sees thus perceives the unageing great Ātman.

66. So far the Yogic school of philosophy has been recounted in essence to you by me. I shall now recount the Sāṁkhya school which is an example of Parisaṁkhyā (Enumeration).

67. They call the great Prakṛti of the soul Avyakta (Unmanifest) and Prakhyāna (Proclamation). From it originated the second principle Mahat, O most excellent king.

68. The Principle originating from Mahat is Ahaṁkāra (Ego). The five elements originated from Ahaṁkāra.

69. These eight are Prakṛtis. The Vikāras (products) are sixteen in number. Five of them are Viśeṣas and five are the sense-organs.

70. Those who are conversant with the arrangement of the followers of the Sāṁkhya school, those who perpetually abide by the path of the Sāṁkhyas, those who are learned scholars in the Sāṁkhya school say that the number of principles is only this much.

71. Everything gets dissolved in its respective source of origin wherefrom it has been produced. These principles get dissolved in the reverse order and they are apprehended by the immanent soul.

72. The Guṇas (i.e. all evolved things) get dissolved in Guṇas like the waves of ocean. They are produced in the ordinary order and get dissolved in the reverse order.

73. The creation and annihilation of Prakṛti, O excellent king, is this much. In the process of creation it has diversity and unity at the time of annihilation.

74. This is what, O great king, should be understood by the experts. The presiding deity is the unmanifest.

75. It has unity and diversity in the same manner as in the case of Prakṛti. It has unity at the time of annihilation and multiplicity due to activity.

76. The Ātman shall evolve Prakṛti at the time of creation in various ways. The great Ātman, the twenty-fifth principle presides over that group.

77. It is called the presiding deity by ascetics. It is that because it presides over the group.

78. It knows the Kṣetra or the Avyakta. Hence it is called Ksetrajña. It lies down in the Pura (city) of Avyakta. Therefore it is called Puruṣa.

79. The Kṣetra is separate from Kṣetrajña. The Kṣetra is called Avyakta and Jñātṛ (knower) is Puruṣa.

80. Jñāna (knowledge) is separate from Jñeya (that which should be known). Jñāna is Avyakta; Jñeya is Puruṣa.

81. The Avyakta is Kṣetra, Sattva etc. Puruṣa is Anīśvara (having no other master) and Atattva (devoid of Tattva).

82. In the school of Sāṁkhya there is no fixed number. The Saṁkhyā creates and explains Prakṛti only.

83. The number can be forty or twenty-four. After enumerating factually (the principles are to be understood). The Sāṁkhya has a thousand processes. The twenty-fifth principle is beyond the other principles.

84. The twenty-fifth principle is mentioned in the Vedas as the Enlightened soul and knowing one. When he realises Ātman he becomes Kevala (The single one).

85. Thus the Sāṁkhya school of philosophy has been described to you briefly. Those who know thus attain liberation.

86. What is called perfect knowledge is the perception of Prakṛti. It has been already explained how that which possesses Guṇas could be produced from Nirguṇa (that which is devoid of Guṇas).

87-90. There is no return to this world to those who realize this. Nor do they turn to the state of mortality. Those who are non-intelligent do not perceive the distinction between the changeable and the unchangeable. In regard to them the vision is not perfect. O king, they are born again and again. The Avyakta is called "Sarva" (the whole). The twenty-fifth principle is the part thereof. People comprehend Sarva not by Sarva. They comprehend Sarva by following Asarva. Those who know thus have no fear.

CHAPTER ONE HUNDRED AND THIRTYSIX

Dialogue between Vasiṣṭha & Janaka (contd.)

Vasiṣṭha said :

1. The Sāṁkhya school of philosophy has so far been recounted unto you, O excellent king. Now listen to me and understand Vidyā and Avidyā in the proper order.

2. They say that Avyakta is non-differentiated during creation and annihilation. Twenty principles are called Vidyā and Avidyā and they are characterized by creation and annihilation.

3. Some principles are Vidyās and some are Avidyās; understand them in their proper order. O dear one, understand the recapitulation of the school of Sāṁkhya, as mentioned by the sages.

4. The sense-organs are Vidyā of the organs of action. Similarly (Tanmātras?) are the Vidyā of the sense-organs.

5. Learned men say that the mind is Vidyā of the objects of pleasure. They say that the five elements are the Vidyā of the mind.

6. Ahaṁkāra is the Vidyā of five elements. So, O lord of men, Ahaṁkāra is Vidyā and Buddhi is also Vidyā.

7. Prakṛti is the Vidyā of Buddhi. Avyakta, the Unmanifest, is the Vidyā of principles. O excellent one among men, Vidhi is also Vidyā.

8. They say that Avyakta is Apara (having nothing greater than it). It is the twenty-fifth principle and it is Vidyā. Every-

thing is mentioned as the Vidyā of Jñeya (which should be known) and Jñāna (knowledge).

9. Avyakta is mentioned by the word Jñāna while the Jñeya is the twenty-fifth principle. Similarly, Jñāna is Avyakta and the twenty-fifth principle is Vijñātṛ (knower).

10. Vidyā and Avidyā have been briefly mentioned by me. What is known as Akṣara and Kṣara, understand that from me.

11. Both of these are called Kṣara. Both of these are Anakṣara. I shall mention the reason thereof in relation to knowledge.

12. Both of them are without beginning and without end. Both of them are supreme. Both of them are known as Tattva by persons who think about Jñāna.

13. Due to the function of creation and annihilation they call Avyakta as unchanging. For the creation of Guṇas it undergoes change again and again.

14. The origin of Guṇas and Mahat etc. is mutual. They call Adhiṣṭhāna (basis) the Kṣetra (field). This is the twenty-fifth principle.

15. One shall reduce the cluster of Guṇas within, into the manifest Ātman. Therefore the ego gets dissolved in the twenty-fifth principle along with its Guṇas.

16. Guṇas get dissolved in Guṇas. Therefore, Prakṛti shall be one. Even the Kṣetrajña is made Kṣetrajña (i.e. the individual soul).

17. When Prakṛti characterised by Guṇas gets into the Akṣara there is Nirguṇatva (state of being devoid of Guṇas) in the body because of alteration in Guṇas.

18. It is in this very same way that Kṣetrajña (gets disolved) by the decrease of the knowledge of Kṣetra. We have heard that it is naturally devoid of Guṇas.

19. When this becomes Kṣara it knows Prakṛti possessed of Guṇas, among Guṇas and also Prakṛti devoid of Guṇas of the Ātman.

20. Morever, he becomes pure avoiding Prakṛti and realising "I am different from Prakṛti".

21. Then he attains freedom from pain. It does not get

mixed with Prakṛti, O great king. It is quite a different one that is mixed and that is seen by others.

22. When he treats with contempt the Guṇas, pertaining to Prakṛti, he sees the great one.

23-25. "What has been done by me so far ? I have been immersed in the ocean of time. Just as the fish in the sea identifies itself with the water and adapts itself to it, so also I identify myself with the different persons due to delusion. The fish does not understand its difference from water due to ignorance. Since I slight the Ātman I do not understand it or anything else.

26. Fie upon me whose intellect has become vitiated and who have become immersed in this. Due to delusion I have followed it up, I have followed different persons (?)

27-30. This fellow is my relative. He may experience my decline in strength. I have attained similarity and identity with this fellow. I am of the same type as this fellow. I perceive equality here. I am like him. Indeed this fellow is free from impurities. It is clear. I am also like this then. Due to ignorance and delusion I have acted like this along with the ignorant Prakṛti. I have remained all this due to this contact. So I have been captivated by it and I did not become enlightened so far with regard to persons of noble nature, middlings or lowly ones. How can I associate with it ?

31. Due to the state of not being enlightened I had associated with Māyā. Now I have become free.

32-33. Now I shall not associate with it. The fact that I who am free from aberrations have been deceived by Māyā which is an aberration, is not its fault. It is my fault for I had been attached to it and I had been approached by it with face turned away.

34. Therefore, I have been stationed in this in multifarious forms. Though, really I am devoid of form I assume forms. Though devoid of form, though actually unembodied, I have been overwhelmed by my-ness.

35-36. Therefore aberrations have been created by that Prakṛti in the course of different births. Though I am devoid of my-ness (actually) aberrations have been created by the same my-ness. I have been born in various wombs and while remaining there, my mind had been devoid of consciousness. Equality has not been achieved by me due to Ahaṁkāra (Ego).

37. After splitting itself into many he joins me once again. Now I am enlightened. I am devoid of my-ness. I am devoid of egoism.

38. The evil quality of my-ness is always generated in the mind and caused by Ego. After abandoning this which has clung to me I shall resort to the state free from ailment.

39. I shall identify myself with this (i.e. the soul) and not with Prakṛti which often misleads. My welfare is with the soul and not with Prakṛti."

40. Thus by addressing the greatest, the twenty-fifth principle is awakened. After abandoning the Kṣara he attains the state of Akṣara devoid of ailment.

41. (He attains the state Akṣara that is Avyakta (unmanifest) and Nirguṇa (devoid of Guṇas) after abandoning the Kṣara that is Vyaktadharmā (whose attributes are manifest) and Saguṇa (possessed of Guṇas). After seeing the Nirguṇa first, O king of Mithilā, he becomes similar to it.

42. Thus the example of Akṣara and Kṣara has been explained to you by me as it has been expounded in the Vedas. It is richly endowed with knowledge.

43. It is free from doubts. It is subtle, pure and free from impurities. I shall explain it once again in the manner heard by me. Understand it.

44. The philosophy of the schools of Sāṁkhya and Yoga has been recounted by me with examples from the two systems. What is stated in the Sāṁkhya is the same which is stated in the Yoga system.

45-48. The Jñāna of the Sāṁkhyas, O ruler of the Earth, is conducive to the awakening (of the soul). It is clearly explained with a desire for the welfare of disciples.

Moreover, scholars say that this system is very comprehensive. In this system, O lord of men, a principle other than the twenty-five, viz. Rebirth is included.

The greatest principle of the Sāṁkhyas has been duly described. That is Buddha (enlightened), Apratibuddha (unenlightened), and Budhyamāna (that is being enlightened).

They say that Budhyamāna Buddhatva (the state of being enlightened that is being understood) is the Yogic principle.

CHAPTER ONE HUNDRED AND THIRTYSEVEN

Dialogue between Vasiṣṭha and Karāla Janaka concluded

Vasiṣṭha said :

1. Prakṛti creates and seizes the unenlightened unmanifest storehouse of Guṇas even as Guṇas hold the Tattvas.

2. In a playful manner, O king, Aja the unborn attains the state of modification; splitting itself into many it is perceived as though it is really multifarious.

3. Budhyamāna that disturbs and stirs this up like this, is not comprehended. It creates, seizes and practices Guṇas.

4. They call this Budhyamāna because it enlightens Avyakta. Avyakta is not comprehended in any other manner whether it is Saguṇa or Nirguṇa.

5. It is only sometimes that it is so, so they call it Pratibuddhaka (Enlightened). If the Avyakta is comprehended it is the twenty-fifth principle.

6. The Budhyamāna certainly becomes one with myness for its characteristic feature—so says the Veda. By becoming enlightened due to mutual endeavour it becomes Avyakta that never swerves—They say thus.

7-8. They call this Budhyamāna because it enlightens Avyakta. It is the twenty-fifth principle. It is the great Ātman. It does not comprehend the twenty-sixth principle, the Buddha (enlightened), devoid of impurities, the eternal, one that cannot be perceived. It comprehends the twenty-fourth and twenty-fifth principles always.

9. The perceptible and the imperceptible, O king of great lustre, follow its nature. The Avyakta, O dear one, comprehends that Brahman which is non-dual.

10-12. It comprehends the Ātman, the twenty-fifth and the twenty-fourth principle. At the time of comprehending the

Ātman, when he considers "I am another" he becomes one with the Avyakta as his eyes and so endowed with Prakṛti. When he comprehends the pure Buddhi without impurities, O mighty king, he comprehends the twenty-sixth principle. Contented, he proceeds (ahead). Thereafter he abandons Avyakta with creation and annihilation as the characteristic features.

13. It comprehends Prakṛti which is devoid of consciousness and which is endowed with Guṇas. It becomes one with the features of lonely Ātman by virtue of realizing of the Avyakta.

14. After coming into contact with the Kevala it shall attain the liberated soul. They call this Tattva (principle) and (the soul) that is without old age and death, Nistattva (one that is beyond the principles).

15. Only by duly listening to the description of the Tattvas does the soul, O king, become conversant with the principles. Learned scholars speak about twenty-five principles.

16. Never does a person conversant with the Tattvas get immersed in the ocean of worldly existence, O dear one. The Tattvas approach these persons quickly. Now understand their characteristics.

17. Prājña free from old age and death is understood as the twenty-sixth principle. Undoubtedly it attains equality with Śakti, it itself being Śakta.

18. Abuddhimān (that which has no intellect) is being awakened by the Buddha (the enlightened one) that is the twenty-sixth principle. This is called diversity, Nānātva, as explained in the Sāṁkhya scriptures.

19. When it is comprehended by the intellect the twenty-fifth principle, accompanied by conscious one, Cetana, shall have unity.

20. It attains equality, O king of Mithilā, with (the enlightened one) that is being comprehended. Although the Ātman is devoid of attachment, O ruler of men, it has the features and characteristics of what is being attached.

21. They underst and that the twenty-sixth principle is evolved out of Karman, after attaining the Ātman that is free from attachment. When this is enlightened the omnipresent soul abandons the Avyakta.

22-24. The twenty-fourth principle is very subtle due to the enlightenment of the twenty-sixth principle. Thus the Apratibuddha (non-enlightened), Buddha (the enlightened) and the Budhyamāna have been briefly described to you, O sinless one, in the manner explained in the śāstras. The difference between these two is the same as between Maśaka (mosquito) and Udumbara (the fruint of a particular tree). The difference obtained between the two is the same as between fish and water. The unity and diversity of the two should be thought of in this manner.

25-26. What is mentioned as salvation is this much. It is termed Jñāna and Vijñāna. The desire, viz. "This person should be liberated" is suddenly originated in the body of the twenty-fifth principle, they say, within the view of the Avyakta. It is certain that he will be liberted thus and not otherwise.

27-30. The soul acquires the characteristics of another object by associating with it. It becomes pure when associating with the pure one and not with the impure one. It becomes free from attributes while associating with the enlightened, O bull among men. While associating with one with the feeling of detachment the soul becomes liberated. While associating with the liberated it becomes Liberated. One with unlimited intellect becomes pure and of pure activities while associating with one of pure activities. While associating with the soul free from impurities it becomes pure; while associating with the single it becomes single soul. While associating with the independent it becomes independent.

31. O great king, the truth and the truthful reality have been recounted so far. By grasping with your intellect the eternal Brahman, the first pure one, you have become Amatsara, devoid of jealousy.

32. O king, this great truth should not be imparted to a person not abiding by the Vedas. It imparts enlightenment in regard to a person who is desirous of acting according to it. It admonishes one who bows down for enlightenment.

33. This truth should not be imparted to a liar nor to a rogue, nor to an impotent person nor to a person of crooked intellect. It should not be imparted to a person who harasses scholars devoted to knowledge. It should be imparted for the enlightenment of the disciples.

34. This should be imparted to a disciple who is equipped with faith and good qualities, who refrains from slandering others, who possesses pure Yoga and who is a learned one equipped with forbearance and sympathy.

35. This secret should be imparted to a person who has discrimination, who is fond of injunctions, who is devoid of quarrelsome dispute, who has learned much, who has humble dress and demeanour and who has no selfish motive.

36. They say that knowledge of this great Brahman should not be imparted to a person who is devoid of these qualities. The narration of virtue in regard to such person is not conducive to welfare, because it is like charity accorded to a person who does not deserve it.

37. This should not be given to a person who has no sacred rites even if the entire earth full of jewels were given away. O leader of men, this great thing should be imparted to a person who has conquered his sense organs, who observes pure rites and who knows reality.

38. O Karāla, let there be no fear at all in you. This great Brahman has been heard by you today. It has been duly recounted. It is extremely sacred. It is fully free from grief. It has neither beginning nor middle nor end.

39-40. It is unfathomable. It is free from old age and death. It is free from ailment. It is auspicious. It is free from fear. In view of the erroneousness of the argument of others, the eternal Brahmā had been propitiated with great effort. That eternal Brahmā of brilliant splendour had been propitiated and this had been acquired in the same manner as this has been acquired by you.

41. I have been asked by you, O leader of men. So this has been recounted to you exclusively as it had been obtained from Brahmā. It is the great knowledge, the utmost resort of those who are conversant with salvation.

Vyāsa said :

42. This great Brahman, the twenty-fifth principle, from which one does not return has now been recounted in the same manner as it had been recounted, O excellent sages, by Vasiṣṭha formerly.

43-44. He who does not completely and accurately understand the great unchanging knowledge, free from death and old age, even after striving for comprehension, returns.

O brahmins, this Jñāna that is conducive to salvation, has been truthfually described by me after listening to it (and under standing it) from the divine sage.

45. This was derived by sage Vasiṣṭha from Brahmā. Nārada the greatest among sages obtained this from Vasiṣṭha.

46. This eternal doctrine has been recounted to me and it has been obtained by me from Nārada. After hearing about this great doctrine, O excellent sages, you will not feel sorry.

47. He has no fear who has understood that Kṣara and Akṣara are different. He has fear certainly who does not know this accurately.

48. Due to the absence of perfect knowledge a person of confounded soul undergoes hardships again and again and attains thousands of births ending with death.

49. Or he may go to the heavenly world or to the realm of low creatures or to the human world. Or perhaps he is released from that ocean of ignorance.

50. In the terrible ocean of ignorance the unmanifest is called the unfathomable one. O brahmins, it is here that the living beings become immersed day by day.

51. Hence due to the destruction of the unfathomable Avyakta, the eternal one, all of you, O brahmins, have become free from Rajas and Tamas.

52. Thus, O excellent sages, the great Liberation, the essence of essences, has been recounted by me. On realising it one does not return.

53. It should not be imparted to an atheist or to a person who is not a devotee. O brahmins, it should not be imparted to an evil-minded person nor to a person who has no faith and who is averse to everything good.

CHAPTER ONE HUNDRED AND THIRTYEIGHT

In praise of the Purāṇa

Lomaharṣaṇa said :

1-3. Thus, O brahmins, sage Vyāsa recounted the Purāṇa to the sages formerly in smooth voice. His words were pregnant with meaning. His statements were free from eighteen defects. They were free from impurities. They were pure. The Purāṇa is full of the gist of different scriptures. It is fully endowed with pure words of good quality embellished with the principles of the systems of Sāṁkhya and Yoga. It contains the prima facie views of the opponent and the finally established doctrines. The highly intelligent sage Vyāsa stopped aftre recounting this duly.

4-5. After hearing the first Purāṇa named Brāhma which is on a par with the Vedas and which bestows the desired fruits, they became delighted and pleased as well as surprised again and again. Then they praised sage Vyāsa, Kṛṣṇadvaipāyana Vyāsa.

The sages said :

6-12. O excellent sage, the Purāṇa that is on a par with the Vedas, which bestows all wished-for fruits, which dispels all sins and which contains wonderful words and letters has been recounted by you and heard by us. O holy lord, there is nothing unknown to you in the three worlds. O extremely fortunate one, you are omniscient like Bṛhaspati among Devas. We shall bow down to you, the great sage of excessive intelligence, closely adhering to Brahman. O great sage, who can recount good qualities since the meanings of the Vedic passages have been explained in the Mahābhārata. After learning the four Vedas with ancillary subjects including Grammar you have composed the sacred book Bhārata. Obeisance to you who have the characteristics of perfect knowledge. Obeisance to you, O Vyāsa, of vast knowledge, of eyes resembling the wide petals of a full-blown lotus. It is by you that the light of knowledge has been made to burn filling it with the oil of Bhārata. By the collyrium-rod of perfect knowledge the eyes of persons blinded by the darkness of ignorance, going astray due to evil visions, have opened up.

Lomaharṣaṇa said :

13. After saying this they honoured and worshipped Vyāsa and went back in the manner they had come to their respective hermitages. They were contented.

14. In the same manner, O excellent sages, the eternal Purāṇa that is highly meritorious and which destroys all sins has been recounted by me.

15. O excellent brahmins, whatever has been asked by you all, has been expounded by me by the grace of Vyāsa.

16. This should be listened to by householders, ascetics and religious students. It bestows wealth and happiness to men. It destroys all sins.

17. Moreover this must be attentively listened to by brahmins devoted to Brahman as well as brahmins and others who are well-disciplined and who desire welfare.

18. (By doing so) a brahmin acquires learning; a Kṣatriya victory in battle; a Vaiśya everlasting wealth; and a Śūdra happiness.

19. If a person of great purity listens to it meditating upon a particular desire he acquires the same whatever be the desire.

20. This is a Purāṇa belonging to Viṣṇu. It destroys sins. It is more excellent than all other scriptural texts. It is conducive to the fulfilment of all aims of life.

21. This Purāṇa that is on a par with the Vedas has been explained by me to you. When this is listened to the heap of sins arising from all defects, is destroyed.

22. What a man obtains after fasting at Prayāga, Puṣkara, Kurukṣetra and Arbuda, he obtains the same by listening to this.

23. The great merit that a man obtains by performing Agnihotra extremely well for a whole year, O brahmins, is obtained by listening to this once.

24-25. The benefit that a man derives by taking bath in the waters of Yamunā on the Dvādaśī day in the month of Proṣṭhapada, or by visiting Hari at Mathurā is obtained if the devotee dedicates his mind to Keśava and recites this Purāṇa with great concentration, O brahmins.

26. He who reads or listens to this Purāṇa obtains that benefit which a person derives by visiting ŚRĪ.

27. The man who reads and listens faithfully to this Purāṇa which is on a par with the Vedas goes to the abode of Hari.

28. A brahmin with mental control who recounts this on holy Parvan days and on eleventh and twelfth days of the lunar fortnight goes to the world of Viṣṇu.

29. This is conducive to fame and long life. It bestows happiness. It increases fame. O brahmins, it bestows strength and nourishment. It is conducive to wealth. It destroys bad dreams.

30. A scholar who reads this excellent narrative during the three joints (i.e. dawn, noon and sunset) with faith and great concentration shall obtain all desired things.

31. He who is distressed due to sickness is liberated from sickness. He who is in bondage is liberated from bondage. He who is frightened is released from fear and he who is caught in adversity is liberated from adversity.

32. He obtains ability to remember births, learning, sons, intelligence, animals, courage, virtue, wealth, love and salvation.

33. If a man reads this with pure mind he obtains all those desired things which he must have kept in his mind.

34. He who listens to this Purāṇa which bestows heavenly pleasures and salvation after bowing to Viṣṇu the preceptor of the worlds, with great devotion in the mind and purity in mind and body, becomes free from sins. After enjoying happiness here and divine happiness in heaven he goes to Hari's region without impurity afterwards. He is freed from the Guṇas of Prakṛti.

35. This excellent Purāṇa that yields much benefit and bestows virtue, wealth and salvation should be listened to everyday by excellent brahmins who are devoutly engaged in their own pious activity and who are desirous of attaining the sole path of salvation, by leading Kṣatriyas of self-control and discipline who always seek welfare, by Vaiśyas born of pure family, and by virtuous Śūdras.

36. You are all excellent men. Let your mind be diverted to virtue, that alone is favourable to one who has gone to the other world, like a relative. Riches and women though resorted to by clever persons do not attain power and stability.

37. A man acquires a kingdom through virtue. A man acquires longevity, renown, austerity, piety and salvation through virtue.

38. Dharma is both mother and father. Dharma is friend and companion to a man both in this world and in the other. Dharma is a saviour here. It is the bestower of salvation. There is nothing (of consequence) except Dharma.

39. This secret and excellent Purāṇa that is on a par with the Vedas should not be imparted to an evil mind, and particularly to an atheist.

40. This excellent Purāṇa has been narrated by me and listened to by you. It dispels sins and increasses virtue. It is extremely secret. O sages, permit me I shall go.